CONSECRATED LIFE TODAY

UNION OF SUPERIORS GENERAL

CONSECRATED LIFE TODAY

Charisms in the Church for the world

International Congress
Rome, 22-27 November 1993

ST PAULS

248.2
USG

Maccise

PRINTED IN ENGLAND

ST PAULS
Middlegreen, Slough SL3 6BT, United Kingdom
Moyglare Road, Maynooth, Co. Kildare, Ireland
60-70 Broughton Road, Homebush NSW 2140, Australia

Distributed in Canada by EDITIONS PAULINES
3965 Boul. Henri-Bourassa, Montreal, QC, H1H 1L1

© Edizioni San Paolo srl, Cinisello Balsamo (Milano), Italy 1994

English edition © St Pauls (UK) 1994
French edition © Médiaspaul, Paris 1994
Italian edition © Edizioni San Paolo srl, Cinisello Balsamo (Mi) 1994
Spanish edition © San Pablo Communicación SSP, Madrid 1994

ISBN 085439 482 6 (UK)

National Library of Australia
Card Number and ISBN 1875570 42 X

Printed by The Guernsey Press Co. Ltd, Guernsey C.I., Europe

ST PAULS is an activity of the priests and brothers of the Society of St Paul
who proclaim the Gospel through the media of social communication

Contents

Introduction

Flavio Roberto Carraro, OFM CAP
President of the Union of Superiors General

The last twenty-five years have seen an extraordinary development in consecrated life, comparable perhaps to the great innovations of the thirteenth century, and in other aspects, to those of the nineteenth century. The impetus for this development came from the Second Vatican Council with the documents promulgated, especially with *Lumen Gentium* and *Perfectæ Caritatis* – but perhaps even more with that new attention to the breath of the Holy Spirit that is still characterizing our times.

On the wave of this new situation, the Union of Superiors General thought of the timeliness of promoting a Congress on the international level on the theme of consecrated life, addressed in particular to Superiors General and their Councillors.

They were studying this possibility when, unexpectedly, on January 11, 1991, at the end of a Eucharistic celebration in his private chapel, the Holy Father announced that the theme of the next ordinary assembly of the Synod of Bishops would be *consecrated life in the Church*.

This news accelerated the preparation of the Congress and determined its profile. In practice, it maintained its initial finality and opened the invitation to theologians and representatives of feminine consecrated life.

The organization went through several phases, it met with difficulties, but it was not arrested. And, thanks be to God, we arrived at the celebration.

Fr McSweeney presented the brief history of this important event whose animator he was. To him and to his collaborators, especially the members of the Secretariat, we owe a debt of gratitude.

It is the desire of the Superiors General that the fruits of the Congress reach the hands of the greatest number of persons possible, especially the Bishops of the Church of the Lord, and all consecrated persons. That is why the publication in four languages was entrusted to ST PAULS.

Now we hope that there will be a serious commitment on the part of consecrated persons to clarify all the more – even with the help of this humble instrument – their own identity and together rediscover new ways and means of consecrated life, expression of that creativity of the Holy Spirit which is always new.

May Mary, Mother of the Church, guide those who are called to live this vocation and enlighten the Bishop who will study the theological and ecclesial aspects of this great gift of God to his Church and humanity.

The design of the Congress

Fr Anthony McSweeney

The design of the Congress reflected the option to take a largely inductive approach to the reality of consecrated life today, beginning with the reality as it has been studied with the help of the sociological disciplines, then moving on to deal with the theme according to three major concepts on which the Congress was built, namely mission, communion and identity, and concluding with an effort at synthesis. Thus the Congress proceeded according to three clearly demarcated phases.

Phase 1: Reality

The findings of two major studies from different cultural and geographic areas were presented as samples in order to stimulate reflection on the current reality of the consecrated life.

Phase 2: The three core-concepts or nuclei

Three core-concept or nuclei of the consecrated life were identified, namely identity, communion and mission. These were seen more as three aspects or facets in continual interaction among themselves rather than as quite separate one from the other. We decided to present the reflections on these aspects, moreover, inverting the usual order, that is to say beginning with mission, proceeding through communion to identity. It was felt that in this way a more concrete and historical approach might be possible rather than an abstract one. In other words, we felt that by beginning with the current understanding and experience of mission and communion we might be able to pose the question of identity in a more nuanced way, thanks to a sharper awareness of the complexity, the charismatic diversity and the historical dynamism of the consecrated life in our time, which is one of a major, even epochal historical change. In each case we decided to proceed by means of a major conference which would deal in more depth with the essential points, followed by a series of shorter communications in the form of a panel having the purpose of illustrating further facets or aspects of the theme and permitting a greater variety a viewpoints.

1. *Mission* – We wished to look at the question of the mission of the consecrated life, from two distinct viewpoints. The first is that of the challenges which arise from the variety of geographic and cultural situations – thus we looked at Africa, Asia and the Pacific, Latin America and the First World. The second is that of the diverse responses being given on the basis of the different charisms of the consecrated life; thus we heard something from the contemplative life, from an apostolic congregation, a missionary institute and a Society of apostolic life.

2. *Communion* – The theme of communion was dealt with in a different fashion. The main conference looked principally at the experience of communion within the consecrated life thus at fraternal life. The question of the consecrated life in the larger communion of the Church was in this instance dealt with by the panel from a variety of viewpoints after an initial setting of the scene by means of a review of the consultation carried out by the USG prior to the Congress. Thus we heard the viewpoint of a bishop, a member of a conventual institute from Eastern Europe, a religious from an apostolic congregation, a lay-brother, a woman major superior and a lay-woman.

3. *Identity* – The principal conference studied the question of identity in some depth, while the panel contributions in this case were aimed at providing a series of carefully articulated perspectives on the question. Thus identity was approached from the standpoint of history and also of culture as well as from a variety of ecclesial experiences, namely the experience of a consecrated woman, of a lay woman, that of a diocesan priest and that of a member of a contemplative order.

Phase 3: Synthesis and conclusions

The synthesis was built on the written contributions as well as the work of the 27 linguistic groups which each day sent a report of their conclusions to the small committee charged with this task.

Each linguistic group was asked to study the theme of the day according to a specific perspectives, either culture, charismatic diversity, future or formation. In this way the refection was enriched and broadened. The final text published here was rewritten in the light of the numerous contributions to the open debate which concluded the congress. This debate brought out issues which some participants felt had been given less attention during the Congress, such as formation, as well as offering comments, criticisms and suggestions.

The Conclusions which are presented here were formulated during the Congress but were not presented in the Assembly; they were offered to a special meeting of the Superiors General (1st-2nd December) which, after reworking and enriching them, approved them as an expression of their point of view. They have been presented to the Synod Secretariat and are being sent to all members of the Synod. They will serve as a point of departure for the contributions of the members of the USG at the Synod. It should be noted that they do not claim to be exhaustive, but rather to highlight matters that are judged to be of particular urgency at the present moment.

In this volume we publish the main conferences, the final document and the Pope's address. The texts of the *Acts* in their entirety are available in the four languages used at the Congress (French, English, Italian, Spanish) at the office of USG (Via dei Penitenzieri 19 – 00193 Roma. Fax: 6-6874317).

1

The reality
of religious

I.
Transforming tradition: Shaping the Mission and Identity of Religious Life in the United States

David J. Nygren, CM
Miriam D. Ukeritis, CSJ

The magnitude of change in religious orders in the United States since the Second Vatican Council has been severe by any standard. Thirty years of renewal has enlivened many orders, seen the diminishment of others and has most leaders today examining carefully the shifts that must happen for religious life to remain a vibrant social institution in the Church and society.

A numerical view of membership in religious orders[1] in the United States since the conclusion of Vatican II indicates a state of constant decline (see Table 1). Statistics indicate that between 1962 and 1992 the number of religious sisters and brothers in the United States has declined by nearly 43% and religious priests number nearly 18% fewer. When considering age, more than 66% of the women who are members of religious orders, and 50% of the men, are aged 60 or older (see Table 2).

Table 1
Religious sisters, brothers and priests: Population changes, 1962-1992

Group	1962	1972	% Change 1982	1992	1962-92
Sisters	173,351	146,914	121,370	99,337	-42.7
Brothers	11,502	9,740	7,880	6,603	-42.6
Priests	21,807	20,694	22,572	17,989	-17.5
TOTALS	206,660	177,348	151,822	123,929	-40.0

Source: Official Catholic Directory 1962, 1972, 1982 and 1992

Table 2
Age distribution of United States Religious in 1992

Age group	Women No.	%	Men No.	%
Under 30	642	0.7	587	2.8
30-34	886	1.0	767	3.6
35-39	1,417	1.6	1,114	5.3
40-44	3,164	3.5	1,658	7 9
45-49	6,437	7.1	1,974	9.4
50-54	8,659	9.5	2,124	10.1
55-59	9,466	10.4	2,223	10.5
60-64	10,615	11.7	2,753	13 0
65-69	9,932	10.9	2,336	1 1.4
70-74	9,689	10 6	2,032	9 9
75-79	11,344	12.5	1,762	8.6
80-84	9,561	10 5	1,002	4 9
85-89	5,785	6.4	407	2.0
90 and over	3,330	3.6	132	0.6
TOTALS	90,927	100.0	20,871	100.0

Source: Tri-Conference Retirement Office, October 1993

Under the present understanding of religious orders in the Church in the United States, and without some significant changes, religious life may move into a period of exponential decline within the next eight to ten years. Such a decline cannot be explained easily. God's will, social and psychological forces, ecclesial changes, intellectual and economic challenges and perceptions of justice each influence the actual path that individual religious and congregations themselves have taken. In the midst of this decline, many religious congregations in the United States also exhibit vibrancy as they refine their purposes and respond to new ministerial challenges. Religious life, though radically different today than when the changes of Vatican II were mandated, reflects enormous generosity, ingenuity and satisfaction. Such is the nature of transforming grace when coupled with the richness of centuries-old traditions of the vowed life.

As members of apostolic orders and as psychologists, we began the Future of Religious Orders in the United States (FORUS) study to examine the factors that will enhance or disable the future of religious life in the United States This project, funded by Lilly Endowment Inc. of Indianapolis, was begun at Boston University and concluded at DePaul University in Chicago. We hoped to provide data by which religious themselves could examine where they are thirty years after the Council and, with the best of scientific information, shape their futures. Our goal was to examine religious life at three levels: the social institution, the religious congregation, and individual members.[2] We did so using a multi-trait, multi-method design that included six components which studied leaders of religious congregations, individual religious identified as uniquely caring, persons nominated in virtue of their vibrant sense of future, scholars and other experts in religious life and members of religious orders at large. The *National Survey*, perhaps the most publicized portion of this investigation, was distributed to a total of 9,999 individual religious. The distribution of those who comprised the population from which the sample was drawn is described by vocation and tradition in Table 3.

Table 3
Distribution of religious comprising FORUS population:
By vocation and tradition

Tradition	Sisters	Brothers	Priests	Vocation Total
Apostolic	79,276	6,459	12,468	98,203
Mendicant	8,951	1,330	4,594	14,875
Contemplative	1,692	211	41	2,144
Monastic	4,250	656	1,535	6,441
TOTAL	94,169	8,656	18,838	121,663

The broad conclusions of this study have been published in Origins[3] and in Review for Religious[4]. The scientific text, *The future of religious orders in the United States: Transformation and commitment,*[5] contains a comprehensive theoretical treatment of the results. And, finally, Focus, a series of three instructional videocassettes, applies the scientific results to practical ways of improving the leadership, spiritual and innovative capabilities of religious orders.

Our purpose here is not to restate the conclusions or to present a thorough statistical report. These sources are now available. Rather, our goals are:

1. to address with you some of the core issues that we believe should be addressed in the Synod on Religious Life; and

2. to identify the methods that are likely to support or inhibit the advancement of religious orders in the Church.

In relation to the goals of this Congress on the Religious Life, we want to explore the dynamics of effective religious orders, the generalized problem of role identity among religious, and the gap between the espoused values of religious life and their expression in the Church. But first, it is important to look at the dynamic processes that have and continue to shape the experience of religious in the United States.

Selected Background Issues

Several historical and sociological factors have influenced religious in the United States. Many of these factors have had significant impact not only on religious but also on the general population of the United States. Some factors are shared in similar forms by religious in many nations and cultures while others tend to be unique to the experience of religious in the United States.

Influence of Catholic Institutions

The United States immigrant population provided a clear focus for religious energy during the late nineteenth and early twentieth centuries. Religious congregations effectively established comprehensive health, education and social service delivery systems under girded by strong Catholic values. Stories abound of those religious, primarily from European countries, who journeyed to the United States with the special purpose of providing for both the corporal needs of their people and their spiritual welfare. These institutions also provided, at one point, the basis for a strong sense of corporate identity among religious.

During these early years, Catholics in the United States were largely isolated and frequently consciously excluded from American cultural and social influence. Over the years, Catholics in the

United States gained in social and political acceptance and influence and emerged, late in the twentieth century, as the most highly educated segment of their country's population. Religious women and men in the United States were, typically, even more highly educated. Concomitant with these shifts, religious separation yielded to cultural and economic assimilation. This assimilation, coupled with the federalization of delivery services and freedom from the cloistered life among apostolic religious, accompanied a shift in the value attributed to independent Catholic institutions.

While religious orders have had historically a profound influence in the institutional life of the Church and the United States, the past three decades have witnessed a steady decline in the number of Roman Catholic institutions. Table 4 shows the general trends for Catholic institutions in the United States, most of which were sponsored or staffed by religious orders.

Table 4
Roman Catholic institutional statistics:
1962 -1992

Institutions	1962	% Change 1972	1982	1992	1962-92
Parochial Elementary Schools	10,177	8,877	7,761	7,176	-29.5
Private Elementary Schools	453	329	318	266	-41.3
Diocesan High Schools	1,566	1,086	882	875	-44.1
Private High Schools	869	729	588	525	-39.6
Colleges and Universities	278	260	237	235	-15.5
Diocesan Seminaries	98	106	86	79	-19.4
Religious Seminaries	447	326	217	156	-65.1
General Hospitals	816	718	635	628	-23.0
Patients Treated	14,140,884	22,895,125	36,723,368	47,635,368	236.9

Source Official Catholic Directory 1962, 1972, 1982, and 1992.

In analyzing this decline, it is also fair to say that many religious orders were no longer willing or, in some instances, competent to serve in the specialized professions or in the administrative roles required to maintain such complex organizations. In addition, the emergence of the Catholic laity as full participants in the mission and ministry of the Church influenced the job market in Catholic institutions and limited the opportunities for work that religious would undertake.

Culture of individualism

After Vatican II, the cultural advantages of individualism also emerged as a strong force that would shape religious life. As much of the "American dream" rests on the assets and liabilities of a rugged individualism, so also among religious has the strength of individualism led to the assertion of individual rights over collective action, a certain privatization of one's role as a religious person and a desire to live apart from one's work, often independent of the group.

These movements were shaped as well by a diminishing institutional identity. Without collective centres of life and mission, individual members sought work where it was available. Gradually, and often subtly, membership drifted from once stable centres of ministerial energy. Frequently, religious found themselves, or positioned themselves, at the periphery. As this migration continued it was clear that many of the orders themselves lost a sense of clear purpose and that individuals, even members strongly upholding the corporate life and ministry, found it difficult to identify the collective work, or apostolate, of the congregation. For some congregations, the mission, transcending any locale, was sufficiently strong to be self-reinforcing. But for many others, the loss of stable work contexts and of the steady and predictable way of life, as well as the dispersion of members, led to isolation of some individuals and the dissipation of energies for the group.

Role of women

Although this Congress is addressing issues related primarily to male religious, the role of women religious in the United

States must be raised if only in a limited fashion. American society is powerfully shaped by an appreciation of the distinctive contribution of women. Women religious in the United States perhaps made their strongest contribution to society and the Church through the development of a comprehensive educational system unparalleled in size, impact and quality. So much of the strength of the Catholic laity today and the Church in general can be traced to the intense sacrifices and ingenuity of tens of thousands of these religious women. These institutions were actually spheres of authority that provided a potent context for formation, the exercise of power and collaboration and achievement. Although their presence in this and other arenas has decreased they often retain influence through various canonical forms of sponsorship.

Today women religious continue to make the second largest contribution, next to the federal government, to health, education and welfare through their sponsored works. Careful stewardship of sponsored institutions has enabled one order, for example, to alone contribute more than $298 million in free health care to the poor in 1992.

Religious women in our country have been highly effective leaders in contributing to the civil discourse on the rights and roles of women in a pluralistic society. They have led society in advocating for justice, calling the Church to examine its assumptions about women, while remaining with the Church that, from their perspective, seems to disregard their unique gifts and contributions. The institutional spheres of influence in Church life have in many ways been less important to many religious who experience direct service or pastoral ministry as critical to their sense of vocation. Institutions were seen to be depersonalizing and bureaucratic.

In addition, many religious women have had to seek employment outside of Church structures to provide financial subsidy for the orders to which they belonged. As the median age increases, the unfunded liability of retirement has increased dramatically. These orders have steadily gone about stabilizing their financial challenges without diminishing significantly their ministerial effectiveness.

Among and within the orders of women religious, considerable conversation occurs about the nature of consecrated life and mission. Thirty years of renewal have led to a spectrum of forms that defies easy categorization. If anything has become clear in this transition, it is that apostolic life and effectiveness in mission have become essential descriptors of their life.

Shifting paradigms of authority

Authority in religious life, as in the Church itself, is under considerable scrutiny by members of religious orders in the United States. While shifts in the understandings of authority began prior to Vatican II, the last three decades have witnessed a disillusionment with authority in American society in general and in the Church by virtue of its diminished impact. Specifically in religious orders, efforts to be more collegial and to practise the best of what members understood to be the requirements of subsidiarity and broad-based consultative decision making have become normative. Consensus is a preferred form of decision making, particularly for women religious, and their successes are further shaping more democratic and collegial forms of governance.

Monroe[6] described the nature of authority to be that of providing protection, direction and order for the sake of the group. The variable interpretations of consensus, subsidiarity, discernment and leadership have complicated understandings and sometimes diffused the conception of authority. This, coupled with the dynamics of individualism, limited understandings of obedience and the separation of one's spiritual life from the life of the Christian community, has made the exercise of authority extremely difficult.

Furthermore, the abuses of authority in the past have made individuals reluctant to endorse authority. Members of religious orders, in particular, are clear in their lowered respect for the magisterial authority of the Church and the U.S. hierarchy. Moreover, within their own congregations, the interpretations of authority vary widely.

An equally strong impact on authority has been experienced in the tendencies toward deconstructionism in American society. Deconstructionism refers to the re-examination of former structures that support a functionalist and hierarchical world view. As it has been experienced in the United States, deconstructionism also questions assumptions regarding external authority and traditional structures of obedience.

Shifting interpretative schemes

Evidence of the power these many influences have had on religious life manifests itself in the shift in language and interpretative schemes used by members of religious orders to describe their experience of God, the Church, the vowed life, and other aspects of their commitment. Interpretative schemes are cognitive constructs that map the meaning of personal life and value. The schemes change as language and meaning structures advance. This issue has been more significant than perhaps any single issue in shaping the experience of religious orders in the U.S.

The use of the vernacular in liturgy, feminist consciousness, and political and geopolitical rhetoric of the 1960s and 1970s shaped emerging generations more powerfully than doctrine advanced by the Church. Personal experience was validated in an era of social unrest, psychological inquiry, and increasing intellectual stature among religious. During these years, religious were quick to resist and rebuff attempts by anyone outside themselves to describe their experience. This was typified in their forceful reaction to the 1983 Essential Elements document.[7] Perceiving it as alien to their understanding and experience of religious life, many members of religious orders reacted strongly to unilateral attempts by external sources to define or describe their lives. In our research, we uncovered data indicating that the fundamental disagreement was twofold: the language did not correspond to the lived experience of religious in the United States and, secondly, religious were suspect of the Church's ability to guide them in a way congruent with their belief.

Thirty years of challenge – thirty years of grace. Today the 117,858[8] Sisters, Brothers, and religious Priests in the U.S. are reaping the fruits of these years of renewal as they elaborate new and fresh approaches to religious life. The suffering-death-resurrection dynamic of the Paschal Mystery has taken on profoundly personal significance as the great majority of religious reflect on both the severe price and their conviction of the appropriateness of renewal in revitalizing the mission. Those persons who continue to be members of religious congregations after grappling with the various dynamics mentioned thus far are, in general, more mature, more able to handle individual responsibility, and, our research would suggest, more actively engaged in effective Church ministry.

Framing the questions

The theme of this Congress, 'Consecrated Life Today: Charisms in the Church for the world', reflects the core challenges to religious life as identified in our research. We would frame the challenges as questions. First, is religious life a structure in the Church or a structure of the Church? In other words, are the charisms accountable to and controlled by the hierarchical authorities of the Church? Or, are they at some level exempt? Secondly, while remaining integrated with the vocations of the clergy and the laity, what is the unique contribution of religious to the life of the Church? Finally, since many communities emerged historically to serve the poor, the question arises: "Is the preferential option for the poor the most important distinguishing mission of religious life?" Allow us to elaborate upon facets of the questions drawn from our data that may be relevant in these deliberations.

Religious life: in or of the Church?

Molinari and Gumpel[9] were first to ask, "Is the consecrated way of life a structure in the Church or a structure of the Church?" The latter construct implies a singular structure of divine origin, namely a hierarchical one, while the former implies the existence of multiple structures in the Church. At the core of this distinction is the degree to which the hierarchical structure governs the pneumatic components, typically understood to be the structures of religious orders in the Church. The former canonical distinctions that located religious structurally in the Church, for instance, as the "state of perfection", provided a vastly different sense of identity than *Lumen Gentium* which states that from the point of view of the divine and hierarchical structure of the Church, the religious state of life is not an intermediate one between the clerical and lay states. Rather, the faithful of Christ are called by God from both these states of life so that they may enjoy this particular gift in all the life of the Church and thus each in his own way can forward the saving mission of the Church.[10]

Embodied in these linguistic shifts are both subtle and profound alterations of identity which, however intentional or unintentional, have had the effect of dispersion of identity among various populations of religious orders.

Our second question, "what is the unique contribution of religious life to the Church?" is related to role clarity. This is one of the most compelling issues to be addressed by religious orders in the United States. Role clarity operates at two substantive levels. First, at the level of the social institution, it pertains to the extent to which religious life is seen as contributing uniquely to the life and the mission of the Church when compared with the laity and clergy. Secondly, the concept of role clarity refers to the individual religious' perceived level of understanding concerning his or her purpose or function in the Church.

Religious life as a social institution. Religious life operates as a social institution within the Church and society. By social institution we refer to its distinctive attributes, outcomes and life-style. Religious orders have boundaries that make them relatively stable over time and rather reluctant to change. With the initiative of Vatican II inviting religious congregations to up-date in accord with their charisms and the signs of the times, religious orders embarked on a path which, according to organizational research, is accompanied by a series of predictable events and powerful dynamics. The organization authorizes change with some clear end state in mind. Movement begins, boundaries and normative policies shift and, after a protracted period of change, stabilization of organizational forms occurs.

In religious orders, however, the trend since Vatican II has been for the range of interpretations about the fundamental nature of religious life to widen rather than to stabilize. The previously well-defined apostolic traditions have been largely homogenized, boundaries continue to blur and, despite the strong contributions by canonists to distinguish societies of apostolic life and institutes of consecrated life, such distinctions have had little practical consequence to either. Many women and men religious, for example, increasingly describe themselves as "lay persons with vows who choose to live in community" and who are otherwise no different from their married or single peers who are not members of religious orders. We believe the lack of meaningful and clear distinctions has led to confusion.

If the forms of religious life were envisioned by the Council, they remain to be articulated. The transition to new forms has evolved to the point that some monastic groups, for instance, are practically indistinct from apostolic congregations. And equally common, many apostolic orders continue with monastic practices rather than develop a distinctive apostolic spirituality and life-style. Yet, in some contexts, the efforts to clarify organizational forms has led to revitalization of spirituality in mission. Tables 5 and 6 suggest some of the identity concerns by vocation and age groups.

Table 5
Views of religious life
Percent of agreement by vocation

Item	Vocation	Level of agreement (%)		
		Agree	Neither	Disagree
Religious life is a	Sister	67.2	23.6	9.2
permanent	Brother	76.9	16.6	6.6
element in the Church.	Priest	78.0	15.8	6.2
Religious life is	Sister	26.6	9.0	64.4
not as important	Brother	29.1	9.9	61.0
as it once was to	Priest	28.3	8.2	63.5
the Church.				
My life as a religious	Sister	72. 6	13.8	13.6
is more meaningful to	Brother	61.7	20.6	17.7
me today than it was	Priest	61.9	19.5	18.6
in the past.				
Women religious are				
essentially lay women	Sister	59.4	11.6	29.0
who choose to live	Brother	59.1	13.7	27.2
the common life and	Priest	44.8	15.2	40.0
to profess vows.				
Religious Brothers are				
essentially lay men	Sister	58.7	21.8	19.5
who choose to live	Brother	67.6	7.2	25.2
the common life and	Priest	48.8	13.1	38.2
to profess vows.				
In my experience as a	Sister	40.5	40.9	18.5
religious, I see that	Brother	38.1	29.8	32.0
there is seldom, if ever,	Priest	65.0	9.1	25.8
any real conflict for men				
religious between being				
a member of a congregation				
and being an effective Priest				

Table 6
Views of religious life
Percent of agreement by age group

Item	Age group	Level of agreement (%) Agree	Neither	Disagree
Religious life is a	19-45	69.5	21.1	9.4
permanent element to	46-60	68.8	21.3	9.8
the Church.	61-73	74.2	18. 8	7.1
	74-96	76.9	19.0	4. 1
Religious life is not as	19-45	25.9	10.6	63.4
important as it once was	46-60	32.0	7.8	60.2
to the Church.	61-73	26.3	9.0	64.6
	74-96	23.8	9.6	66.5
My life as a religious is	19-45	60.1	23.6	16.3
more meaningful to me	46-60	65.8	16.3	18.0
today than it was in the past.	61-73	68.0	16.0	16.0
	74-96	77.9	10.9	11.2
Women religious are	19-45	52.0	13.9	34.1
essentially lay women	46-60	59.8	12.1	28.1
who choose to live the	61-73	52.4	13.3	34.4
common life and to	74-96	57.7	12.7	.29.6
profess vows				
Religious Brothers are	19-45	54.3	13.5	32.2
essentially lay men	46-60	60.9	15.6	23.5
who choose to live the	61-73	55.8	16.9	27.3
common life and to	74-96	61.4	19.0	19.6
profess vows.				
In my experience as a	19-45	33.5	27.4	39.0
religious, I see that	46-60	41.4	30.1	28.5
there is seldom, if ever,	61-73	53.0	31.3	15.8
any real conflict for	74-96	60.4	30.3	9.3
men religious between being				
a member of a congregation				
and being an effective Priest.				

The individual religious and role clarity. As the Church gave a compelling mandate to laity to assume their rightful role as members of the Christian community and expanded the call to holiness in explicit ways to the entire Church, a comparably clear mandate for religious identity was not evident. When religious were asked to undertake the serious study of their founders and charism and to adapt to the times constitutionally and ministerially, the desired end state was not imagined. Thus, not surprisingly, the mandate for change has in part legitimated change as a normative condition. As a result, while some orders have a clear sense of identity and mission to which members respond excitedly, others are adrift.

Our data indicates that a significant proportion of religious in the United States, particularly women and those younger in age, indicate that they do not have a clear understanding of their purpose or function in the Church today. Percentages may be found in Tables 7 and 8.

Table 7
High, moderate and low role clarity:
Percent by vocation

Role clarity	Sisters	Brothers	Priests
Low	33.1	24.3	22.2
Moderate	12.3	10.6	9.4
High	54.6	65.1	68.4

Table 8
High, moderate and low role clarity:
Percent by age group

Role clarity	19-45	46-60	61-73	74-96
Low	37.5	33.2	24.3	17.0
Moderate	10.6	10.2	11.7	12.1
High	51.9	56.6	64.0	70.9

In considering the effects of low role clarity, research indicates that ambivalence regarding one's role can lead to anxiety, reduced ability to meet role requirements, decreased ministerial satisfaction, lower trust and self-confidence, an increased sense of futility and a greater propensity to leave a religious order.

Our data indicates religious experience each of these states in varying degrees. Ultimately, the lack of clarity among U.S. Religious may contribute to further diminishment in both numbers and vitality.

Roles are controlled by at least two factors: the expectations of those affected by the role and the context within which the role is lived. Broad-based dialogue among religious, the laity and the clergy will help to identify the uniqueness of religious life in the Church. Addressing the context within which religious life in the United States is lived is far more complex at this time in history. The larger frame of institutions which practically controlled or at least supported the role has grown progressively smaller. As a result, the social role is less evident. Similarly, without the pervasive institutions to both contain and elaborate the identity, the question of corporate focus and mission become more salient

Religious have in many instances been assimilated into the diocesan structures. It seems that as the parish has become identified increasingly as the primary locus of ecclesiology, religious orders have been assimilated into that context. While this is not necessarily an undesirable end for some, it raises the question of the uniqueness of religious life in the Church, of the structural alignment with the diocesan Church and what, if anything, should characterize the life and missionary efforts of, to use the canonical categories, societies of apostolic life and institutes of consecrated life.

As apostolic religious are assimilated increasingly into closer alliance with either the diocesan clergy or the laity, their distinctive impact may be diminished. Already in the United States there exist loosely federated congregations of women with vague membership boundaries that promise to evolve toward quasi-secular forms such as the YWCA or the Salvation Army. Further demise of a charismatic presence of religious could move toward what some would call the "protestantization" of the roles in the Church precisely at a time when the Protestant denominations are examining the need for structures whereby religious virtuosi can be identified and supported.

The stress accompanying role transitions produces various reactions. These reactions can include an inclination to mimic old roles, to compartmentalize conflicting life spheres, or to engage in passive or active withdrawal. The response chosen is likely to depend on the perceived legitimacy of the new role, respect for those advancing the role, the personal capacity to implement the role and the existence of a context or form of life that corresponds to the mission. The combined satisfaction of the meaningfulness of the role and corresponding life-style can yield role fulfilment. While seemingly paradoxical, the findings suggest that involving religious themselves in the clarification process, including those alienated and lower in role clarity, may lead to a resolution of both role ambiguity and conflict among themselves and with others in the Church.

Resolving these role issues will be difficult. Several factors should be kept in mind in deliberating on these matters. First, the data indicates that lower clarity among some groups of religious may be a function of a high degree of alienation from the Church as indicated by their increasingly diminished respect for the magisterial authority of the Church due, in part, to the past abuses of ecclesiastical authority. Others believe that the primary cause of the unravelling of religious life is the result of limited vision among the hierarchy as to the unique gift that religious life is to the Church. Tables 9 and 10 present some of the data suggesting significant alienation from the hierarchy but neither resentment about nor a desire to retreat from the clear role of the laity in the Church. Religious are clear that they want to determine their future and that any external influence will not be received easily. While curious to some in light of the above, religious in the United States do remain committed strongly to the Church's mission and want to assist in shaping its future.

Table 9
Relationships with other segments of the Church:
Percent of agreement by vocation

| Item | Vocation | Level of Agreement (%) | | |
		Agree	Neither	Disagree
What happens in the	Sister	75.9	13.3	10.8
institutional Church	Brother	71.8	15.1	13.0
is very important to me.	Priest	82.8	9.3	7.9
My respect for the	Sister	26.0	28.9	45.1
Magisterium of the Church	Brother	21.8	36.2	42.0
is more than it was when	Priest	30.0	33.1	36.9
I took my vows.				

In general, members of the laity are easy to work with.	Sister	74.9	21.1	4.0
	Brothers	76 6	18.9	4.5
	Priest	79.3	15.0	5.4
In general it is easy to work with the hierarchy in the Church.	Sister	31.4	24.3	44.3
	Brother	37.2	28.7	34.1
	Priest	47.3	22.7	29.9
In general, there is conflict between religious and the laity.	Sister	5.2	18.3	76.5
	Brother	8.7	22.3	69.0
	Priest	6.0	14.6	79.5
In general, there is conflict between religious and the hierarchical Church.	Sister	42.1	30.0	27.9
	Brother	30.8	33.2	36.0
	Priest	24.4	29.0	46.6
In general, members of the laity have a clear picture of what religious do.	Sister	11.6	20.8	67.6
	Brother	13.5	18.0	68.4
	Priest	10.1	19.0	70.9
In general, members of the Church hierarchy have a clear picture of what religious do.	Sister	19.7	29.5	59.8
	Brother	22.9	24.9	52.1
	Priest	22.6	25.0	52.5
It is necessary for religious to work together with laity so that the mission of the Church can be accomplished.	Sister	95.8	3.3	0.8
	Brother	93.0	5.2	1.8
	Priest	94.5	3.8	1.7
It is necessary for religious to work together with the hierarch of the Church so that the mission of the Church can be accomplished.	Sister	77.9	13.1	9.0
	Brother	81.7	12.8	5.5
	Priest	89.2	6.2	4.6
The institutional Church must clarify the role of religious for religious life to remain viable.	Sister	36.9	24.3	38.8
	Brother	45.8	23.7	30.4
	Priest	39.5	26.7	33.8
The bishops of the Church should be influential in determining the future of religious life.	Sister	20.7	23.9	55.4
	Brother	24.1	24.3	51.6
	Priest	24.5	23.6	51.9

Table 10
Relationships with other segments of church
Percent of agreement by age group

Item	Age group	Level of agreement (%) Agree	Neither	Disagree
What happens in the institutional Church is very important to me.	19-45	64.9	18.2	16.9
	46-60	68.8	14.8	16.4
	61-73	85.1	9.8	5.1
	74-96	90.2	7.4	2.3
My respect for the Magisterium of the Church is more than it was when I took my vows.	19-45	15.2	32.4	52.4
	46-60	15.7	27.9	56.4
	61-73	32.3	32.1	35.5
	74-96	45.7	35.4	18.9
In general, members of the laity are easy to work with.	19-45	81.2	15.0	3.8
	46-60	78.9	17.4	3.7
	61-73	74.1	20.2	5.6
	74-96	70.5	24.2	5.3
In general, it is easy to work with the hierarchy in the Church.	19-45	24.2	22.3	53.5
	46-60	26.1	22.2	51.7
	61-73	44.0	27.2	28.7
	74-96	56.1	28.9	14.9
In general, there is conflict between religious and the laity.	19-45	7.6	16.6	75.7
	46-60	6.2	16.0	77.8
	61.73	5.1	19.8	75.1
	74-96	5.6	20.7	73.8
In general, there is conflict between religious and the hierarchical Church.	19-45	43.0	28.7	28.2
	46-60	43.5	28.2	28.4
	61-73	29.6	31.7	38.8
	74-96	20.7	34.4	44.8
In general, members of the laity have a clear picture of what religious do.	19-45	10.1	15.2	74.7
	46-60	10.6	17.0	72.4
	61-73	10.8	20.2	69.0
	74-96	16.4	28.1	55.6
In general, members of the Church hierarchy have a clear picture of what religious do.	19-45	15.5	19.1	65.3
	46-60	13.7	17.7	68.7
	61-73	22.8	26.1	51.1
	74-96	36.2	29.4	34.4

It is necessary for religious to work together with the laity so that the mission of the Church can be accomplished.	19-45	95.6	3.5	0.9
	46-60	95.0	3.7	1.3
	61-73	94.7	3.7	1.6
	74-96	94.1	4.7	1.2
It is necessary for religious to work together with the hierarchy of the Church so that the mission of the Church can be accomplished.	19-45	76.2	14.1	9.7
	46-60	77.3	13.4	9.4
	61-73	85.0	9.4	5.6
	74-96	89.4	7.7	2.8
The institutional Church must clarify the role of religious for religious life to remain viable.	19-45	76.2	23.9	45.9
	46-60	32.2	23.9	45.4
	61-73	43.7	26.2	30.1
	74-96	55.4	27.9	16.8
The bishops of the Church should be influential in determining the future of religious life.	19-45	16.4	20.2	63.4
	46-60	15.7	19.7	64.6
	61-73	24.9	27.7	47.5
	73-96	36.1	29.5	34.4

Commitment to working with the poor, vowed life and prayer

This section addresses briefly three clusters of attitudes relating to service of the poor, the vows and patterns of prayer. They are offered for consideration since they are viewed as powerfully shaping identity.

The leadership conferences of religious in the U.S. identified prophetic witness and a contemplative attitude as two dynamic components that will transform religious life. For many religious, one of the unique expressions of prophetic witness is found in their commitment to the poor. With this awareness we explored the extent to which the "preferential option for the poor" was viewed as the focal identity of religious. The data suggests a gap between what is espoused and what is real. A moderate percentage of religious do not intend to work with the poor even though they believe that doing so is somehow important. Interestingly, the younger religious are more likely to intend to work with the poor than the older members.

Table 11
Working with the poor:
Percent of agreement by vocation

| | | Level of agreement (%) | | |
Item	Vocation	Agree	Neither	Disagree
Although there is	Sister	28.2	16.3	55.5
increasing talk about	Brother	36.0	18.7	45.2
religious working with	Priest	31.8	17.9	50.3
the poor, I feel little				
commitment to that.				
I feel adequately	Sister	41.1	21.6	37.3
prepared to work with	Brother	39.2	24.1	36.7
the poor.	Priest	45.4	21.9	32.7

Table 12
Working with the poor:
Percent of agreement by age group

| | | Level of agreement (%) | | |
Item	Age Group	Agree	Neither	Disagree
Although there is	19-45	26.5	16.0	57.5
increasing talk about	46-60	30.7	14.7	54.6
religious working with	61-73	33.3	19.0	47.7
the poor, I feel little	74-96	32.2	20.8	46.9
commitment to that.				
I feel adequately	19-45	43.7	20.1	36.3
prepared to work with	46-60	41.4	18.1	40.5
the poor.	61-73	39.9	23.8	35.3
	74-96	41.9	27.8	30.3

We interpret these findings in several ways. The ideal outpaces the action and the intention. Secondly, perhaps the identity of religious is not so isomorphic. In other words, perhaps all religious orders are not intended to have such a singular focus on the poor. The charisms of the Church have always emerged in response to ever-intensifying need, but the needs understood, perhaps, more broadly.

Furthermore, the debate in the United States between mission and consecration has at its centre this concern with a focus on the poor. Many apostolic religious believe they are consecrated by mission, specifically in service to the poor.[11] They believe that the action of God is most evident in mission.

The durability of commitment is also an issue. Considering the population as a whole, fewer than half (42%) of those surveyed indicated their belief that permanent commitment will be normative in the future. Several dynamics since Vatican II help to explain the population's ambivalence about permanency. First, alternative forms of membership are evolving to allow temporary commitment or affiliate membership. Secondly, they have witnessed constant resignation among their members. It may be that those who believe permanency is not expected may simply be making their judgement based on the actual practice of the significant proportion of the population who have exited over the past 30 years.

In addition, questions have surfaced regarding the role of the classical vows of poverty, chastity and obedience. For example, many who hold strongly to the view that consecration precedes mission often see these traditional vows as non-negotiable. Others, however, do not. Those holding this latter view often suggest alternative vows, for instance of solidarity, cosmic reverence and creativity,[12] as most strongly relating to the mission.

Table 13
Beliefs concerning vows and permanency:
Percent of agreement by vocation

Item	Vocation	Level of agreement (%)		
		Agree	Neither	Disagree
The vows have been a	Sister	75.1	18.7	6.2
great source of freedom	Brother	67.8	21.8	10.4
for me.	Priest	67.3	21.9	10.8
I believe that in the future	Sister	19.8	39.6	40.6
other vows will substitute	Brother	17.8	28.9	53.3
for the traditional vows of	Priest	13.8	25.6	60.7
poverty, chastity and obedience.				

In the future, temporary commitment will be the norm for religious life.	Sister	21.7	40.3	38.1
	Brother	20.8	32.7	46.5
	Priest	13.6	31.8	54.6
In the future, lifelong commitment for religious life will be the norm for religious life	Sister	33.9	40.9	25.2
	Brother	45.4	34.4	20.2
	Priest	56.1	30.1	13.8

Table 14
Beliefs concerning vows and permanency:
Percent of agreement by age group

		Level of agreement (%)		
Item	Age group	Agree	Neither	Disagree
The vows have been a great source of freedom for me.	19-45	64.2	24.6	11.1
	46-60	64.9	23.7	11.5
	61-73	76.5	17.8	5.7
	73-96	82.8	13.1	4.1
I believe that in the future other vows will substitute for the traditional vows of poverty, chastity and obedience.	19-45	19.2	27.7	53.1
	46-60	21.3	35.4	43.3
	61-73	16.0	35.0	49.0
	74-96	13.2	36.3	50.5
In the future, temporary commitment will be the norm for religious life.	19-45	19.6	30.0	50.4
	46-60	21.3	35.7	43.0
	61-73	19.5	38.9	41.5
	74-96	15.8	41.2	43.0
In the future, lifelong commitment for religious life will be the norm for religious life.	19-45	46.4	31.9	21.6
	46-60	38.5	36.5	25.0
	61-73	40.9	39.2	20.0
	74-96	45.1	38.8	16.1

But how do those currently living the vows regard the discipline of the vowed life? When asked about the meaningfulness and difficulty of living the vowed life, male religious, overall, indicated that chastity was most difficult and least meaningful. Women religious reported that poverty was most difficult and chastity most meaningful. Ongoing formation in the vows in the context of U.S. culture is an obvious necessity.

Table 15
Meaningfulness and difficulty of vows:
Rankings by vocation

Vocation	Rank	Meaningful	Difficult
Sister	1	Chastity	Poverty
	2	Obedience	Obedience
	3	Poverty	Chastity
Brother	1	Obedience	Chastity
	2	Chastity	Obedience
	3	Poverty	Poverty
Priest	1	Obedience	Chastity
	2	Poverty	Obedience
	3	Chastity	Poverty

Table 16
Meaningfulness and difficulty of vows:
Rankings by age group

Age Group	Rank	Meaningfulness	Difficulty
19-45	1	Poverty	Chastity
	2	Chastity	Obedience
	3	Obedience	Poverty
46-60	1	Obedience	Chastity
	2	Chastity	Obedience
	3	Poverty	Poverty
61-73	1	Obedience	Obedience
	2	Chastity	Poverty
	3	Poverty	Chastity
74-96	1	Obedience	Obedience
	2	Chastity	Poverty
	3	Poverty	Chastity

Tables 17 and 18 provide data regarding members' general practice in patterns of prayer, including participation in Eucharistic liturgy as well as private and group prayer. While the survey format did not allow for the investigation of causal relationship, our research did surface a strong positive correlation between frequency of prayer in each of the forms presented below and role clarity.

Table 17
Prayer patterns:
Frequency percents by vocation

Item	Vocation	Daily	Frequency (%) Several times a week	Once a week	Less than once a week	Seldom or never
Over a typical week,	Sister	62.8	28.4	7.3	0.7	0.7
how often is	Brother	58.2	33.9	6.6	1.1	0.3
Eucharistic liturgy	Priest	69.7	27.3	2.6	0.4	0.0
a part of your routine ?						
How often do you	Sister	81.5	14.2	2.0	0.9	0.7
pray or	Brother	67.2	22.3	4.6	2.2	3.0
meditate privately?	Priest	69.7	22.5	3.0	2.6	1.9
Other than celebration	Sister	52.1	24.1	5.9	10.6	4.7
of the Eucharist,	Brother	56.5	22.4	4.7	7.7	7.3
how often do you	Priest	41.8	23.7	9.8	13.5	9.4
pray with a group?						

Table 18
Prayer patterns:
Frequency percents by age group

Item	Age group	Daily	Frequency (%) Several times a week	Once a week	Less than once a week	Seldom or never
Over a typical	19-45	44.6	43.7	9.5	1.5	0.7
week, how often is	46-60	50.4	38.9	9.1	1.0	0.7
Eucharistic liturgy	61-73	75.2	21.0	3.3	0.2	0.2
a part of your routine?	74-96	87.7	10.7	1.3	0.1	0.2
How often do you	1945	62.3	28.0	4.8	2.0	2.2
pray or meditate	46 60	68.5	22.4	3.7	2.6	2.0
privately?	61-73	82.2	13.4	1.7	0.9	1.2
	74-96	90.8	7.2	1.0	0.3	0.4
Other than celebration	19-45	49.0	26.8	7.7	8.6	6.2
of the Eucharist,	46-60	42.3	27.5	7.6	13.0	7.9
how often do you pray	61-73	51.9	22.0	6.2	11.4	6.1
with a group?	74-96	65.0	15.7	4.4	7.3	4.8

Transforming tradition

We believe that the factors that will most enable the transformation of the rich traditions of religious life are threefold. First, the formula of fidelity to purpose and responsiveness to absolute human need must be understood in the contemporary context. Secondly, religious congregations must focus their energies collectively toward mission. Finally, outstanding leadership must emerge to carry the process of transformation to completion.

Our research indicates that the orders that seem to be stabilizing in membership and direction are those that attend to two fundamental dynamics. First, they are faithful to their founding purpose. Secondly, and in some ways more importantly in this time, they are responsive to new and emerging human needs. Vatican II called all orders to attend to this latter dynamic in their process of *aggiornamento*. Responsiveness to absolute human need is an equally complex spiritual and organizational dynamic. As new forms of poverty, new populations of immigrants, unmet human needs and utter desperation among those who, for instance, are homeless or infected with the AIDS virus, emerge in society, what is the Church's response? What we observe is that orders that are indeed attentive to these and similar concerns in the external environment and willing to assess and alter current commitments with the intention of serving the most pressing needs are, indeed, increasing in internal cohesion around an intensified mission. Collaterally, they are often the groups that attract newer members. Responsiveness to need addresses the direct relevance of the charism to the world in which it is lived.

Literature of the last decade has invited us to "refound," "revitalize," and "give birth" to new expressions of religious zeal. Much of the literature speaks to the importance of vision in this process. It is probably true that all of our founders had some vision as the charism took shape. But in our age, we believe that "focus" may better describe the pointed, specific and strategic orientation required to intensify our action in mission. Vision has a nearly unlimited horizon and it often leads to vague outcomes. Charisms in the Church must be focused to have a measured effect, without which groups drift or feel ineffective in mission.

Part of the necessary focus relates to those distinctive attributes or competencies required in those called by God to religious commitment. Religious in the United States have been known

41

historically for their charity. Even today, the impulse to generosity has not been eclipsed among most. In order to examine this behaviour, we studied those who were identified by their fellow religious as extraordinarily caring.[13] These religious, known for their love of God and charismatic intensity, were found to have a rare profile. They engage in the life of another reflexively, moved by compassion and with little need to protect themselves from the discomfort of the immediate needs of others. As compared to typical caring people, they do not feel anxious in the face of suffering. While typical caring people attempt to alleviate human pain to minimize their own anxiety, the caring religious moves comfortably into the presence of another without the barriers of fear. This immediacy is born of trust and a view of authority that is benevolent. These religious are neither imposing nor avoidant. They are present in simple and direct ways. They are motivated by a love of God whose authority they experience as profoundly benevolent and by a selfless concern for others.

In addition to the profile of authentically caring people, we believed that articulating those qualities which marked excellence in leadership could also be helpful toward the advancement of religious life. By studying outstanding leaders to determine if there were core abilities, personal qualities and motives that brought leaders to focus on both the charism and pressing human needs in an effective manner, we were able to develop a profile of the competencies required to effectively lead religious congregations today.[14] This profile describes men and women grounded deeply in faith who consistently communicate the centrality of God in their lives. They have a high need to achieve personally and have a clear sense of the impact that the congregation could have. Moreover, they are characterized by objectivity and compassion

With all these attributes, the outstanding leaders do not have an exceptionally strong need to belong to the very groups they are attempting to lead, and yet they find meaning precisely in that context of faith, membership and impact. The outstanding leader has a clear vision of the future and successfully employs the means to both gain the support of the congregation for the direction and implement the decisions of the group.

Outstanding leaders, on the other hand, are rooted in an awareness that they act with, and on behalf of, God. They treat members as though they were equally responsible for the life of the

42

congregation yet do not compromise the clarity of their role as leaders. These leaders understand how to position the congregation strategically to be responsive to human needs, and they generally are granted authority by their members. Whether in apostolic, mendicant, monastic or contemplative congregations, outstanding leaders understand the importance of focus and a clear identity in order to transform the tradition with optimism and productivity among the members.

Conclusions

In this brief review of the FORUS project, we have attempted to frame the issues that our research suggests may be relevant to the Synod on Religious Life. The critical challenges relate to identity, focus in mission and leadership.

The orders exhibiting resilience in the United States context are those that are faithful to the founding purpose and responsive to absolute human need, defined broadly to include spiritual and physical deprivation. Changes since Vatican II have focused fundamentally on founding purpose and charism and less significantly on new forms of poverty and collective responses. Given the collateral decline in personnel during this 30 year period, religious have been forced to alter drastically their sponsoring relations to institutions.

Vital orders have resisted focusing solely on maintenance and decline. They have sought aggressively to implement a Gospel response to various needs commensurate with their resources. The key for both the apostolic and monastic vibrancy is focus. Such groups go about strengthening their respective missions systematically through planning with broad-based involvement of the members, a willingness to relinquish some ministries in order to go where they are being led, and a clear determination in the leader to have an impact. The categorical structure of societies of apostolic life and institutes of consecrated life do not seem to address yet adequately the perspective that the mission of both groups may be the same and that the "preferential option for the poor" relates in some way to the identity of both. Similarly, the traditional categories of the apostolic, mendicant, monastic and contemplative traditions do not reflect with specificity the self understanding of the members. In fact, when self-identifying their tradition on our national survey many who belong to groups defined historically as mendicant now define themselves as either apostolic or evangelical.

The research also indicates low role clarity among a fairly significant number of religious. The youngest among us are, percentage-wise, the least clear. The vocation of the religious woman is experienced as the least clear in the current Church environment, followed by that of the Brother and then the religious Priest. Lack of identity often leads to a blurring of membership categories, responsibility diffusion and a weakened sense of self-efficacy. Each of these issues becomes a serious threat to the vocation of the religious to the Church.

Effective leadership will be critical to the future of religious life. Leaders must advance Jesus Christ as the source and end of prophetic action and mystical awakening. With their own drive for making things better and a concern for impact, the generosity of members will be increasingly focused. Outstanding leaders expect more rather than less of their members, and provide the framework for constant expansion of the mission. Vision leads to a focused sense of purpose through careful planning so that congregations can actually effect what they intend. Narrowing the gaps between the espoused values of an order and their behaviour as organizations also can have a potent influence in transforming the rich tradition of religious orders in the Church.

NOTES

1. Throughout this text, use of "religious life", "religious orders" and "religious congregations" will include those members of and groups typically designated as institutes of consecrated life and societies of apostolic life. Furthermore, religious "orders" and "congregations" are used equivalently in this document.
2. A total of 816 congregations or provinces of congregations based in the United States participated in the *National Survey*. The groups accounted for the 121,439 individual religious considered in the random sample.
3. D.J. Nygren & M.D. Ukeritis. (1992). Research executive summary. Future of religious orders in the United States. *Origins*, 22 (15), 257-272.
4. D.J. Nygren & M.D. Ukeritis. (1993). Future of religious orders in the United States. *Review for Religious*, 52 (1), 6-55.
5. D.J. Nygren & M.D. Ukeritis. (1993). *The future of religious orders in the United States: Transformation and commitment.* Westport, CT: Praeger Publishers.

6. Personal communication at Leadership Panel Convening, April, 1991, Boston, MA.
7. Congregation for Religious and Secular institutes. (1983). Essential elements in the Church's teaching on religious life as applied to institutes dedicated to works of the apostolate, May 31, 1983: Vatican City.
8. *Official Catholic Directory*, 1993.
9. Molinari, SJ, & Gumpel, SJ. (1987). *Chapter VI of the Dogmatic Constitution "Lumen Gentium" on Religious Life*. Rome.
10. *Lumen Gentium* (1964), § 43.
11. N. Foley. (Ed). (1988). *Claiming our truth: Reflections on identity by United States women religious*. Silver Spring, MD; Leadership Conference of Women Religious.
12 . A. Kovats. (1992). Reflections on the vows from a cosmic/ecological perspective. *InFormation* (Silver Spring: Religious Formation Conference) *146*, (November/December 1992), 1-4.
13. D.J. Nygren & M.D. Ukeritis. (1993). The motivation of people who care. *The future of religious orders in the United States: Transformation and commitment*. Westport, CT: Praeger Publishers.
14. D.J. Nygren & M.D. Ukeritis. (1993). Religious leadership competencies. *Review for Religious, 52* (3), 390-417.

II.

The present reality of the religious life: Basic data on the evangelical life and mission

Fr Julian Lopez, SJ

INTRODUCTION:
A GOSPEL ATTITUDE IN ORDER TO CONTEMPLATE THE REALITY OF THE RELIGIOUS LIFE

We would like to ask you to approach this report on the "Reality of the Apostolic religious life" with a *"Gospel attitude"*, in order to be able to *listen* to it. The same attitude that we usually ask each family or religious congregation to adopt when we go to talk to them about the findings we have gathered on their life and mission, following one of our surveys.

We are asking you to adopt an attitude that is grounded on one of the great convictions of our faith: *God speaks to us through the facts of daily life and history* (it was through those daily events that Israel gradually discovered God). Jesus invited us to listen to what events tell us, and to read the "signs of the times", as Vatican II reminded us. For 28 years, D.I.S. (our 'Department of Sociological Research') has taken stock of the "facts of life" of over 200,000 religious men and women of different nationalities and from different continents. This interior approach to re-reading the facts relating to the lives of these religious men and women that we are about to examine in this report, seen in the light of the faith, will help us to listen to *what God is telling us*, and sometimes *what God is shouting at us*, through this information on the lives of the religious enumerated for the survey. And this attitude of faith is perhaps the best way of overcoming the prejudices which some people may sometimes have against using the science of sociology as a form of "mediation" to become acquainted with the wonderful and mysterious reality of the consecrated religious life.

The sources of our report

As we indicated earlier, the sources on which our report draws are the "facts of life" (attitudes, experiences, motivations, situations, difficulties, etc.) of over 200,000 religious men and women enumerated since 1965 on an ongoing basis, through *anonymous questionnaires* inviting them to reply with genuine and humble sincerity. One very important point must be borne in mind here: the first thing that D.I.S. does when setting out to study a religious congregation is to carry out *an open, written, consultation* with the religious concerned regarding the things that they themselves feel should be studied. For this consultation no questionnaire is used in advance; we let the religious tell us what they experience and what they feel to be the important points that we should be studying, expressing themselves in their own way, freely and spontaneously. D.I.S. has received thousands upon thousands of reports over the years, and in this free and ever new flow of communications from the religious we have learned, and are still learning, what the religious life is, what it does, and how it is experienced. Our Questionnaires simply set out the past experiences as they are expressed by the religious themselves, and the things which they are interested in knowing about and studying, in a sociological form.

The interviewees have all been religious, men and women, belonging to orders and congregations, most of them European foundations which subsequently spread beyond Europe and became established in all 5 continents, with religious provinces for indigenous vocations, some of which are extremely numerous. This has enabled us to find out about the life of religious in widely differing countries and cultures, and to identify the constants and differential variables.

We have selected the sociological data on the religious life that we are presenting here using a scientific criterion: we have used the data which, on account of the correlation coefficients of relevance to other fundamental facts about the religious life, emerge as being particularly significant. In other words, we have presented *the facts or data which make the religious life function, or which present it from functioning, in the manner of the Gospel*. It is evident that we have not been able to give all the fundamental data (in view of the time allocated to this paper). However, it does contain the most important findings that have emerged repeatedly across the years in surveys conducted on religious, and data which, because of variations across time, reflects the situations that have emerged as being most relevant to religious above all during the past five years. In both cases, all the data given here is sociologically sound, mostly on account of the consistency of occurrence, and because the same findings are generally repeated in many religious congregations, for both men and women.

What this sociological report on the religious life sets out to achieve

At this Congress we shall be examining the key issues of the religious life, from various points of view. This paper is intended to provide a framework through which to approach the real life situation of religious today. The angle from which the analysis is made is *sociological*, which is why we would like you to interpret it in the light of the faith.

As you all know, the sociologist studies reality, and the "facts of life" of a particular group: the facts which are both internal to the individual members, and external to them (in so far as they are affected by them). This is what we have being trying to do over the 28 years of studying the religious life: to try to understand how religious live as persons consecrated to God, to discover their great experiences, how they live together and how they relate to one another, what they do, how they work, how they carry out their evangelising mission, where their fears, difficulties and hopes lie, and how they see their future. In other words, we have endeavoured to become acquainted with what their life really is, in order to be able to support and assist these men and women who are a source of such great Gospel ferment in the life of the Church.

Now, the sociologist is concerned with the whole of reality, and seeks to "photograph" it as it is. This is one of the reasons why we normally use the stark and objective language of mathematics. Reality, for sociologists, equals 100. This means that 60% is a part of this reality, while the other 40% will be the other part of this reality. What is not of sociological relevance is negative, or pessimistic, while the other part is positive or optimistic. However this appraisal is not what constitutes the specific element in the sociologist's work. What is important to the sociologist is to ensure that *the facts are true*. He is concerned with the truth of the total reality and not only what is positive or negative. The reason we mention this is that at this time of "epoch-making night", as it has been called, and with today's sensitivities, in a period of marked changes followed by far-reaching upheavals, it seems that the only major things happening today are negative (just see what is happening in the mass media, and even at times in the Church's own communications). For the sociologist, positive data is as important as negative data, *provided that it is true*. What is important is to know reality as it is, with all its objective dimensions, in order to be able to act on that reality and try to transform it.

This knowledge of reality, within and outside the religious life, is acquired by our Team as a *means* of carrying out *a Gospel-oriented discernment*. For there can be no real discernment unless one knows the objective reality and truth about what is being discerned. In other words, we use the modern resources of social enquiry and research in order to study the facts of life of consecrated persons, with all their potential and their limitations, problems, needs, etc., Now for the believer, reality is total and whole *when the facts of life are enlightened by faith*. It is through faith, in discernment, that one discovers *God at work* and the paths of God for our future in these facts of our daily lives. This is the way in which we approach the internal and dynamic knowledge of the religious life (and this is the approach that we shall be taking in this paper). We shall be using a sociological methodology in order to become thoroughly acquainted with the situation that consecrated religious experience, as an essential means of carrying out true Christian discernment, seeking to listen to the "Word" which God is "speaking" to us in these facts of life.

This report on the Apostolic religious life is *a report which sets out to be conclusive and concrete. Conclusive*, because it claims to provide a systematic and synthetic account of all the main trends, which transcend a multitude of data, which repeatedly emerge in the religious belonging to the congregations we have surveyed. It is also intended to be *a practical report*, in the sense that it sets out these great realities which it has studied in *quantitative* terms as frequently and as far as possible, using percentages, which is the way in which these facts are expressed and the language which is used in order to be able to study them. Nevertheless these figures will not be the sum total of frequency of occurrence, but *experiential percentages* which are repeated so consistently in the various groups of religious we have studied, that they may be reliable constants of proven empirical value.

Through these conclusions, sometimes expressed in percentage terms, *real-life processes* emerge, and it is possible to see *the present reality of the Apostolic religious life* from within the dynamism of its faith and the new demands of the apostolic vocation of consecrated persons in the contemporary world.

The wealth and the limitations of the field surveyed

This report sets out some important facts that have been identified in relation to this large group of congregations that *wish to have a scientific knowledge of the reality of the interior life of their individual members and various groups and groupings,* in order to be able to grow in faithfulness to Our Lord and to his mission. We are referring here to religious congregations for men and women which we have studied, most of which are the main religious orders and congregations of pontifical right, for men and women, that have become internationally established. They are therefore an extremely valuable source of data on the religious life in the Church and in the world.

But this also implies a limitation. Our experience is mainly based on the congregations that are willing and keen to know their reality (setting aside all forms of dogmatism, ideology or facile intuition), and which have managed to overcome prejudices about the help that science is able to give them (in this particular case religious sociology) in existential terms. There are also congregations that are capable of reading the Word which God is speaking to them through the events that all their members are experiencing (which presupposes that the individual person is appreciated as such, and not so much in terms of the functions that people perform within the group or, to put it another way, it presupposes that they genuinely rely on "each of their members", and not only on their government). And they are also congregations that have already made progress along the path of discernment, seeking the light of Our Lord in the realities which they experience, and hence which underpin the decisions taken by their government, and their options, etc., in the light of reliable, scientific knowledge of their real-life situation as a group at any particular moment.

In view of this particular type of openness, we cannot extrapolate this data to apply to the other religious families that we do not know, and quite probably those other religious families do not know this data themselves, either. However we have recently been studying a large number of congregations that had formerly shown less readiness to open up, in human and theological terms, until very recently, but which have finally decided to use this means of becoming acquainted with the reality of their congregation as a result of a number of internal situations that have occurred (for life's events sooner or later affect the whole of the Apostolic religious life as well). This new experience has confirmed the great soundness and the existential impact of the values and factors that we have been discovering in our research across the years on these congregations. Sooner or later, these values and factors create a crisis which, if it is tackled, leads to a process of "vital growth" in the religious congregations.

1. CHANGE IN THE RELIGIOUS LIFE AS A RESPONSE TO A CHALLENGE: TO BE "MEANINGFUL" MEN AND WOMEN OF CHRIST AND HIS GOSPEL IN THE CONTEMPORARY WORLD

Over the past few decades the religious life has changed as a result of a difficult and tense process that has occurred in most congregations. But it has also been a process which has been full of Gospel impetus, realism and hopeful utopia, in the face of a challenge: the challenge of becoming meaningful men and women of Christ and his Gospel in the world and in society today.

It would take too long to describe all the stages in these real-life processes. But we must recall the human and social factors, or at least the most fundamental ones, in order to paint a complete picture of the present state of the religious life from a sociological viewpoint. We will examine a number of factors, both external and internal to the religious life, which have had a considerable effect on its present state, which will give us a better understanding of the enormous impact which social change has had and is still having on the religious life.

1.1. External factors: The changing scenario of mankind and its impact on the religious life

The changes that religious have experienced over recent years have not occurred in a vacuum, but have taken place in the "changing scenario" of a world undergoing accelerated transformation. As *Gaudium et Spes* noted, a great reality had been present within this process: the ecclesial community and the religious life within it, acting in solidarity with mankind and its history, has been affected by major changes. Everything that affects men and women has also affected the religious life and each of its members. The process of renewing the religious life, encouraged by Vatican II, took place against a human scenario that was being buffeted by continual and accelerated changes. Changes that have been described as "the awakening of a new civilisation, in terms of its breadth and universality". The religious life has been, as it were, a sounding box for this enormous change and has very largely experienced it too, and is still experiencing it, in its own flesh.

1.1.1. *The impact of a dynamic society in a constant state of flux, on the religious life which had defined itself as 'restored' in order to change no more*

In order to gain a better understanding of the shock and the impact of social change on the religious life, we must bear in mind the fact that after the French Revolution the religious life was restored, and acquired a new splendour. But this was done with a static and unchanging awareness of what the religious life really is. The result was that it defined itself by establishing, once and for all, what the religious life was and was to be; it canonised itself as a "state of perfection" and made its religious values and customs absolute in themselves. But the nineteenth century religious life did not realise how far it was under the influence of the social and religious values of its age, which were therefore relative, temporal and perishable.[1] Here is one concrete example: 90% of today's apostolic sisters in Spain belong to congregations founded between 1800 and 1929.[2] But that nineteenth century, in which such a great boost was given to the apostolic religious life for women, was unaware of the fact that it was designing women's evangelical consecration in terms of a sociological model of nineteenth century woman (and of nineteenth century man, too) which, by its very nature, was changeable and was soon to disappear before the great historic transformation that was to occur in the twentieth century.

The fact that the religious life is evidently experiencing the symptoms of human, social and religious change (and every real change inevitably creates traumas, pain and bewilderment) must be interpreted as a sign of life, and not of death, as it sometimes is. The changes that are taking place in consecrated men and women, in the way they live and relate to one another, and the way they work and perform their mission, are the vital reactions of the organic body of the religious life that wishes to continue living in a fruitful and meaningful way in the world, and not merely vegetate without hardly having anything to say to the men and women of today, because it lacks the vital force to spread and communicate the Gospel message.

And that is not all: just as we accept the great changes that are taking place in vital areas of society (for example, education, the family, business, etc.) to be normal and necessary to life in order for them to be able to survive and respond to the demands of change, we should consider it to be equally normal and not at all extraordinary that the religious life, as an entity which is, and is striving to be, evangelically meaningful to society, should also be implementing changes in a similar way, and of similar importance, to those that are being or which still have to be implemented, by the institutions that we have just called vital social entities.

These changes and transformations are the ones which are inculturating the religious life into our world, and they are making the religious life comprehensible to mankind (or could do so, if they really wish to) just as Jesus inculturated his "message" into the world and made it comprehensible to his own age. Many religious, as we have often seen from their reports, see these changes as stemming from the vital need to be brothers and sisters of the whole of mankind which has already been changed and is changing constantly; a mankind to which they feel committed to accompany with a form of religious life which is understood and meaningful in Gospel terms for a society which is constantly evolving.

1.1.2. *What change is not, and what it means to change vitally*

In order to discern which individual religious and which Religious institutes have really changed in order to be Gospel "signs" to the contemporary world, we must remember what change is in life, and what it means for a human being or a human group or for an institution such as the religious life to change vitally. Because change is deeper and more transforming than one imagines, and less spectacular than people sometimes expect. Change does not mean taking on new external things, and society's latest innovations. One can go on living surrounded by the most modern facilities and use them, but without changing a single thing; what radically transforms men and women, institutions or society and the religious life, is the change made to the *hierarchy or scale of values.*

Let us take a few concrete examples with which we are familiar in the religious life, and which D.I.S. has discovered abundantly in all of its surveys, in relation to what it means to change the scale of values and what happens when this axiological scale does change. When a religious community holds the person as its paramount value it sets itself completely apart from any other community which places work as its primary community value on the scale of values, judging from the way it works and lives. When continuing (or ongoing) formation becomes a priority value on the scale of values of a religious brother or sister, that religious becomes a totally different person from any other whose scale of values continuing formation is a secondary, and not a fundamental value. When a congregation takes its mission love for the poor as its primary value undergoing aggiornamento, it is obliged to change virtually everything (formation, type of work, institutions and activities, etc.) in comparison what the same congregation had formerly done when it used to practise indiscriminate charity to all as the primary value of its mission. These few examples show the transforming power of change in a scale of values, while at the same time they topple the myth of change as something spectacular. For it is not so much a matter of external aspects changing, but of an internal transformation of the values of the individual persons and groups concerned.

Unless the scale of values is transformed, and if one only lives through a new experience of changing external facts and realities, what is "new" will be used out of pure convenience, but there will not be any real change; if the scale of values of individual persons and Institutions remains intact, one cannot talk about any personal or collective change; the setting may change which, in our case, is the background surrounding the religious life, but the religious or their congregations will continue living on the sidelines of this world, as distant alien beings.

1.2. The configuration of Religious institutes and their members as the result of change

What does the data on religious reveal? Has the religious life changed in order to make it more evangelically meaningful to our brothers and sisters in today's world?

Our Department, the D.I.S., has thoroughly analysed the correlations between the essential factors of the religious life repeated across the years, and in a large number of congregations, in order to eliminate randomness or coincidence, and has noted the changes taking place and their effects on Religious institutes, considered collectively, and in religious brothers and sisters taken individually. Its analysis of the data has brought out the factors or the means which lead or cause consecrated persons to change, and consequently being about changes to the Religious institutes to which they belong. By analysing and weighing up these means and factors affecting consecrated persons, it is possible to estimate, to a certain extent, the real change that has occurred in one's own Religious institute.

When applying all this data to concrete reality (and this involves trying to simplify complicated analysis processes) we have to express it in terms of institutional and personal typologies. The typologies for the Religious institutes are: those that have accepted change and taken it on board, those whose attitudes to change are ambiguous, and those that are not accepting change. These three typologies also apply to individual religious. The means whereby individual religious undergo change can be summarised in terms of an attitude: *the attitude adopted by the religious to continuing formation*, which is manifested and takes shape in terms of five specific dimensions: human/personal, social, theological, catechetical and congregational formation.

1.2.1. Institutional typologies and change

A. Religious institutes that have accepted and taken on board the historical changes of our age, in terms of their evangelical and apostolic life option:

These Religious institutes have accepted renewal without difficulties or tension, with an attitude of sincere receptiveness and out-reach, and genuine Gospel-inspired depth and hope. They have opened up to renewal on the basis of a healthy and critical understanding of historical reality and for evangelical reasons. Christ was also embodied into his age, and everything that was human, in its people, in its history... These congregations have accepted the risks which this attitude implies, and they have tried to live the ascesis that the new life was demanding of them with a sense of responsibility. They have overcome their fear of the difficulties that this process entailed, and the internal tensions that arose in their own religious families, and they have managed to overcome a lack of understanding in their environment which – significantly – frequently came from Christians belonging to a higher social class than theirs, and from official circles that were far removed from their apostolic religious life. They generously accepted the demands which the new situation was making on their life, frequently requiring them to make a break with the past; this meant endeavouring to discover the call of the Faith in the present situation, which was so different from anything they had known in the past, in order to live through an authentic "exodus", to leave the place in which they had become settled for so long, in response to the demands of the Gospel. They have taken to this path with this profound Gospel attitude of persons who believe and who know that they will encounter the presence of God in history; men and women who discover the call of his living Word in the "signs of the times", and in the encouragement they have received from the conciliar Church to undertake this renewal.

B. Congregations which have "adjusted" to *change*:

We are using this expression "adjust" to indicate the attitude taken up by some religious congregations that have made the effort to "adjust" to some of the new realities and situations. This has been reflected in their rules and legislation, etc., but it has not always percolated down to bring about the deep-seated cultural, religious, etc., change that these changes demand; they have therefore failed to tailor the formation of their members to meet the new Gospel demands of their consecration in the newly arising situations and realities. In these congregations the members live with a greater "permissiveness", and have made their organisation of life and contacts with other people, etc., more flexible. But the basis of their life, and the theological framework underpinning it, is still the same as before. Their religious and theological formation and their vision of reality have not changed, with the result that they live their new situation with a certain internal contradiction, frequently giving rise to ambivalence and bewilderment. They are unable to see and accept the human and/or Gospel motivation underlying the new situations, and they find it difficult to take a positive attitude to dealing with them. The result is that they do not live with enthusiasm, because enthusiasm stems from a personal, meaningful, Gospel motivation, and from a sincere discernment of the signs of the times in which the hand of God is discovered in history. These congregations create the impression that it is necessary to grow resigned to living through rough times which, with the help of Our Lord, will eventually pass.

C. Congregations that have "shielded themselves" against *change*:

Lastly, there are religious families *that have shielded themselves against change*, that have rejected it and been incapable of acquiescing to it. They have viewed change as a slackening of the religious life. They have not been able to understand cultural and historic change, or the need and possibility of bearing Gospel-inspired and evangelising witness within this new culture, as religious men and women who have committed themselves to Our Lord. They had made certain temporal values, and/or certain ways of living their lives, or types of spirituality, etc., into absolutes, not realising that they belong to a totally different cultural and ecclesial situation; and they have been unable to grow in the experience and expression of their faith and vocation in a more "aggiornato" form. They have gone onto the defensive, warding off change, new human and social values, the equality of all human beings, the new image of women, the new approach of theology, of spirituality, of new forms of Gospel presence etc., But despite their resistance to change, these congregations have also been affected by it.

1.2.2. Renewal experienced in communion, or in a state of tension?

These three types of situations have been caused by the attitude on the part of individual persons and officials of the congregations. In cases where individual members and their officials have become sensitised in the same direction, the congregation has undergone experienced its transformation (or its static state) with a certain internal consistency, but not without tensions and difficulties. Subgroups have always been formed, varying in the size of their membership, taking up a range of different reactions to the new challenges of life. These subgroups have expressed themselves in various ways, using the institutional channels available to them.

However, when government officials and/or individual religious have adopted polarised contrasting positions, the internal conflicts and tensions have been more intense and have created a sense of acute hopelessness, breaking down the communion of the congregation, wearing people down, and causing others to leave the religious life, etc., On the other hand, renewal has been experienced in a more positive manner, albeit not without difficulties and tension, when genuine dialogue and integrating relations have been established in the same direction, between government (ordinary government at various levels, or extraordinary government, chapters, etc.) and the religious themselves. In other words, when both sides have been capable of identifying the new values, updating the formation of their members so that they are enabled to take on these new values, and have encouraged their congregation to be concerned to undertake evangelical renewal in terms of their commitment of faith and their charism.

When the government of a congregation has opened up and has encouraged this process, the congregation has grown better in a life of new evangelical depth, "updated" in the internal communion of its members, as the findings of our research show. When superiors have encouraged and responsibly and realistically steered the renewal process, there has been a more positive acceptance and adaptation of the charism of the congregation, reflecting the pluralism of individual persons and situations.

The process of congregational change in these cases has led to an authentic personal and institutional maturity. These congregations have set out along an authentic path of self-evangelisation, and have made themselves more faithful and more authentic in bearing witness to the Gospel, which the members now know and put into practice more perfectly, and announce and proclaim in a more "meaningful" way for our age.

1.2.3. Personal typologies and change

Once we know the institutional attitude that the congregation as such has taken towards *change* we can begin to discover the processes through which the congregations have been passing, leading them to their present situation. But there is another factor, which is perhaps more important and of even greater priority, that has occurred in this experiential process (which congregations are continuing to experience) in the religious life: *the personal structure of the members of the congregation with regard to change.*

The human person, which in our case means religious men and women, fashions his or her personal structure in terms of a whole set of factors relating to education, origin, heredity, personal experience, education and formation, environmental factors, cultural influences, etc. When one studies empirical data, particularly through factor analysis, one can find that people take up basically three attitudes to change:

- "dynamic persons": these are the ones who accept change as a dimension of life;
- "static persons": those who dogmatically reject change as an evil (good lies in the past for these people);
- "bewildered persons": those who do not know what attitude to take up, paralysed by their "doubts" regarding the changes taking place in life.

The manner in which individual religious are "structured" and the attitudes they adopt to the changes which they experience have a decisive and vital influence on the behaviour, motivation and attitudes of religious today, in terms of their whole existence and vocation as consecrated persons, and on their mission.

We would like to point out that this personal structure is something that is independent of the will of the individuals concerned, preceding it, and usually helping to determine the decisions they take. It is therefore independent of their good intentions. But because it is something that affects the inclination of individual persons, their structural being has an enormous influence on the life of their congregations.

The findings show that this "structural" manner of being and reacting differs in the same person as between the way they treat what we might call change in the "external" life of the congregation (the media, medical assistance, family relations, etc.) and the way they handle aspects of the faith, and the realities of the religious life. Those who are open to change at the "external" level – enjoying travel, or receiving the latest medical care, if necessary – are sometimes reactionary in their attitudes to the challenge to update a liturgical celebration, or to change their method of prayer, or communicating in fellowship, or living together in a community, or holding dialogue with people who are different from them, etc.

Not only do the personal attitudes of individual members of the congregation to the new manner of living according to the Gospel and evangelising differ, but they are frequently at loggerheads, faced with the changes and demands of renewal; this has made it more complicated and difficult to carry through the renewal process, and has frequently taken up too much time. The tension has worn down many people, who have been incapable of separating the deep-seated evangelical nature of the charism that they have embraced, from the tensions being created by a polarisation of positions held by groups and individuals faced with the new challenges, leading to disenchantment and sometimes causing people to drop out of the group altogether.

In short, the religious life in the past few years has been through an internal process whose outcome has been the present situation of the congregations. The historical scenario and the impact of change on this process have been briefly noted, at a two-fold level, in the two typologies mentioned above (institutional and personal) leading to very different situations today within different religious families, depending upon the path they have been following. However the path continues, just as the History of mankind continues, and the challenge still remains open.

In the majority of congregations, an internal equilibrium is being restored as a result of the process through which they have passed, particularly when they have managed to develop adequate continuing formation for their members and a "climate of conversion" and of "Gospel-based discernment", faced with the events of real life, discovering them to be "signs of the times". The recovery of the internal equilibrium depends on the time and the context in which the process began, the progress that has been made so far, and the evangelical depth of the members of the group.

1.3. Internal factors that have affected the religious life, stemming from its own dynamism: continuing formation, renewal of Constitutions and apostolic planning

It is necessary to emphasise the fact that the transformation through which the religious life has passed is partly the result of the need to adapt to a "changing scenario" and that this has mainly come about under the impetus of the internal dynamism of the religious life, as a response to a vital challenging issue: How to be "meaningful" men and women of Christ and his Gospel in a new historical, human, social and cultural reality, affected by such far-reaching and constant changes.

The apostolic religious life has always believed that Our Lord leads history, and that he is present in it. For this reason, throughout the ages Our Lord has been creating diverse charisms – new forms of presence, witness and service, arising from self-offering to Our Lord and as a response to the different needs of every age. The force deriving from the Gospel that animates the religious life is its great source of creativity and energy, and the findings that emerge from surveys on congregations often speak of this Gospel force, even at moments of crisis, and we discover to our amazement the power of the Spirit that sustains their lives.

1.3.1. Continuing formation as a new value in the religious life

In civil society, men and women very soon realise that they must renew themselves, retrain, or die as professionals or entrepreneurs. The most highly qualified managers as well as the lowest grade operatives or peasants know that if they fail to keep up-to-date they will simply help to swell the queues of the unemployed and the maladjusted.

The same applies to the religious life with regard to continuing formation. This is an internal factor which the religious experience strongly as a new value. Formation today is seen as the awareness by individuals of the need to respond to a series of demands and questions which arise within individuals or within the group; demands that have to be attended to, and questions that require an answer.

Most of the needs and questions emerge independently of the will of the individual, as a result of something external to oneself. They arise from a mankind that is in a continual state of development and change. People feel that the Church, and consequently one's own Religious institute and one's own person, must accompany this world in a state of transformation with the light of the Gospel. And in order to accompany this new and continually changing world, *a new, continuing and permanent formation* is required.

Religious see formation as a means of maintaining personal equilibrium and balance, to avoid becoming, perhaps, an expert in one particular area of life, but ignorant and maladjusted in another.

Continuing formation, which has become a *value* of the religious life today is not merely a continuing series of studies in order to acquire a deeper theoretical education and culture. Neither is it merely limited to updating professional know-how and expertise (which is also necessary for any type of task/mission in the various fields of activities in which religious are engaged). Continuing or ongoing formation, as it is viewed by religious today, is something different, something much more serious, more profound and stable. *It consists of strengthening and sustaining the human, spiritual and evangelical values of the consecrated person, and the "meaningful capacity for living and acting" in terms of humanity, through self-giving to Our Lord and to one's fellow men and women.*

The data we have gathered shows that continuing formation is experienced by religious today as an attitude of life, as an interior strength of the person. It is the patrimony both of simple religious and of intellectuals. More than that, we have discovered that sometimes religious of a high intellectual calibre who have cut themselves off from continuing formation as an attitude of life, have become maladjusted persons.

We can certainly assure them that continuing formation taken on as an attitude of life, makes a radical difference between one religious and another. It creates different persons, and different enthusiasm about life and work. The data has revealed two types of religious: those who have a future because of the way they are responding to the challenges of life; and those who already lack the strength in practice to respond to the present and to the future. Furthermore, it is no exaggeration to say that this group of religious who have taken on continuing formation as an attitude of life is the very same group which is carrying forward the religious life today.

The diagrams that follow set out the most significant and most frequently found data. They refer to all religious, and sometimes give separate figures for men and for women religious. Some figures vary and fluctuate, and we have decided to express this variation in terms of a positive increase of a given item of data, which means that the other percentages must be proportionally reduced.

CONTINUING FORMATION

EXPERIENCED AS A NEW VALUE	33%
CREATING DIFFICULTIES	66%

Source: D.I.S. Diagram 1

The present situation: The data shows that only a *large minority* of religious, around 33%, have discovered continuing formation as a new value; the vast majority, about 66%, particularly those in middle age, are finding it very difficult indeed to accept continuing formation in practice (see Diagram 1). Much of the discouragement, the lack of understanding of reality, insecure attitudes to life and to facing up to Gospel challenges, and the difficulty of coping with the programming laid down by the congregation, etc., stems from a lack of continuing formation suited to the needs of the religious concerned. They do not know how to set aside a certain amount of time to be actively devoted to continuing formation as something of vital relevance to them, or they do not have adequate facilities for this type of formation. Many religious will be ready to agree to any sacrifice, but not to reduce their working hours. And yet the data also shows that if they do not join the continuing formation process, and if they are not given all the appropriate facilities they need for it, devoting sufficient time to it, their own work will be impoverished (even though these religious deceive themselves by thinking that they are enriching their work by devoting more material time to it, while the work is poorer in quality). This also leads to an impoverishment of the human person, and an impoverishment in terms of the Gospel; the religious themselves become a problem, and they frequently impoverish their communities because they are maladjusted.

The institutions which work best today (educational, medical, groups working with the deprived, etc.) are the ones whose members have joined in an intense process of continuing formation. The fact that comparatively few religious have joined in this continuing formation process is one of the most serious reasons why the religious life is not able to adjust to the contemporary world. It will be difficult to make up for this failure to adapt unless the majority of religious manage to take part in a process of adequate continuing formation which will enable them to continue responding to the challenges of life.

It is true that the data gathered over the past few years give cause for some hope, because one-half of the two-thirds of the religious who have not taken up continuing formation as an attitude of life, namely one-third of all the religious men and women, say that "they are entering this process of continuing formation." Let us hope that this is true.

1.3.2. Concrete areas of formation which the findings reveal to be the most important for continuing formation

Here are a few areas of formation (by no means a comprehensive list) which the findings of the surveys have shown to be really important because of the effect that they have on the life and work of religious: human, social and biblical formation, and formation in the sacred sciences, catechesis and pastoral care, and the increasing number of religious with a secular university background

1.3.2.1. Human formation

According to the D.I.S. surveys, the expression "human formation" is defined as "knowledge and acceptance of self, steadiness, responsible use of one's own freedom, the capacity to relate to others, the ability to live together with different people or persons of other generations, etc." The positive response of all the religious is very high: positive percentages revolving around 75% were most frequently found.

HUMAN FORMATION

These percentages vary, and can rise positively up to 10%

POSITIVE	50%
INSUFFICIENT NEGATIVE	50%

However these subjective replies, which are true, are not so high when they are related to the objective facts that demonstrate the extent to which people accept themselves, and use their freedom, their ability to live with others and relate to them, etc. These percentages should perhaps be reduced from three-quarters to one-half. There are quite a number of religious (perhaps one-fourth) who believe that they are well formed in the human dimensions of life, when they are not in reality (according to the data which they give regarding their community life); and this is very dangerous for the life of human relations, within and outside the congregation. If to this 25% who mistakenly believe that they are well formed we add the other 25% who humbly confess their lack of human formation, we have more or less 50% religious men and women, with a serious lack of formation in the human dimensions of life mentioned earlier (acceptance of self, responsible use of freedom, ability to relate to others, etc.) (see Diagram 2).

This proportion does not vary significantly in the various generation groups.

1.3.2.2. Social formation

The D.I.S. surveys define social formation as "the sound and updated knowledge of society and of the people in and among which one lives and works (their history, culture, values...), being aware of living with and for others; cultivating a critical sense of social events, social justice, human rights, etc.".

Training or education in social formation understood in this sense does not normally apply to more than 50% of the religious men and 33% of religious women. The lack of social formation admitted by religious is very high, and is even higher in the older generations (see Diagram 3).

SOCIAL FORMATION

These percentages vary, and can rise positively up to 15% for religious men

	Male	Female
POSITIVE	50%	33%
INSUFFICIENT NEGATIVE	50%	66%

Source: D.I.S. Diagram 3

It is not possible to make a sound evangelical response to a society of such complexity and pluralism, and consequently understand it, unless one knows oneself fully. This is one of the other serious reasons for the failure of the religious life to adjust to mankind-society. It is not possible to dialogue with the contemporary world when the persons involved in the dialogue do not know one another, and it is evident that the initiative for this mutual knowledge must come from the religious life. Progress has been made in this direction, but there is still much more to be done if the religious life wishes to be the "leaven in the dough".

1.3.2.3. Biblical formation

Biblical formation, the rediscovery of the Word of God, its meaning and the revealed message, has been one of the main advances made in the spiritual formation of religious. Many have moved on from a rational type of ascetics and theology towards an ascetics and a theology based on and understood in terms of the Word of God, which makes it possible to read the events of real life. The consequences of this change are enormous.

One of the great silent revolutions has occurred within the religious life: contact between religious and sacred scripture, which is now better understood and is directly prayed by them. The Word of God is commented upon and expressed in community prayer, at meetings, with simple interpretation and exposition based upon personal faith, but full of grace and full of the living experience of those who believe in Jesus and find the original message in his Word, which impacts on their lives and which is judged in their response of faithfulness to the following of Christ.

"UPDATED" BIBLICAL FORMATION

	Male	Female
YOUNG	90%	80%
MIDDLE-AGED	60%	50%
OLDER	30%	20%

Source: D.I.S. Diagram 4

Virtually all generations of young religious have undertaken intense biblical formation, which is the food for their interior life, at a personal and community level. The middle generations, particularly the older ones, are divided between those who have become thoroughly familiar with sacred scripture, and those who have a relationship with it filtered through more ideological and ascetic forms of spirituality, which while good in themselves are not of a biblical inspiration (see the percentages in Diagram 4).

Biblical formation is one of the great achievements of the religious in recent times, despite the fact that it has not yet been fully attained, and has not yet reached every one of them, even though the levels of formation could still be improved upon.

1.3.2.4. Formation in the sacred sciences

To a lesser degree religious have also acquired an updated knowledge of systematic theology (dogmatic, moral theology, spiritual theology, etc.). The average percentages of religious who feel that they have an updated familiarity with the sacred sciences are 50% for men and 33% for women.

FORMATION IN THE SACRED SCIENCES
These percentages vary, and may increase up to 15% in religious men

	Male	Female
POSITIVE	50%	33%
INSUFFICIENT NEGATIVE	50%	66%

Source: D.I.S. Diagram 5

This means that half the male religious and 66% of female religious do not feel that they have an updated formation in the sacred sciences (Diagram 5). But this is an indicator that is dynamically evolving upwards towards more positive data, varying up to 15%. The younger generations have a sounder formation in the sacred sciences, but as the age rises this improvement falls. Religious women, perhaps because the majority of them do not have a systematic theological formation, and also because they are more deeply involved in culture (at all levels), have made the greatest effort at renewal in the sacred sciences. Religious priests of the middle and older generations have renewed their formation to a lesser degree, while many of them still have a rational theological background rather than a biblical one.

1.3.2.5. Formation in Catechetics and Pastoral Care

Theological renewal and an updated theology naturally give rise to the desire to be better trained to communicate the message of Jesus to others using appropriate and effective forms and methods, so that men and women of today can welcome and understand the Good News. Hence the need for formation in Catechesis and the Pastoral Care and the desire to receive formation in the fundamental anthropological sciences connected with the Pastoral Ministry (psychology, anthropology, sociology, etc.) which is very strongly felt in the religious life.

The positive data on those who feel that they have been given updated formation in catechesis and the pastoral ministry are about 33% for men and 40% for women; these figures are lower than for updating in the sacred sciences. These figures are is very closely correlated to social formation. The people have learned a teaching but do not know how to communicate it to the people, partly because they do not know the people well enough (see Diagram 6).

With regard to religious women, perhaps because they started with an initial handicap, enormous efforts have been made to provide training in catechesis and the pastoral ministry, and their average positive percentages are around 40%; quite a number of people in the middle and older generations have missed out on this updating. But a generation of young religious of both sexes, and also quite a few in middle age, are increasingly updating their knowledge of Christ and the Gospel, and are acquiring a better capacity for communication and dialogue with men and women of today in order to hand on to them the message of Jesus.

CATECHETICAL-PASTORAL FORMATION

	Male	Female
POSITIVE	33%	40%
NOT SUFFICIENT NEGATIVE	66%	60%

Source: D.I.S. Diagram 6

However while it is true that membership of one or other generation of religious indicates a difference at the personal level, the findings show that it is not so much age as the various mentalities stemming from a different type of religious-theological formation which is much more distinctive; this training or formation leads to a view of life stemming from a rational type of theology, as opposed to one based on a biblical type of theology more closely linked to the history of salvation and the contributions of the human sciences.

Data gathered in recent years reveals something very important regarding the future of the religious life: basic theological, moral, catechetical and pastoral formation is gradually becoming common to all consecrated persons without discriminating between the men and the women, or those who are training for the priesthood and those who are not.

1.3.2.6. The incorporation of religious men and women more fully in the secular university culture

The religious life has always had people trained in different cultural and professional fields in order to perform their apostolic mission (health care, education, social work, human development, community development, etc.).

Moreover, apostolic life congregations for women in the past, in some countries, were Institutions that were ahead of civil society itself in fostering the advancement of women. Today we can see that women are qualifying on a massive scale up to university level, and this applies in our case to consecrated women as well (the average percentage is as high as 66%, and this figure is higher as the age of the sisters declines).

Even in the developing countries, society is increasingly demanding skills and specialisation for different tasks (education, health care, community development, etc.). Religious are aware of these demands, and sometimes they have thrown themselves fully into completing their cultural preparation and professional qualifications in so far as they are able to, beginning at each one's own starting level, sometimes at very great personal and congregational sacrifice because of the increased workload this has entailed, etc.

In the female religious life, it was initially the teaching sisters who acquired higher qualifications, followed by sisters in the health care and social action spheres (even though the latter two sectors have not had the same numbers of highly qualified sisters). This has had great repercussions on the personal lives of the religious men and women in their renewal process, because of a number of characteristic features that accompany the cultural change that takes places at the personal level, such as:

- the influence of science as a means of assimilating the new current cultural values. Accordingly, the religious have toppled the myths relating to issues based more on the culture of the past than on a Gospel view of these realities which follow the laws of human sciences;

- the formation of a critical mind, which is particularly necessary in order to analyse reality and make committed Gospel-based choices when faced with that reality.

1.3.3. Renewal of Constitutions and the real life of persons in the congregations

Religious congregations have renewed their Constitutions since Vatican II at the behest of the Church. This is a very positive fact because the new Constitutions are generally fine tracts of Gospel-based theology today, and are much closer to an account of what it means to follow Jesus Christ and collaborate in his mission today in a modern experiential manner, than merely developing other aspects of the religious life (such as the purely ascetical, juridical aspects, etc.).

On the basis of these facts, which in this case are the thorough and profound understanding of the Constitutions of a great number of religious congregations and of the main documents that have been issued above all by General Chapters, Assemblies, etc., we must say that in terms of programmes – namely the contents of life and action expressed in their most important documents – the religious life has made, and is continuing to make, an enormous effort to draw up and put into practice the dynamic thrusts of life and apostolic action with regard to what the religious life is and what it wishes to become. This applies both within the religious life itself, and also in terms of the outward aspect it presents to the contemporary world, not only to the People of God but also to the society of believers and non-believers.

We are duty-bound to recognise that within the limits of its strengths and possibilities, the religious life is doing everything it can in order to "spell itself out" in Gospel terms, because it feels called and inspired to do so in order to respond in a dynamic and evangelical manner to what the signs of the times are demanding of it.

When D.I.S. investigates the way in which religious men and women are practising what is planned in the Constitutions and in the Decrees of their Chapters, General Assemblies, etc., through its surveys and questionnaires, it notes that some of the fundamental aspects that have already been programmed are being put into practice, coming to terms, as one would expect, with all the limitations that exist in all ages. But other, equally fundamental, aspects have not been given up by the majority of the ordinary members of Religious institutes. This paper will bring out these fundamental aspects, which are more and which are less commonly practised, as we describe the data gathered from personal Questionnaires, according to the answers volunteered freely and anonymously by religious men and women surveyed.

1.3.4. *Planning life at different levels (congregational, communitarian, personal)*

We are living in a planned world, and planning has become a means of predicting reality, facing up to it, changing it, etc. There is no alternative: "either you plan, or somebody plans you." In the contemporary world it is not possible to improvise, and if one tries to do so the price can be very high.

This value of our world has been taken on by the religious life which has entered a planning process at all levels: congregational, provincial and communitarian. The general and provincial Assemblies and Chapters, most of the time, carry out planning or draft projects for the groups for which they are responsible. And these congregational and provincial plans and projects are gradually "coagulating" and are being implemented.

PERSONAL LIFE PROJECT

POSITIVE	25%
NEGATIVE INSUFFICIENT	75%

Nevertheless it is found almost everywhere that although projects to guide the life and work of a group are being carried out at the group level, very little is being done at the personal level. Comparatively few religious men and women (around 25%) actually have a personal project, which is realistic and sound, to meet their personal needs; a plan which they themselves have discerned, drawing it up in dialogue with another competent person to help them to take on into their own personal lives what they are planning at the congregational, provincial or community levels; the remaining 75% of the religious men and women do not have a personal life project at all (Diagram 7).

The findings show that common, congregational and provincial, and even community plans and projects are not as powerful and as effective as they should be, precisely because the individual persons do not incorporate them into their own personal projects, and do not make them part of their own lives, because in practice they have not worked out a personal project which meets the needs and demands of the Gospel.

No common congregational project can replace the duty which is incumbent upon each individual religious to draw up a personal project. One of the most reliable indicators to show that a religious has responsibly taken up continuing formation is the fact that they have their own personal life project. When this exists, all the indicators on the life of that religious, from every point of view, indicate more positive data. If not, the common projects of the congregations do not function, very largely because the personal projects fail. What is planned at the common level is not integrated at the personal level.

2. DYNAMIC ROOTS OF THE RELIGIOUS LIFE (IN FACTS OF LIFE AND NOT IN "PRINCIPLES")

2.1. The CORE which generates the religious life

The "transformation" through which the religious life has been passing, as we have already mentioned, has always had one internal factor that has been decisive throughout the whole process: the ideal of returning to live what is genuinely evangelical, purifying it of certain aspects that have become "consecrated" but which are very difficult to sustain today for an educated believer (self-evangelisation). This internal force reveals a historical constant: the religious life has a firm base and living roots in the realities of the Faith. It is these which feed its commitment, which make it able to adapt, and which give it dynamism, an evangelical commitment and fidelity, today as in the past. This is its *life-generating core*.

In a world in which a great number of people are non-believers and where there is increasing apathy, the religious life emerges as a counter-culture of faith which encompasses existence. Taken on as a project-utopia for a life based on Jesus and his Gospel, it is capable of moving men and women to devote the whole of their existence to the cause of God and the Gospel, today as in the past.

We can find pointers to this generating core in the following data on the lives of religious: a personal experience of God, a personal following of Jesus Christ and his life-style (as inspiration for their own lives and their option for the poor), personal and community prayer, an updated sense of the identity of the congregation (which is experienced today as a broader reality than the formulation of the charism, as we shall be seeing shortly) and self-giving to the liberating-evangelising mission.

All of these real life realities are those which dynamise the existence of religious. When they are at work, they foster self-giving and give sense to everything that they experience. When they are weakened, the sense of personal-vocational existence is emptied, and the work-mission is impoverished in such a way that it eventually becomes replaced by other inter-human factors.

Religious life therefore has its own *life-generating core*, in realities of the faith. To put it in another way, at the heart of the religious life is Jesus and his Gospel, which inspire a form of existence, for individuals and for the group. This experience is so evident and so irrefutable that it gives rise to critical demands regarding certain inter-ecclesial or inter-congregational situations, and to conscientious objection to certain ways of acting, when they cease to have any meaning after being held up against the Gospel.

There are a number of indicators of this *life-generating core*:

2.1.1. Religious, as strong believers, wish to be witnesses and proclaim their experience of "what we have seen and heard"

One of the indicators that has emerged most frequently in the answers to the Questionnaires, and which is one of the strongest indicators of correlation is the experience of God on the part of religious. An experience of God which means a personal experience of that mysterious, but real, encounter between each living person with the living God.

A simple way of expressing this after years of experimentation is "communicating with God", "feeling God", "relating to God", which has now enabled us to measure this ineffable experience. These expressions perfectly sum up the purpose of the question, which is evidenced from the high index of answers to the question, and the strong correlation which exists with the data from other questions.

Data on the experience of God shows that this reality cannot be replaced by anything or anyone in the religious life, not even self-giving to one's brothers and sisters. One is meaningfully in the religious life only if it is based on God, namely, when one's experience of God is kept alive. When this reality exists positively, the three structural features of the religious life – personal life, life in a fraternal community and self-giving to the mission – are strengthened and determined by the personal experience of God. When this exists, one has the strength to take up the challenges of life from within one's own vocation.

Conversely, as the experience of God in the individual person declines, that person's capacity to pray personally and in a community declines as a result, and difficulties arise in the common life; work and activities become a mere professional task, and the relevance of the faith to the real life of each day fails, and the sense of the work and mission of the Gospel is lost.

The negative percentages for this question taking all the religious groups as a whole, are small, and do not normally rise above about 6%. Conversely the positive percentages are very high, for 70% of religious men and 80% of religious women (Diagram 8). The intermediate zone, indicating a certain weakening in the experience of God, ranges between 24% and 15%.

EXPERIENCE OF GOD
These percentages vary, and can rise positively up to 15%

POSITIVE	70%	80%
INTERMEDIATE RATHER WEAK	24%	15%
NEGATIVE VERY WEAK	6%	5%

This group is very important, because this is the area of those whom we might call the "weak in the faith"; these are the people who are living in a delicate situation which usually has negative repercussions (dropping out or bringing on a congregational identity crisis, etc.). If they do not react in time.

These findings support the contention that the religious are strong believers, and that the experience of God must be united to other fundamental aspects of their religious life. It also reveals the existence of minority groups who experience crises of faith in the religious life.

One might wonder where they find the support they need to underpin this experience of God. Factor analysis links this to the following factors: fruitful personal prayer, a personal experience of the calling to follow Jesus Christ, the Eucharist experienced as a source of fraternity, encountering God in daily life (the union of faith and life), feeling at peace with oneself (the interior harmony of individual persons who accept themselves as they are with their limitations), continuing formation, particularly updating in biblical and catechetical-pastoral formation, and an evangelical sense of one's work and mission. These indicators do not exhaust the whole of the aspects of the life of the consecrated person on which their personal experience of God has an influence, but they are certainly some of the most significant.

2.1.2. *The centrality of Jesus (a personal following of Jesus Christ and his life-style), as the inspiring force and motivation of the religious life*

The consecrated life has always been theologically defined as the life of "the following of Christ". But this definition does not distinguish a religious from a Christian lay person, who must also follow Christ. However, there is no doubt that religious feel called to follow Jesus Christ in their personal lives, with a specific life-style, whose originality stems from the fact that they take up certain values which Jesus lived in a special way. Attraction and devotion to his "person" and to his "cause" occupy the real and the affective centre of the life of a religious; and today, after so many years of carrying out research in this field, we can say that what lies at the root of the vocation to the religious life, and what inspires the most difficult attitudes and commitments in the life of all religious is the following of Jesus, his person and his message.

This great life-experience must be very closely united to the experience of God, and is another source of Gospel energy in the lives of the vast majority of religious.

PERSONAL FOLLOWING OF JESUS CHRIST BY RELIGIOUS
These percentages vary, and can rise positively up to 5%

INTENSE POSITIVE	75%	80%
WEAK INSUFFICIENT	25%	20%

75% of religious men and 80% of religious women experience their personal following of Jesus in an intense and positive manner; the negative data on this question affect 25% of the men and 20% of the women; although these are not many, it is usually these persons who present a more overall negative situation with regard both to their vocation and to their congregational sense (Diagram 9).

This indicator is currently influenced by the more thorough Christological formation given to religious of both sexes, which fuels their free and personal following of Jesus Christ. An updated Christology has led many religious to change the way in which they internally live their vocation of "following the Lord Jesus" and their commitment to the evangelising mission; both of these have been enriched, giving them a greater and better understanding of Jesus Christ in history and of his message, based upon a richer and more updated Christology.

The personal following of the person of Jesus Christ and his message on the part of religious men and women is such a constant factor that even though other important indicators tend to weaken, this one usually remains firm. This is something which also demonstrates the great capacity of the religious life to develop love for Jesus Christ and an active and committed following of him in individuals. Based on this personal experience, Jesus and his life have given a new sense and meaning to various aspects of the religious life, both with regard to the way in which all the religious live their vows, presupposing a concrete and more radical manner of living the values which Jesus himself lived and proclaimed as values of the Kingdom (overcoming an ascetical-juridical concept of those values), and with regard to the style, the fields and the duties of the evangelising mission.

This following of Jesus as a person, and this endorsement of the values of the Gospel help us to understand why it is that religious sometimes come into conflict with certain regulations and/or sections of the Church which are based on another type of religious values.

2.1.3. Men and women of prayer: a prayer as an encounter with God is a unique reality in the life of consecrated persons

Simple Christian people believe that religious are people who "pray". And as soon as they meet us under any circumstances they always ask us to "pray" for them. At various times in the history of the religious life there have been times when people have wished to "enclose" the religious life in the chapel, particularly when the religious have tried to make themselves present in new areas of the mission, or in frontier zones of the faith; difficulties have always arisen, and on frequent occasions people have argued that it is the responsibility of religious to "pray" for this world.

But are religious really people of prayer? Yes, they are.

The findings of the surveys show that personal prayer is a genuine source of interior energy in the life of consecrated persons today. This is a reality which, like the experience of God, cannot be replaced by anything else, like the air we breathe. Without a prayer life, and indeed without a fruitful prayer life (by this we mean prayer which gives a sense to everything one is and lives) it is not possible to live positively the various aspects of the religious life: the vows, fraternity, Gospel criteria and commitments, the mission, etc.

Every religious needs this unique and personal experience of meeting God in prayer; an experience which must be intimately linked to the experience of God mentioned earlier. Prayer always emerges in our findings as the necessary means of attaining an experience of God; more than that, it is like the other side of that experience, it is the time and the place where we can personally and ineffably meet God in a very special (albeit not the only) way. The correlation between the experience of God and personal prayer becomes all the more exact as personal prayer increases the experience of God and vice versa.

One thing is certain: while it is not only in personal prayer that we manage to experience God, the findings show that without personal prayer our experience of God in our brothers and sisters and in daily life, etc., is eventually weakened, or cannot be sustained.

What is the position of religious before this indicator of personal prayer? A great many congregations have been through moments in which many of their members have experienced a crisis in their personal prayer life, and many others are still doing so. This is normally coupled with a higher level of conflict in other aspects of the consecrated life. It is normal for there to be a reaction within the group, when others become aware of their situation and help them, or provide appropriate ways in order to help them overcome.

PERSONAL PRAYER
These percentages vary, and can rise positively up to 17%

WITH DIFFICULTIES WEAK	52%	45%
NEGLECTED	15%	
NOT PRACTISED	5%	

The data show this: a large number of religious ranging from 33% of religious men and 40% of religious women have a positive personal prayer life which helps them and enriches their attitudes and their evangelical life commitments. These positive percentages can fluctuate upwards up to 17%. Another large group (hovering around 52% and 47%, respectively) find personal prayer difficult to practise (either because they do not harvest the fruits of prayer or because sometimes they give it up, or do not remain faithful to it, or because they have not managed to establish a balance between prayer and action). A third group, generally a minority group of around 15% are those who hardly practise any personal prayer, or have virtually given it up altogether (Diagram 10).

Both the group with difficulties in their personal prayer life and those who hardly pray at all, or those do not pray at all, clearly have difficulties in experiencing God, in living their vocation positively, in taking upon themselves the demands of the Gospel in their community life, and viewing their membership of their congregation positively.

However the majority of the population of consecrated people (men and women) are a praying population. In recent years the tendency has been for the positive percentages of personal prayer life to increase, and in particular there has been an increase in the "Gospel quality" of their prayer lives.

2.1.4. *The experience of a historic faith*

The indicators reveal that there are many religious who have grown up with a prayer life which is more fully integrated into life (overcoming dualism and spiritualism) and which fuels their experience of historic faith. Today the groups of religious who have made the greatest progress in the renewal of their lives tend to pray on the Word of God and to enlighten their daily lives with the dynamic of revealed saving events through which Our Lord continues to be present and active in our history. These religious pray the Word of God and with its message they enlighten the events of ordinary life and try to discover in them the hand of God. The religious in every congregation who have managed to establish this unity of faith and life are those who reveal more positive indicators in everything which refers to their personal situation as consecrated men and women, and the changes experienced in their congregation, and they are the ones who have a greater impetus as a result of the new "prophetic" commitments of their mission. This unification of their life of faith is helped when the religious have a sound biblical formation.

HISTORIC FAITH (INTEGRATING LIFE)
These percentages vary, and can rise positively up to 15%

POSITIVE UNITING FAITH AND LIFE	65%	75%
ABSTRACT FAITH NOT UNITING	35%	25%

The findings show that the vast majority, namely 65% of the religious men and 75% of the religious women (this figure shows the great influence of renewal on the biblical/theological formation of individuals) experience a unified spirituality which unifies their real life, and they have a historic faith, which also means that they have the capacity and the habit of cultivating "Gospel discernment", seeking to discover the "signs" of the presence and the will of God in the facts of daily life. These positive percentages vary, and can reach as high as 10%. The remaining 35% of religious men and 25% of religious women have not managed to acquire this experience of unifying faith (Diagram 11). As we have already mentioned, those who gave negative answers to this question are more disoriented, and take up negative attitudes with regard to many other aspects of their consecrated and apostolic lives.

Activism is a great stumbling-block to the interior life of a religious. The great demands of the religious life throughout the world, coupled with the fact that the numbers of religious is declining all the time (both because of those leaving congregations and the smaller number of new entrants) have caused the phenomenon of "activism" – by which we mean the predominance of action over reflection-contemplation-action – to become a constant "temptation" today which spoils the interior life of individuals and jeopardises the fidelity of religious to a life of prayer, particularly the younger generations. This prevalence of action, where it exists, impoverishes the interior life and undermines the source of energy which sustains the experience of God.

ACTIVISM (PREVALENCE OF ACTION IN LIFE)
These percentages vary, and can rise positively up to 15%

BALANCE ACTION-CONT	50%	60%
ACTIVISTS MORE ACTION	50%	40%

The findings show that 50% of the religious men and 40% of the religious women are, to varying degrees, affected by activism. The other half of the religious men and 60% of religious women strike a balance between reflection-prayer and action. Sometimes these positive percentages may rise by up to 15%. These are people whose situation is more positive as far as the full set of indicators of the evangelical life is concerned (personal, communitarian and apostolic) (Diagram 12).

Sometimes activism appears to be a means of evasion in the life of some religious. This evasion is usually coupled with:

- in their personal lives, a greater lack of interior harmony and a weakening of evangelical motivation;
- in the community, personal independence of the community commitments and in general with individualistic attitudes;
- in the tasks of the mission, a certain professionalism with a loss of the evangelical sense of their work, creating difficulties in their team work and in their evangelical discernment.

Activism also affects the members of the government in congregations. Activism always impoverishes personal life, community living, and the updating of the apostolic mission.

2.1.5. The congregational identity (as an all-embracing sense of the charism)

The religious institutes which opened up to the process of change during the early years of renewal sought out their own identity amid the great changes that they were experiencing in the world and in the Church. They attempted to discover this identity, to a large extent, on the borderlines of the charism of their own religious family, within the "People of God" whose awareness re-emerged very strongly in the wake of Vatican II in the more dynamic and living local Churches.

At the end of a decade (more or less) a healthy reaction occurred. This was mainly to do with the work carried out by the congregations in drafting their new Constitutions and rediscovering the spirit of their founders at the present moment in the history of mankind. All the congregations made a great effort to reformulate their charism in modern terms, enriching it with new calls of Our Lord (the option for the poor and commitment to justice which stems from the faith, greater inculturation in local peoples, etc.) without losing the Gospel core of the charism as the tradition of the congregation had always experienced it.

The situation has changed radically. In the process of living the new Constitutions we have been given a source for renewing our charism and we have endeavoured to become better acquainted with the spiritual heritage of our congregations, to adapt it to the modern world. The majority of the congregations have opened up to the dynamic power of the updated charism in their programming documents already. However, the process under which people identify with them and make these new evangelical proposals their own is still ongoing.

INTERNALISING THE NEW CONSTITUTIONS
These percentages vary, and can rise positively up to 10%

POSITIVELY WELL	35%
INADEQUATELY LITTLE	65%

The findings show that, generally speaking, only a large minority, namely 35% of religious men and women, have internalised the Constitutions and incorporated them into their lives. Another large group, 65%, have deepened them and are intending to take them into their own lives, but inadequately. Within this percentage there is another minority, which is decreasing (largely people of the two older generations, who are perhaps encouraged today by a number of regressive tendencies) who cling on to the charism with the same view that they had always had of it in the past, to which they look back with great nostalgia and with which they are extremely familiar (Diagram 13).

The findings show that the sense of the identify of the congregation today encompasses a much broader and all-embracing reality than the "theological formulation of the charism" in a more or less updated vision of it. The sense of congregational identity, from what we have found, comprises the following factors: affective membership of the group, knowing and taking on the proposals of the congregation and integrating them into one's personal life, a sense of responsibility to group commitments, living the realities of the congregation as something proper to them, taking on the one mission of the apostolic body of the congregation, in communion with and ranging beyond the pluralism of duties and commitments of the mission and work currently being performed by the members of a congregation. If all of these existential attitudes are practised meaningfully in a climate of communication, they are the present source of the congregation's identity, which is a much broader reality than merely a theological/evangelical proclamation of the charism, and staking out preferential areas of action and concrete tasks.

2.2. Fraternal community living and its decisive influence on the life of religious

Living in relation to others is the key to the existence of every person. And the best possible environment for relating to others is living with them. Living with others, in marriage, in the family, in politics or civil society, or in the Church and in one's own religious family, is either a source of riches for the self-fulfilment of every human being, when one is capable of tackling and overcoming the difficulties stemming from one's own and others' limitations; or it can be a source of suffering and personal trauma.

Living together "as brothers and sisters" who have come together voluntarily to share an evangelical life project belongs to the very core and essence of the religious life. For this reason community life has a decisive and essential influence on the lives of all religious.

Now, in any sphere whatsoever, living together is one of the spheres of human existence in which the human aspect of social change has a very far-reaching impact. We are referring here to the change in the scale or hierarchy of values.

2.2.1. A new scale of values in religious community life

Here are a few of the significant factors of social change that have affected community living:

- a new sensitivity towards the value of the freedom and equality of all human beings;
- the far-reaching change in relationships, due to new knowledge about identity-otherness and to a greater appreciation of interpersonal communication (which has so many repercussions on the quality of life of a human being);
- the democratisation of ways of living: a different concept of authority and of the exercise of authority, greater participation of members in the life of the group and particularly in the decision-making processes which affect the members.

The community life of religious has been affected by this new scale of values in society, which is based upon a view of the person. But the community life of religious has not only been affected by the scale of values of the social environment, but also by what has happened "within the community itself", through a serious reflection on these values in the light of the faith, which has revealed them to be full Gospel values, proclaimed and practised by Jesus of Nazareth.

As a result of the impact of social development and from the viewpoint of an updated commitment to the Gospel, religious community life has changed and has become humanised in terms of its internal dynamics, making it more "evangelical". The religious have discovered that the person is the primary value for Jesus and his Gospel, and that therefore the person must be the primary value in the life of any community which lives its life centred upon Jesus Christ. And it must do this not with the "theory" of principles, but in the concrete reality of day-to-day living together. Every religious community that has renewed its scale of values wishes to be "prophetic". In other words, they wish to be a sign and witness of a type of existence in which the freedom and equality of its members, brotherly and sisterly love, and interpersonal communication are tangible indicators which make the charity and the Gospel-based fraternity which the group experiences credible *today*. How can one believe today that charity is being practised in a group if there is no mutual trust, for example? Or if people cannot dialogue about their conflicts, whether great or small, that arise as a result of their life and work for the Kingdom? How can one bear witness to the fact that all the brothers and sisters are equal as persons (and not in terms of roles and functions) if there are class differences within the community, or if some persons are not fully accepted?

2.2.2. *The real and ideal typology of communities*

According to our findings the ideal of community life is the "fraternal community" for the majority of religious (65% of the men and 80% of the women). In other words, they want a community in which people live united by bonds of trust, communication, and friendship; persons who share the faith, prayer, the vocation and the mission, and who bear witness to Christ through their mission and through their practice of the congregation's charism (Diagram 14). This type of community, whose primary value is the person, is the ideal for the vast majority of the religious, and for virtually all the generations under 40 years of age. 35% of the religious men and 20% of the religious women consider their work and observance to be their primary value (Diagram 14).

THE IDEAL OF COMMUNITY LIFE
(FRATERNITY-WORK-OBSERVANCE)
These percentages vary, and can rise positively up to 10%

PRIME VALUE: FRATERNITY	65%	80%
PRIME VALUE: WORK	20%	13%
PRIME VALUE: OBSERVANCE	15%	7%

This is the ideal. But what is the reality in which this ideal is actually lived? The findings reveal a situation in which religious community life is not uniform, when one takes into account the personal experience of the brothers and sisters of what actually happens in their communities.

Within the constant process of change, community life in most congregations creates a threefold typology of communities depending upon the value which is most prominent in the life of the group (in reality, not in ideas or written projects):

a. communities which are teams of apostolic work: groups whose bond of union is above all that of their work/mission, and the apostolic task which they perform;

b. communities of regular life and observance: whose bond of union is above all the conventual value of the order, the regular life and observance;

c. fraternal communities: whose bond of union are above all persons: persons who live together in a climate of trust, of mutual respect and closeness, who share their faith, their vocation and the mission which they are performing.

In every community the three values we have mentioned exist: apostolic work, observance and persons. But the fact that one of these values takes priority and stands out over the others in day-to-day community life creates very different types of communities. This may be due, inter alia, to the fact that these three types of values provoke one or other type of interpersonal relations: functional relations, when the primary value of the union is work, or the order and observance; affective relations, face-to-face, person-to-person relations, when the primary bond of union are the members of the group, as persons.

Data on different types of communities

A. One group which accounts for 52% of religious men and 43% of religious women, usually says that they live in communities whose primary bond of union is their apostolic work. These people are the ones with the lowest percentages: in their relational life, in the help they give to others in serious difficulties, in interpersonal communication, these are the ones who share their faith and life to a lesser degree, who live their lives more individualistically, and frequently show "activism" in their apostolic responsibilities.

B. A minority (15% of religious men and 12% of religious

women) describe the life of their community as hinging around observance. However this type of community is usually the ideal of community life which is sought after above all by those who are over 65 year of age. This is very understandable in view of what they have experienced in the past, the formation they received and their present-day needs (the pace of life, difficulties in adapting to new ways of relating to others, of communicating, of praying, etc.).

C. The others describe their group as a "fraternal community" (33% of religious men and 45% of religious women); this percentage varies and can be increased by up to 15%. Those who experience this type of fraternal community usually represent almost all the religious who wish to go on living this reality in the future. And these are the ones whose indicators are more positive on all the other aspects of the consecrated life: living the vocation, experiencing God, trusting their fellow brothers and sisters, a higher level of sharing the faith, the vocation and the mission, greater balance and personal harmony, and a more intense living relationship with God (prayer), etc., (Diagram 15).

PRIORITY VALUE LIVED IN THE RELIGIOUS COMMUNITY
These percentages vary, and can rise positively up to 15%

FIRST VALUE: WORK	52%	43%
FIRST VALUE: OBSERVANCE	15%	12%
FIRST VALUE: THE PERSON	33%	45%

The figures show that in a fraternal community in which the persons constitute the bond of union, there is an evangelical community life which strengthens the life of the religious at all levels (vocation, following Christ, fraternity, mission, etc.). In this type of community the people live their lives centred more closely around their vocation and they are given greater strength in their mission.

There are frequently communities in congregations that describe themselves as being places of "tension"; these are the groups which give the least help to living the Gospel ideals and those which most dispel any joyful expectations about the consecrated life and those who have chosen it. The human person, in the long run, cannot live positively in an environment that is full of tension (which is internal violence). Even if the tension is caused by different views or demands in the evangelical life (poverty, the self-giving of persons to one type or other of service/mission, etc.) these tensions are always negative, and they always destroy the ideals of the religious life which their members have chosen.

2.2.3. Attitudes which fashion a fraternal community

What enables us to become best acquainted with the religious community is not the number of the members or the place where the group lives (these two factors, numbers and locality, only have an indirect effect). What most reveals the state of a religious community are the human and Gospel attitudes of its members and the degree of communication that exists between them.

The findings show that a fraternal community is one in which the common life is based upon mutual trust, friendship, sincere communication, sharing and mutual forgiveness. The brothers and sisters managed to deal with one another on a very deep personal level and subsequently this is where the fruits of the Gospel are usually borne automatically, leading to the sharing of the faith and the group search for God's will (community discernment). The members live as brothers and sisters, they pray as brothers and sisters, they share the joys and the difficulties of each other's lives; each person knows that they can rely on the help of the others when they meet serious difficulties in life, and they experience mercy and mutual pardon, and manage to overcome individualism. The community is converted into a true theological place.

This type of community already exists for a large number of religious in every congregation, and the vast majority aspire to it for the future of their community life.

The factors which most easily foster these Gospel attitudes for community living must be linked to those mentioned in part 2, when we spoke of the "generating core" of the religious life: a personal experience of God, positive and shared prayer life, the positive practice of the vocation to consecration in the religious family, and the sense of belonging to the congregation. The interdependent nature of these indicators in individual persons shows that the religious community is quite different from just a group of friends, who meet together in order to work for some good or even Church objectives. The transcendental dimension of following Jesus, taken on personally as a vocation and mission is a very decisive reality in every religious community. In the religious community the members desire to share both realities (vocation and mission) with their brothers and sisters in a climate of trust and positive relationships. By so doing the community is transformed into a "prophetic sign" of the Kingdom.

After studying so many thousands of religious men and women it is amazing to note from the findings the high Gospel quality of their personal zeal and their community lives and the clarity of their Gospel ideal.

Community limitations and difficulties. The factors that make it difficult to live positive and Gospel attitudes in community life include the following: work/mission, when it becomes the first bond of union in the community; individualism, as the fruit of a variety of causes including the formation of a spiritualist/vertical tendency which expresses serious reservations regarding deep human relationships; a different view of the congregation's life at a particular moment in its history; and above all the lack of healthy, sincere and loyal communication between the members of the community (which is an issue that will be examined separately because of the influence it has today on the religious life.

The vast majority of communities, particularly of men, and also most of the women's communities, are usually groups in which people with different values regarding the life of fellowship or fraternity live together. This pluralism often creates many situations of conflict, stemming from the different "expectations" of the persons involved in relation to what they expect and desire of their group life.

CONTENTMENT AND PLEASURE IN ONE'S OWN COMMUNITY
These percentages vary, and can rise positively up to 5% in men
and 10% in women

CONTENTED	75%	85%
NOT VERY CONTENTED	25%	15%

Despite the difficulties of living together, an average of 75% of religious men and 85% of religious women (percentages which vary and can rise by up to 10%) have said that they are content in the community in which they live (Diagram 16). This indicates something which is very important: the great human qualities of these consecrated persons, whose joy and satisfaction at living with their brothers and sisters in the congregation is not lost due to the shortcomings they experience "rubbing shoulders" every day.

2.2.4. Communication-participation

The exceptional importance of communication at all levels in the contemporary world is evident to all. The development of the mass media and their great impact on society are clear indicators of the importance of communication in contemporary society. Moreover, we all have a better understanding of the influence which communication has on the process of personal maturity. No-one is therefore surprised at the fact that the "value of communication" constantly emerges as something which encourages or hampers the dynamic of the internal life of congregations, and more specifically the life of fellowship within communities and participation in the life of the religious family.

Communication, whether at the level of information, dialogue, ability to express oneself and to share what one is and does ("sharing" is a utopia if intercommunication does not work), is a factor which encourages all the human and Gospel attitudes of a fraternal religious community. Conversely a low level of information-communication, or its absence (which can exist for a wide variety of different causes) hampers the experience of these attitudes and is usually a source of tension, whether latent or manifest, emerging under the guise of respect which conceals interpersonal distance and the lack of communication.

Intercommunication encourages the weakening of a sense of belonging, individualism and seeking out other environments outside one's own community, to make up for the void which one feels within it.

An appreciation of true interpersonal communication is a great value to religious (men and women of their age). A value which has marked a break with the past for many people, a past in which they lived the culture of "silence" and non-communication. The religious life has opened internal channels of communication-participation between its members, and has also opened them up to receive the inflow of communication from outside, through which they now have a better understanding of reality and the environment in which people live and perform their mission.

POSITIVE NORMAL   50%
INSUFFICIENT WEAK   50%

Communication is a good, which strengthens the lives of religious; but it is also a reality which many people need to be trained in. The findings show that about 50% of all religious men and women find difficulties in communicating within their communities, while the other 50% do not (Diagram 17).

2.3. The role and the exercise of Government in the religious life

In the religious life, as in any institutional group, government (superiors/government at all levels) is a key factor in maintaining the direction and the achievements in the life of the group.

In the process of transforming the religious life which many congregations have been through (and specifically those on which we have data) the superiors have had a very decisive influence. Part of this influence has been already analysed when we described the "typology of congregations that have accepted and undertaken change". But the influence also covers other aspects of life, depending on the type of leadership these persons have exercised, which is very closely related to the type of relations they have established with the others.

2.3.1. Different types of government leadership (experienced by religious men and women today) in local government

a. Authoritarian and/or managerial leadership. This does not allow individuals and groups to participate in the decision-making process affecting them. The authoritarian local superior is now in the minority (15% for men and 10% for women religious have mentioned it) in congregations that have undergone the development process and the self-evangelisation within the group. Managerial leadership of the community, under which there is a tendency to be more occupied with activities and administrative

91

tasks than with people, was reported by similar percentages of religious as authoritarian leadership. This type of leadership usually creates individualism, dissatisfaction and difficulties in the life of obedience amongst the religious (Diagram 18).

b. Conciliating leadership. This is expressed through kindness and understanding towards all the members, allowing them to act, but not directing or guiding group life. It does not clarify options, objectives or the strategies to attain them. It creates bewilderment amongst people (because "everything goes") and it creates a vacuum of authority in the group, either because responsibilities are not being undertaken or because the members give up their responsibilities in order to create a bogus "peace", which is disconcerting to more clear-sighted people. 35% of religious men and 30% of religious women report this type of leadership. The function of these leaders does not combine with any positive data on community life and obedience.

c. Leadership of animation and service. 40% of the religious men and 40% of the women report this. This is a more renewed and more evangelical style of exercising authority. It is the authority which encourages participation and discernment (rather than imposing personal decisions); the authority which is exercised as a brother or sister over other brothers and sisters, and is expressed by being close to others and through trust in others. This type of authority usually promotes the involvement and participation of the religious, encouraging team work and a process of involving all the members of the communities in decision-taking regarding matters of importance to their lives (even though the superior always has the last word). The findings indicate that this is a more evangelical type of authority because it reveals greater respect for the person, and it relies on others, and is therefore a means of strengthening the life of individuals and the group, clarifying their choices and objectives which they take upon themselves (Diagram 18).

TYPES OF LEADERSHIP IN THE LOCAL GOVERNMENT
These percentages vary, and can rise up to 10% in each typology

AUTHORITARIAN	15%	10%
MANAGERIAL	10%	15%
PERMISSIVE-NO GUIDANCE	35%	30%
ANIMATION AND SERVICE	40%	45%

The percentages for the three types of leadership mentioned above (authoritarian, managerial and conciliatory-permissive) show that over 50% of all religious report a great void in local government at the level of animation and service, and it is precisely to this that the religious life is tending today, and which strengthens the religious life.

2.3.2. Types of relations: their influence on the type of authority and on obedience

The exercise of one or other type of leadership must be linked to and determined by the type of relationships that exist between the person exercising government powers and the members of the group:

- A minority (about 10%) have a relationship of inferior to superior with the government, with a clearly servile sense of obedience.
- Another equally minority group, or 20% of religious men and 15% of religious women, have purely functional relations with the government (work, etc.).
- Most religious, 70% men and 75% women, have a relationship of fellowship (trust, closeness, brotherly and sisterly relations). We have also included in this brotherly/sisterly relationship a number of persons who would describe their relationships as "filial", which also indicates a trusting relationship. This type of filial relationship is typical of older people (and is not found in the under-Forties) (Diagram 19).

RELATIONS WITH SUPERIORS
These percentages can rise up to 10%

FROM INFERIOR TO SUPERIOR	10%	10%
FUNCTIONAL, WORK	20%	15%
BROTHERLY/SISTERLY	70%	75%

These figures show that the exercise of authority in the religious life has been profoundly transformed, in the direction of greater Gospel authenticity in the vast majority of congregations – "let the greatest among you be your servant" (which has not happened to the same extent in other spheres of the Church). With the change in the way authority is exercised, obedience has also changed as a consequence, into more active, responsible and participatory obedience. The change in the exercise of authority is also a factor that has greatly modified the dynamics of the life of religious communities and of whole congregations.

In those congregations where the exercise of authority has been transformed, there are fewer conflicts regarding obedience. And when these conflicts do exist they are nearly always due to the fact that the superiors have not taken account of others when taking decisions, since people are generally convinced today that the Will of God must be sought among everyone concerned.

OBEDIENCE-RESPONSIVENESS TO INSTRUCTIONS
These percentages can vary up to about 10%

TOTAL RESPONSIVENESS	40%
RESPONSIVENESS WITH DIFFICULTY	55%
NOT RESPONSIVE	5%

The responsiveness of religious to obey instructions (to being posted elsewhere, being moved to other communities, or allocated different work, etc.) is higher than one normally thinks; only 5% of all religious (and these percentages are not normally exceeded) are not responsive, and they represent a minority of persons who have lost the sense of obedience. About 40% said that they were totally willing to go and to do whatever they were told. 55% were willing, although they indicated provisos or difficulties, because having to move or change created serious or very serious personal situations. But they were nevertheless willing to obey despite the difficulties this might cause. These findings show that it is frequently not easy to obey and to accept postings in the religious life, but it also shows that those who are not disposed to obey are tiny minorities (Diagram 20).

2.3.3. *The government of congregations, a prophetic vision and strategies for action*

United to this substantial and evangelical change in the exercise of authority-obedience, there is also another fact that emerges from the findings: the tendency of the government of congregations to lay down objectives without taking account of the strategy of the "means" which they must use to obtain them.

The religious life certainly comes into being as a result of a Gospel call, and is rooted and draws its most authentic internal strength from the "ideal" to live as Jesus lived, sharing his mission. Perhaps because the "ideal" is identified with some sort of idealism (which is not related to reality) or because the superiors are ill-prepared for a new style of animation-service leadership, the fact remains that we are constantly having to make congregations aware of the need to "take account of reality, and with the means within their reach" in order to carry through their Evangelical Project, which usually only appears to be a fine-sounding statement of values and Gospel objectives. Any real planning must be based first and foremost on the means that one has in order to attain objectives. Objectives cannot be laid down without providing the means to attain them. Very frequently, only objectives are proposed, and the means are almost completely forgotten. If no means are provided, if the means are not planned, and if they are not there, the evangelical leaders who govern religious institutes can frequently create confusion, making their planning ineffective, and in the end create frustration within the religious group when it sees that the objectives that are laid down are not being realised, and that everything remains the same as before, and that everything that has been programmed is inaccessible to individual persons or to communities.

The findings indicate that a great deal of evangelical progress has been made, that the Will of God is being sought more, but there still remains much to be done before all religious have an evangelical experience of authority. A great many superiors have been changed into much more evangelical leaders, but many of them must bring their ideas further down to earth, to be closer to the reality of individuals and groups for which they have governmental responsibility. In addition to being people with a "vision", what the religious needs today is that they should be people of "action" with adequate "strategies", which are concrete and functional, in order to bring this vision to focus on the real life of their congregation.

3. THE GOSPEL MISSION OF THE RELIGIOUS LIFE TODAY

The personal life of an encounter with God, lived in a fraternal community, and commitment to the mission are the three key points of the religious life. In this third section we will comment on a number of realities regarding the mission, which emerge in the lives of the religious enumerated in the surveys.

3.1. The religious life as "The prophecy of the Kingdom"

3.1.1. Religious men and women as witnesses, in addition to being evangelising agents

For a long time the religious life in the Church has been identified with the mission, and this was defined in the Constitutions as being the purpose of the congregation. The mission included apostolic tasks of one kind or another, generally (but not exclusively) carried out in their institutional work (education, health care, welfare, charity work, Pastoral Ministry, etc.).

When we study the evangelical mission of the religious life (for men and women) today, we can see a new factor: the awareness of their members of a new aspect of their mission, namely to be witnesses to Jesus and his Gospel, "you shall be my witnesses". The religious see their mission in the Church today not only as evangelising agents, but primarily as witnesses through their way of life. The "witness" of their lives is a mission in itself for them. The religious life is felt to be a "living sign of Jesus and his Gospel", by taking on a specific way of living the values that Jesus lived, the vows and the life of "fraternal communion", being considered as a prophetic sign of the new humanity in Christ.

This "prophetic-witnessing" awareness of their existence is seen today in the mission of the religious life as the "task" specific to the religious life. This does not mean that in the past there were no religious who lived this dimension of their apostolic life. But what we do find is that in view of the new awareness of the value of "being" above "having", and the fact of greater "discernment of their evangelising work" (another factor which has been incorporated into the fulfilment of the mission) there has been an increased awareness and an enhanced specific ideal of the religious life to be "witnesses" of Jesus and his Gospel in the lives that the religious lead today. This awareness has encouraged new forms of life which are more simple and closer to the life of the people, and this has led to new forms of presence and commitment in new spheres of action. At the root of all these changes, of apostolic zeal and action, is the ideal of living more closely to men and women as "witnesses" of him who became one of us, and for whom he gave up his life. From this evangelical ideal, religious cannot see just any form of presence as being specifically that of a witness today; neither do they see just any kind of work, in the various tasks which they perform, as being evangelically significant and meaningful to the modern world, for the same reason.

This prophetic awareness of "being witnesses", through their own lives has brought about a shift in emphasis on the charism/mission of the congregations. In this change, one outstanding point is the decision to live more deeply involved in the environment, together with an appreciation of, and an effort to acquire, the values of the people (inculturation).

THE INCORPORATION OF THE RELIGIOUS COMMUNITY INTO THE ENVIRONMENT
These percentages vary up to about 10%

POSITIVE INCORPORATION	15%	50%
WITH DIFFICULTIES	40%	35%
NONE	45%	15%

These figures show that 15% of religious men and 50% of religious women already live the value of incorporation positively and evangelically, as well as the updating/"aggiornamento" of their charism-mission, in order to accompany people in their liberation process; 40% of religious men and 35% of religious women find it difficult (on account of their age, mentalities, lack of adequate preparation for the new life, or the style of working, etc.). The remaining 45% men and 15% women do not live incorporated into the environment. Progress is being made along the path of "evangelising embodiment", and many highly qualified religious with a powerful sense of their vocation, are joyfully pursuing this path, and wish to continue to do so increasingly (Diagram 21).

3.1.2. The religious life in the ecclesial community

Over the past two decades the religious have played an increasingly active part in cooperating in the life of the ecclesial community (at local and diocesan level). There are various reasons for this: the opening up of religious to being more actively involved in the life of the People of God, drawing on the ecclesiology of Vatican II; the decline in the number of priests, which has made it much more necessary to seek help from other pastoral workers of both sexes.

But this is frequently accompanied by a negative experience, contrasting with the greater awareness of the religious life, since religious see themselves as a "prophetic sign" through their lives, while they are sought out and in demand in the local and diocesan Churches, etc., with the religious women always at a subalternate, second tier level, frequently just because of the work they can do. In other words they are needed only as pastoral workers, or to carry out miscellaneous and financial services. The charism which inspires their lives is ignored. And this is a fairly constant and widespread fact, with few exceptions.

The failure to match the awareness of a Gospel-based prophetic existence, their charism in the Church and the real demand for them by the local Churches (as apostolic agents, who are needed only because of their "work") frequently creates tension, misunderstandings and frustration in all religious men and women, because it "cheapens" the religious life in their eyes. Local Churches (diocesan, etc.) frequently show that they are substantially ignorant of the religious life. This is understandable because the clergy in all spheres, do not generally study the theology of the religious life nowadays. But what is even more deplorable, when these situations arise, is the fact that the ecclesial role of the religious is reduced merely to "working" at one level or another depending upon requirements, and depending upon how deeply involved or not the lay people are (if there are trained lay people, these are usually given preference to religious). This lack of understanding of the prophetic mission of the religious life in the Church impoverishes the life of the ecclesial communion, which could be greatly enriched if people were to properly appreciate and incorporate the prophetic value of the various charisms of the religious life into the dynamics of Church life.

There is another situation which arises regarding religious

clerics. Increasingly more and more of these religious are fully involved in diocesan work (parishes, different areas of the pastoral ministry, etc.). For these people and for their congregations the challenge that arises is how to establish a balance between the diocesan pastoral work and the institutional charism as religious. They cannot always manage this, but they have a healthy sense of concern in order to harmonise the responsibility of their priestly ministry without ceasing to live the charism of their congregation.

3.1.3. The mission and the "preferential option for the poor"

The prophetic mission of the religious life has been enriched in many congregations by the "preferential option for the poor".

This "preferential option for the poor" is one of the evangelical constants which has emerged very forcefully in the religious life over the past few decades. On a personal and institutional level, religious men and women have made this preferential option for the poor. In other words, they have felt called to place themselves within the life of the poor, the marginalised, and the weak members of society and the world, standing by their side, as Jesus did.

This has been another one of the main silent revolutions that have taken place within the religious life, and is one of the greatest gifts of God which the religious life has received in recent times. Like all serious changes, this "preferential option for the poor" has created upsets in the lives of consecrated people, in the works of the religious institutes and in the criteria of life, and in financial terms, as well. All told, despite suffering and tension, the balance has been positive, and today the religious life is carrying out much more "meaningful" work, based on the Gospel, to help the disadvantaged of this world.

The preferential option for the poor has been the Gospel locomotive force which has done the most to stimulate many congregations to change their forms of presence, to open communities to becoming involved in new areas of work (the third world, suburban sprawls, marginalised human groups, abandoned rural zones, etc.). This call is also the one which has most challenged, from within, the historical works specific to the religious congregations.

The findings indicate that the vast majority of religious are moving in terms of this ideal, and that in the developing countries they are committed to the poor and work with them. In the developed countries, the findings show that some are committed to the poor in their own environment: 25% of religious men and 35% of religious women. Over 20% of the men and 25% of the women wish to become more committed still. Lastly, 50% of religious men and 35% of religious women feel solidarity for the poor, from where they are living as the present mission of their congregation. In the religious institutes surveyed by D.I.S., very few religious (5% or less) are not sensitive to the option for the poor in one way or another (Diagram 22).

THE OPTION FOR THE POOR IN THE DEVELOPED COUNTRIES
These percentages vary up to 10%

COMMITTED	25%	35%
WISHING TO BE COMMITTED	20%	25%
DISTANT SOLIDARITY	50%	35%
NOT SENSITIVE TO THE POOR	5%	5%

The preferential option for the poor has frequently created tensions in the internal life of congregations for a variety of reasons. There have been groups of people who are more aware than others of this option, governments have given greater or lesser support to some persons or to others, and different approaches to the apostolic field or the type of commitment, etc., have emerged. The tensions have been strongest when individuals or groups have become "polarised" around one or other approach to the commitment to the poor, or when they have acted within their congregations as pressure groups. Conversely when the Gospel motivation of individuals or groups has not worked as an exclusive factor but to establish dialogue, and when communion has been lived in the "plurality" of the different commitments within the same charism, the preferential option for the poor has come about with greater internal harmony in the changes that this required, and new areas of witness and evangelical work have been opened up.

Furthermore, the urge to become more embodied, the "revealed" sense of salvation in history and the whole process of self-evangelisation (already mentioned) that has been experienced in the religious life as a whole, have all converged in this direction, and have led religious men and women to opt to stand by the poor, the disadvantaged and the marginalised and to work on their behalf. Another factor that has had a profound influence on this option has been the critical-historical awareness which is typical of our own age, and which today has been acquired as part of the heritage of most of our better formed and trained religious. It is a fact that, regardless of all the processes that have taken place, the religious are much closer to the poor than they were before. The mission has generally enhanced their fidelity to the Gospel, and this has had many positive evangelical consequences for the religious life. Here are a few of them: the religious are living the beautiful experience of "being evangelised by the poor"; the educational centres of congregations which have made a preferential option for the poor have moved (to the districts lying on the outskirts of cities, into the rural environment, etc.) or they have opened up to all social classes, particularly to the least well-off; the religious life has been sending out highly qualified religious men and women to poor areas and zones; the congregations have changed their financial and administrative criteria and they are now more consistent with the preferential option for the poor; great solidarity is being shown to the less favoured at the level of persons, resources and facilities inside congregations. These are some of the indicators, of the many that we might have mentioned, regarding the religious life and the preferential option for the poor.

3.1.4. Fostering justice on the basis of the Gospel

The religious life is more committed to fostering justice today on the basis of the Gospel. This commitment is very closely linked to the preferential option for the poor, and forms a great unity with it.

The commitment to struggle to combat the injustices which are oppressing men and women today (poverty, unemployment, economic and social abuse, racism, male chauvinism, immigration, etc.) has strongly marked the apostolic approach taken by many congregations, and has been taken up in their Constitutions. Proof of this is the fact that so many religious of both sexes are committed to fighting for justice on the basis of their evangelical option of life: communities of religious have become embodied in the poor districts and disadvantaged areas of the cities, the rural world and the third world, defending the disadvantaged, showing solidarity with other movements working to combat injustice, with religious intellectuals working through their teaching and their publications in order to sensitise contemporary society to act with justice.

THE PROMOTION OF JUSTICE BASED ON THE GOSPEL
These percentages vary up to 5%

ALREADY COMMITTED	35%	55%
NOT VERY COMMITTED	65%	45%

The findings show that 35% of religious men and 55% of religious women are already practising this commitment to some extent, while the rest feel more dissatisfied with the way they are experiencing it, and have expressed the desire to become more committed to fostering and promoting justice. The people and groups who are more incorporated into the poorer environments are also generally speaking those who are more committed to promoting justice (Diagram 23).

3.2. Work/Mission

Work is another key point in the existence of every human person, and this is also true of religious. Work, which for religious is the mission to which they have been sent, is also a source of personal fulfilment, of Gospel demands and realism. The vast majority of these people are hard workers, who responsibly take upon themselves the task committed to them. And this work, this service and commitment to others, in one area or another, is a source of personal, human and evangelical fulfilment for each one of them.

Work is also a source of "realism". As a group, religious live a sober life, living on the fruits of their work which they share with one another. This way of living means that they are realistic with regard to the necessities of life, which they share with other human beings, because they see the law of labour as a means of subsistence, like the simple people of this world.

SATISFACTION WITH PERSONAL WORK
These percentages vary, and can rise positively up to 10%

HAPPY AND CONTENTED	90%
LITTLE CONTENTED OR DISCONTENTED	10%

The findings on the working lives of religious are extremely positive. The work they perform is one of the sources of great personal satisfaction for 90% of all religious, men and women (Diagram 24).

In most cases problems with personal work and the difficulties with the institutional work they perform is due to causes that are external to the religious themselves. In other words, they come from society (for example, the authorities) or other spheres, including areas of the Church, which give rise to negative situations. This is all the more evident when they are denied their rightful support, as in the case of education, healthcare work or welfare, etc., by the civil authorities.

Let us recall that there is a certain tendency today to overlook certain positive situations and data because people sometimes only feel that negative data is interesting. However reality can only be understood when the negative and the positive data are taken in just measure; we must be objectively aware of our limitations, but also of our strengths and our possibilities. This is the only way that, with an objective knowledge of our reality, we can be effective in human and Gospel terms.

In this section dealing with the working life, as indeed in the rest of this report, we are only concentrating on a few of the most important aspects of the evangelical mission of religious, as they emerge from the findings, and which acquaint us with what they are experiencing and how.

3.2.1. Human quality of work

The findings reveal that about 90% or more of all religious are content with their work, and that the same 90% say that they are also content in the Institutions and/or activities in which they work. Only a small percentage, which is normal in any group, of 10% (or less) are not content (Diagram 24-A).

SATISFACTION IN THE INSTITUTION OR ACTIVITY
IN WHICH ONE WORKS

HAPPY AND CONTENTED	90%
LITTLE OR DISCONTENTED	10%

These very important figures show that the religious are content with their work and with the places in which they work; and they also show from the outset that the problems facing the religious life do not stem fundamentally from work, nor from the types of work or institutions.

Where problems with work and with the Institutions exist, it is not because the people are not happy with what they are doing, but as a result of external circumstances to these Institutions and to the religious life itself, as we have already indicated.

As far as the working life is concerned another important fact has emerged: the great capacity for hard work that the religious have. Most of them are hard workers, and only a minority are not. But in present-day society it is necessary to note not only what work one is doing, but the yield from that work. In other words, we must reflect upon whether the fruits of the work are proportional to the effort and the human energy put into it. This largely depends on the training and the professional skills of the persons carrying out the work.

The figures show that the results of work, based on the human-evangelical aspects of the person (such as self-giving to others, solidarity, outreach to others, generosity, etc.) is one of the values which the religious practise more than all others, and at the same time it is one of the values most highly appreciated by the lay persons who work with them, even though this does not apply to all.

3.2.2. Professional quality of work

Another aspect of the performance of individual persons and Institutions is professional performance. This performance is based on the professional quality of the persons and on the technical facilities they use in the works they perform. The main institutions in which the religious work are educational (universities, secondary schools, primary and infant schools), health facilities (hospitals, clinics, dispensaries), welfare centres (homes, rehabilitation centres, etc.), the media (mass media, publications, etc.) and specifically pastoral activities. As indicated above, 90% of the religious are content with the Institutions in which they work, despite the fact that they recognise that the Institutions could and should improve.

The majority judge the work carried out by religious favourably and positively. Since they use technicians and facilities, their performance is generally good or very good, and certainly superior to what one would otherwise expect of the facilities, equalling or even exceeding the performance and the results of other centres equipped with more powerful and costly facilities. Throughout the years we have studied many educational and healthcare centres, and we have seen the importance of the human element, both in terms of the religious themselves and their lay colleagues, just as we have also seen the shortcomings and lack of other facilities, and the way in which the human element manages to make up for the inadequacy of technical facilities. This great human quality, due to generous and constant self-sacrifice, as the expression of charity, is the great "prophetic" dimension that we have already mentioned, and which emerges in the work carried out on behalf of others. This is the mission which is entrusted to every religious.

TRAINING FOR PROFESSIONAL WORK
These percentages vary, and can rise positively up to 10%

SUFFICIENT TRAINING	65%	45%
LITTLE OR NO TRAINING	35%	55%

One of the questions that we must always ask in our surveys is whether the religious feel that they are properly trained in professional terms (as educators, healthcare workers, social workers, etc.). 65% of the men 45% of the women answer that they feel "sufficiently" trained. But 35% of the men and 55% of the women say that they are not sufficiently trained (Diagram 25). This data shows the great need that exists for training on the part of a large number of religious men and women in terms of their professional work, and this is a training that cannot be made up for by good will or generous devotion to work, which has already been mentioned.

3.2.3. The evangelical quality of work

The work of a religious has a two-fold dimension (which has nothing to do with any form of dualism): a professional dimension, and professional effectiveness (which we dealt with in the previous question) and the apostolic-evangelical dimension, or Gospel fruitfulness. A very large proportion of the religious expressed self-fulfilment through their professional work, varying between 65% for men and 70% for women; however, while there are very low percentages of religious who say that they do not feel evangelically fulfilled in their work, around 5% of those questioned, there are still a fairly large number who experience ambiguity in their work, 30% of the men and 25% of the women religious. These partly live the evangelical dimension in their work, and partly they do not. This is a situation which occurs more frequently amongst teachers (Diagram 26).

PERSONAL EVANGELICAL FULFILMENT IN
PROFESSIONAL WORK
These percentages vary, and can rise positively up to 10%

POSITIVE FULFILMENT	65%	70%
PART FULFILMENT	30%	25%
NO FULFILMENT	5%	5%

The factors explaining why not all the religious fully discover the Gospel power of their work relate very closely to their experience of God, personal prayer and the indicators relating to the way in which they live the congregation's charism. This data shows that however admirable, the work-mission on its own is not sufficient to fully discover the evangelical power of what one is doing. It is also necessary to have "the enlightened eyes of the heart", the living faith, which is kindled in the experience of the interior life of the individual religious.

3.2.4. Teamwork

Personal work is still valuable in the religious life today, when this work is fully incorporated into the apostolic body of the congregation, the local Church, etc., and when the religious are not 'free-lancing' and do what they please, in the manner they choose, as it were "using" their religious family. While this manner of work-ing alone, or working together but not as a team, was very frequent in the past, today it has become essential to work as a team.

TEAMWORK
These percentages vary, and can rise positively up to 10%

POSITIVE	50%	45%
JOINTLY BUT NOT AS A TEAM	40%	45%
NEGATIVE INDIVIDUAL	10%	10%

Teamwork among religious men and women has greatly improved in the past few years, but it nevertheless comes up against serious difficulties. The present situation is as follows: 50% of the men and 45% of the women religious have already joined in the dynamics of teamwork. 40% and 45%, respectively, of the two groups find it difficult, recognising that they work "together", but not as a team. About 10% work on an individualistic basis, doing "their own thing". This noticeable lack of teamwork on the part of quite a number of religious seriously impoverishes the action-mission of religious today (Diagram 27).

3.2.5. The critical sense of reality in religious

The critical sense of events, the capacity to analyse reality and to understand the positive and negative aspects, and the causes and effects of reality, forms part of contemporary culture, and it is therefore part of the patrimony of the vast majority of the religious (about 90%) (Diagram 28). This value of contemporary culture is a source of discriminating knowledge, which is necessary in order to be able to make responsible, personal and group choices, in a plural culture and society. This critical sense has given religious a better understanding and ability to analyse reality, and on the basis of this knowledge to conduct a more realistic evaluation both of the mission which they perform and of the facilities and resources with which they carry out that mission, in response to the needs they discover in reality. This value has enriched and updated the mission of the religious life.

Because of this critical sense, whenever teaching or authority, etc., are practised or exercised in a bullying or absolutist manner, this clashes with the critical attitudes of individuals. For today people tend to assimilate something (formation, training) or to obey (authority) not so much because of the person who issues the orders or on the strength of arguments based on authority, but by virtue of an analysis of the "contents" and the "meaningfulness" of what is being ordered. This gives rise to obedience based on active co-responsibility, dialogue and well-informed cooperation. And this is why ongoing evaluation of what is being performed is so valuable.

THE CRITICAL SENSE OF REALITY

DO HAVE A CRITICAL SENSE	90%
DO NOT	10%

The state of religious congregations in terms of their critical sense of life varies widely and is largely determined by the educational and formation levels of the persons concerned and their participation in the life of the congregation. The findings show that the broader the participation of individual religious in the planning and decision-making processes, the richer these decisions and plans will be, but also the greater the commitment to them of everyone concerned.

This critical sense has been actively incorporated into the life of a great many religious, as a value that makes it possible to "know reality" and to "evaluate the Mission".

3.3. New data on the mission

In the present evangelising task of the religious life new findings have emerged regarding the way in which the mission is performed. We have already indicated some of these (a critical sense of reality, teamwork, etc.) and we are mentioning others, even though they cannot be developed as fully as they deserve in view of the limitations of this paper.

3.3.1. Preferential approaches to life-mission

The call to the religious life to give one's life to evangelisation and to serve the poor is nothing new. The vast majority of congregations had this call at the very source of their charism. But what has been rediscovered, as something new, is the style or manner of this self-giving and this service today. This new style or manner has the following features:

a. Working for the total liberation of persons

We wish to carry out the evangelisation of the poor with an attitude of closely sharing their situation: living among them (incorporation) and with them, moving beyond the provision of external aid or protectionism. The mission is directed at the total liberation of persons, which is quite different from any other type of aid under which one merely educates and instructs them, practises charity to them, or helps to keep them, etc. The internal dynamic of evangelisation, seen as the total liberation of the person, is the one which has led to new commitments to justice and human rights, based on the faith, according to the various charisms.

b. Active cooperation in the task of transforming structures which are the causes of poverty, injustice and the marginalisation of men, women and peoples

As the critical awareness of religious has grown, and as this has led them to carry out "a critical analysis of reality", there has also been an increased awareness of the unjust structures which oppress human beings, thwarting God's plan for mankind and for nature. This awareness has led religious to enrich their "evangelising mission" by actively cooperating in the task of transforming these unjust structures (active denunciation, supporting movements working in this direction, taking part in various actions, etc.).

3.3.2. Gospel discernment

More and more religious are carrying out "Gospel discernment" of the dynamic of the mission they perform. In other words, they are seeking to analyse and judge what they are

109

doing in the light of the Gospel, in order to relaunch their mission with the conviction of faith of people who are seeking the will of God, often involving difficult and complex choices. Gospel discernment is bringing great maturity to the action and mission of the religious life.

Gospel discernment, or to put it in another way, the active search for the will of God in a group, is one of the best guarantees of a sincere evaluation and "inspiration" which relaunches this action in response to the new calls of Our Lord in the work of evangelisation, when it is incorporated into the dynamic of the mission being performed.

GOSPEL DISCERNMENT IN THE APOSTOLIC WORK GROUP
These percentages vary, and can rise positively up to 15%

EXPLICIT	8%	10%
IMPLICIT	25%	35%
NOT PERFORMED	67%	55%

These findings show that at the present time only 8% of religious men and 10% of religious women explicitly carry out discernment of their apostolic work. 25% of religious men and 35% of religious women perform it, to a certain degree, when they evaluate their projects (albeit only implicitly). The remaining 67% of religious men and 55% of the religious women have not yet begun to carry out a Gospel discernment of the work they perform (Diagram 29).

3.3.3. *A new level of collaboration between religious and the laity*

In the many surveys which D.I.S. has conducted on the laity who collaborate with religious, and particularly lay teachers in universities and other educational establishments, the following overall findings have emerged, which are fairly reliable as a whole, and can be extrapolated fairly safely:

a. About 35% of these lay educators and teachers are persons who identify with the mission and spirit of the religious with whom they work. They work with this apostolic spirit, and not only because it is their job. But it is very important to note that this identification by lay collaborators with the spirit of the congregation is, in the majority of cases, by osmosis, and not explicitly formulated. It is something they acquire by rubbing shoulders and working together, but it is not normally expressed and put into words as such, due to a certain modesty on the side of the religious as well as the laity themselves.

b. 44% of these lay collaborators are good people, who work with the religious because they have to work to live. The aspects of the mission and the apostolic spirit is somewhat distant, even marginal, and they think that the Christian mission of work is of concern only to the religious, even though the vast majority of these lay persons are not opposed to this apostolic spirit. Quite a few of these educators could discover the Gospel mission of work according to the spirit of the congregation if they were to be cultivated.

c. As for the remaining 20% of the lay colleagues, we simply have to learn to put up with them, but it would be better if they did not work in our institutions (Diagram 30).

LAY IDENTIFICATION WITH THE CHARISM OF RELIGIOUS
Lay teachers in schools and universities

IDENTIFIED	35%
GOOD PEOPLE NO IDENTIFICATION	45%
APATHETIC OR HOSTILE	20%

These overall findings on one sector of the action-mission of the religious life are the ones we can use for what we might call the conversion of religious to greater involvement of the laity in their charism. Each age in history has its own particular features. Perhaps one of the historical features of our age will be the need for the explicit integration of lay persons into the spirit and charism of the religious institutions, from their choice of the lay state, and not merely implicitly, or by osmosis, as occurs in most cases at the present time. This integration will have, as an important consequence, the human and Gospel enrichment of our lay collaborators, and will strengthen the work of the religious and of their Institutions through working with lay persons who share the same spirit and the mission as their religious companions.

Collaboration with the laity demands a change in structures and roles or functions within the religious life. These changes include some which affect the management of the institutions. It will be necessary to govern jointly with lay persons, and the religious will have to work in teams with lay persons and under their direction.

The main work and role of the religious in our institutions will tend to be that of persons who foster Gospel values and the Gospel spirit of work rather than specialised workers in education, nursing, etc., which will increasingly become the province of the lay workers. This does not mean that the religious must stop acquiring adequate vocational and professional training. On the contrary, university qualifications or other qualifications will be more necessary than ever before in this work of cooperating in the lay world where qualifications are so necessary. But the work will tend to be directed towards more direct dedication and to proclaiming the Gospel and getting others to live the Gospel.

This integration of lay collaborators into the evangelical work of the mission alongside religious is a great task. Our findings show that considerable progress has already been made in this direction. There is already a very high level of collaboration and integration of lay people, even though in most cases their involvement is still only potential or implicit. It is necessary to go on working at this duty of the human and Gospel enrichment of many people, and in many cases shore up the future of some of our institutions with their cooperation, in order to make them truly respond to what the world expects today of the religious life, and for which there are often few religious available. The congregations that have fallen behind in the involvement of lay collaborators in their charism/mission must now make haste in this direction.

3.3.4. The challenge of living in communion with pluralism

One of the greatest difficulties in the process of transforming the religious life has sometimes been the loss of the internal communion of the congregation between the people committed to different spheres or ways of living and evangelising. Internal pluralism has grown, and this has thrown down a challenge to our ability to live communion in pluralism.

At various levels, from government to grassroots, religious today are faced with a great challenge (the same challenge that faces society and the Church as a whole): the need to learn to live, and manage to live, a communion of Gospel and congregational ideals, internal, sincere and Gospel-based communion, in a plural world (different generations, different forms of community life, different peoples and cultures, different degrees of incorporation, the preferential option for the poor, etc.).

It appears at the "theoretical" level that religious are convinced that pluralism is a fact, that it can be a source of great wealth. But in the congregations that have experienced the processes analysed above, there are many religious who are still harking back nostalgically to the "uniformity" that they once experienced (although only about 12% consider pluralism to be bad). But as far as the attainment of pluralism is concerned, about 38% experience congregational pluralism as a source of richness, and 50% recognise pluralism as a fact and say that they "would prefer" to live it in a spirit of dialogue, fellowship and mutual support in action (Diagram 31).

APOSTOLIC PLURALISM IN WORKS/INSTITUTIONS
These percentages vary, and can rise positively up to 10%

GOOD, SOURCE OF RICHNESS	38%
GOOD, WITH DIFFICULTIES	50%
BAD	12%

These findings confirm the many internal tensions, divisions and conflicts that exist and which destroy the enthusiasm and the commitment of individuals and congregations who fail to strike a balance between cordial internal communion and pluralism.

The most wonderful charisms are nothing without mutual love and understanding; they split the energies of the religious family (of the Church...), they cast a shadow over the witness of fellowship and consequently they do not build up the Kingdom. They are a great evil for the religious life, for its prophetic witness and its mission. With the aid of Gospel discernment it is possible to move ahead in the internal unity of the congregations.

3.3.5. Evangelisation and education

Within the wide range of work carried out by the religious life, we would like to mention a few figures which refer to the presence of religious in the world of education, because this is one of the apostolic areas in which this presence is strongest.

Today, educational work for all religious covers a much broader spectrum than straightforward classroom teaching (with which it was sometimes identified in the past). This is the first fact which has opened up new types of presence and work in the field of education to many congregations (family education, community education, street educators, rehabilitating drug addicts, and working with other types of marginalised people, etc.).

However, the presence of the religious life continues to play an important role in educational establishments. D.I.S. has studied the Christian dimension of education in religious educational establishments with great commitment over the past few years, particularly in primary and middle schools. From the professional point of view of education, the vast majority of religious schools are of a high quality, and indeed very high quality.

From the point of view of the Christian dimension of education, namely seeing whether the values that are transmitted through education in these Institutions are truly Christian, and whether the pupils and students not only learn to know the human person but also learn to know God and direct their lives according to the Gospel values, we have to say that over the past ten years or so, we have noted a considerable improvement in the findings of our surveys of schools.

One of the main reasons for this improvement has been the educational projects drafted in former years which have gradually percolated down to all the members of the educational community. Many ideas held by the religious themselves, and lay teachers, parents and students and pupils about what Christian education is all about today have become clearer.

And yet this improvement in the Christian dimension of education is not evenly spread. There are some teaching congregations that have made much more progress and improvements than others, and are now learning to overcome the difficulties which are facing the Church as a result of the lay-oriented educational system in so many countries. Other congregations have improved, but they still have to solve quite a few difficulties, particularly with regard to the catechetical-pastoral formation of the religious and their lay collaborators, and the need to find an appropriate space for Christian formation within academic and school life.

It should be noted that in democratic countries it seems that the schools run by religious are now moving away from a neutral type of education, with Christianity being implicitly present, where it was formerly taken for granted that it was sufficient to give children a good education without hardly mentioning the message of the Gospel at all.

3.4. Activism

In section 2.1.4. we dealt with activism from the point of view of its effects on the interior life of the religious and its repercussions on community life. We will now view activism from the point of view of work and the mission.

The apostolic religious life is based on three fundamental pillars: the person, the community and the mission/work. When these three factors are balanced, the religious life of the congregation as well as the personal life of each religious will be harmonious, balanced, fruitful and productive.

Falling prey to activism means emphasising the pillar of work, action, to the detriment of personal and community life, damaging the dimension of contemplation and community living. The presence of activism tends to stifle both the personal life of the religious relating to his or her experience of God, prayer, reflection, study, formation, and the internalisation of life experiences and the realities of community life, the quality of living in fellowship, service to the community and the congregation; there is hardly any time left for these things. All the values that make up the contemplative side of the religious life take on a lesser importance than is due to them, and they lose the great value which they really possess in the existence of each religious.

This activism, living absorbed by action and the consequent lack of balance between *being and doing*, is not only something which affects the world of religious who are consecrated to God, but also the secular world and society in general. This is a very typical limitation of our age, which affects virtually everyone and everything. One should not therefore be surprised that it also affects the religious.

The average percentages of activism among religious men and women are worrying, ranging from a minimum of 50% to a maximum of 60%. This indicates that even in congregations under the best conditions, the number of persons caught up in "activism" is still high, ranging between 50% and 40%. Age tends to put a brake on activism, which is more common in the younger generations. But even in the middle-aged generations activism is very strong and can even extend to 75% of the members of those generations. This is understandable, because the middle generations are the ones who undertake the main burden of the work and the Institutions. Even the government of congregations is frequently affected by very high percentages of activism, of between 40% and 50% (Diagram 32).

EFFECTS OF ACTIVISM (IMBALANCE BETWEEN
ACTION-CONTEMPLATION)
These percentages in some groups can rise to 10%

ALL THE RELIGIOUS LIFE	50%
RELIGIOUS BETWEEN 35 AND 55 YEARS	75%
RELIGIOUS GOVERNMENT	40%

These findings show that activism impoverishes people in their human and Gospel dimension. It impoverishes prayer life, which it replaces by action. Many religious men and women have to reorganise their lives in order to avoid becoming impoverished by their activism, and impoverishing the groups to which they belong. Sometimes, however, activism cannot be blamed on individual persons, but on the organisation of their group work, even community work, or the work of the institutional province to which they belong. The government should be concerned to ensure that their best brothers and sisters do not end up in a state of activism, and they must also ensure that they are not polarised by the concerns of their institutions, to the detriment of the attention given to persons and to their internal religious community life.

The figures for activism by religious men and women are worrying, and in a sense they help to explain why the religious life is lacking in effectiveness in our world, by failing to project the contemplative dimensions of the religious life which men and women of our age so dearly need. Frequently they are only accompanied in action, whereas they have more than enough of this already.

4. THE RELIGIOUS LIFE AND YOUTH: VOCATIONS

4.1. Youth pastoral ministry: an urgent and vital challenge to the religious life

The issue of youth pastoral ministry has always been present throughout these years of research in practically all the surveys carried out by D.I.S. on religious. Our department has also conducted major specific surveys into religious vocation, of young lay persons and young religious. At the end of this report we would therefore like to offer a brief but important summary of the findings, conclusions and sociological experiences regarding vocations to the religious life.

The data studied here show that the religious life needs to draw up a pastoral ministry geared to contemporary youth as a matter of urgency, and ensure that it is effective. This must include a specific vocational pastoral ministry directed at young people including children and adolescents under 14. This is not only an urgent challenge but it is a matter of life and death. On it may depend the future life of many congregations.

For the last two decades the religious life has been preoccupied with the problem of identity and internal congregational renewal, and at the same time it has been committed to undertaking many evangelising tasks, with admirable self-sacrifice. And many religious institutes in general, and with certain exceptions, have not known how to, or have been unable to create and put into practice a "new" pastoral ministry for adolescents and young people, even though there is a shortage of young vocations. The facts confirm that the models of youth pastoral care which used to exist in the past no longer work and are not effective, at least in the Western developed world, and that this is also true for other countries, since the changes that are taking place among young people are so far-reaching that this pastoral care must now be tailored to cater for the present world situation.

THE ATTITUDE TO THE PASTORAL MINISTRY OF
YOUTH-VOCATIONS
These percentages vary, and can rise positively up to 15%

ACTIVE ATTITUDE   20%
PASSIVE INAPPROPRIATE   80%

The findings show that quite a number of congregations are behaving as if they did not even know what it means to have a shortage of vocations, partly because they still have a fairly large number of religious who are of working age. They are busy and happy with their commitment to the poor and the marginals, and their institutional works, etc., but their groups are already suffering from the consequences of having abandoned the "pastoral ministry" of young people, and of the ageing of their group and consequently the lack of a generational turnover. A minority of 20%, reaching as high as 35%, of religious are usually aware of the need for this pastoral care and want to work at it, by taking "concrete measures" namely: devoting more people to it and planning pastoral and vocational ministry properly, tailored to suit present-day youth (Diagram 33). The remaining 80% of the religious, which can even rise as high as 85%, take up the following inadequate postures:

- Passivity: wait for the young people to come along to them, it is sufficient to pray, bear good witness of life and the "vocations will come on their own".
- Maladjustment: for too long an unsuitable pastoral ministry has been practised with young people, which hardly has anything to do with their human and Gospel concerns.
- Wait-and-see: more time must be spent to internally clarifying the life and mission of the congregation and "when everything is clear to us", we can start this pastoral ministry.

A survey that we carried out in Spain a short time ago on young Christian believers between 19 and 26 years of age, who had some contact with religious, showed how much they appreciated the religious life, and it also revealed the capacity of these young men and women to respond to the call of Our Lord to the religious life. But no-one loves or becomes committed to what they do not know. And the religious life, at least in many congregations, has always lived its charism in a kind of "underworld", without telling others about it and without offering young people the ideal to share in it.

Moreover, quite a few, if not many congregations frequently carry out vocational campaigns (with folders and pamphlets, etc.) for reasons, and with arguments and using types of approach, which actually achieve the opposite effect to the one intended, because they do not tell young people what the religious life is really all about. In most cases what they say is incomprehensible, and has no attraction to young people today.

4.2. The age in which the religious vocation emerges

The figures we are offering here are given by way of example, and show the importance of intensely cultivating young people, adolescents and children in an evangelical manner to live a Christian life which will enable vocations to the religious life to emerge.

AGE IN WHICH THE VOCATION TO THE RELIGIOUS LIFE BEGINS
Data on Spanish religious ages 29 and under

UNDER 14 YEARS	37%
FROM 15 TO 18 YEARS	50%
AFTER 19 YEARS	13%

These are the results of a recent D.I.S. survey on all the young Spanish religious men and women under 29 years of age. 87% of these young religious said that they felt their "first" call to the religious vocation before they were 18 years old. Within this 87%, 37% felt their first concern regarding their vocation before they were 14, and 50% between the ages of 15 and 18. Only 13% of these young religious men and women felt the "first call" to a vocation when they were still young adults over 18 (Diagram 34).

These figures show the great need for a pastoral ministry for children, adolescents and young people. Children, adolescents and young people must be evangelised to enable them to live their faith, to follow Jesus Christ and his Gospel, without ceasing to be persons of their own age. They must be helped to find the way to realise their ideals and their life project based on the faith, and those who are called by Our Lord must be helped to find the ideal of the consecrated religious life. This conviction is clearer today in the religious life than it was several years ago, but frequently it remains a well-formulated "objective", but it is not striven for and it is sterile, because the "means" are not provided whereby to attain it.

4.3. Religious and their direct pastoral contact with young people

"PERSONAL PASTORAL CONTACT"
WITH YOUNG PEOPLE
These percentages vary, and pastoral contact can rise up to 10%

PASTORAL CONTACT	35%	20%
OTHER CONTACT OR NO CONTACT	65%	80%

When congregations are asked how many of their members have *"personal* pastoral contact directly with young people" the answers do not exceed 35% for men and 20% for women. The rest have contacts with young people in an educational capacity or for pre-evangelisation, etc., but they do not have personal and direct pastoral contact with young people. This means that 65% of the religious men and 80% of religious women have no direct pastoral personal contact with young people (Diagram 35). This data speaks for itself, and is one of the several causes for the lack of vocations to congregations and to the religious life in general, and particularly to the women's religious life.

4.4. The features of vocational and youth pastoral ministry for our age

The findings of our surveys have brought out the features of a youth-vocational Pastoral Ministry which make it functional and effective:

- Active pastoral ministry: it is necessary to reach out to young people. Today it is very difficult for young people to reach out to the religious, from the pastoral and apostolic points of view; if religious do not reach out to them (particularly in the Western world) the two worlds will increasingly become more distant: the religious life on the one hand and the world of young people on the other. The religious life must take a step towards them.

- A formative pastoral ministry: when religious make contact with young people, their meeting must be "formative" in the human and evangelical dimension. This means that it must be a permanent and extended encounter, in the long term, and must therefore be organised and stable. Young people say that their vocation was a process, a personal path.

- Pastoral ministry teamwork: it is necessary to dedicate the best religious to carry out a combined Pastoral Ministry with young people, adolescents and youth, giving it preference over any other apostolate. Moreover, this is a task which must be carried out on a team basis today. There is no room today for "free-lancers" in this pastoral ministry, or for the vocational recruitment officials that used to exist in the olden days. A team is needed, both because of the complexity and the demands of working with today's young people, and also because of the greater value of pastoral work when several people join forces to carry it through.

- The pastoral ministry with a clear congregational identity: the youth pastoral team must work according to their congregation's evangelical project clear-sightedly and enthusiastically. Young people want to know what the religious institute has to offer them in terms of life and action (not only action, which is what they are normally offered most of, but they also want to know the evangelical life-style of the group, as a "prophecy" of the Kingdom). Only religious who are enthusiastic and excited about their lives can attract others to choose it.

- Community support: it is very important to have the cooperation and support of the communities in this pastoral action with young people. Today, young people are very sensitive to the values of relationships, and they therefore wish to know how the religious live. Young people today form a social group and they need the group more than they used to in former times. This is why they wish to know "how people live in communities", and hence the need for the witness of the community, the welcome, the joy, the way of life, to be evangelically "meaningful" to young people who are called by Our Lord to the religious life today (Diagram 36).

COMMUNITY SUPPORT FOR YOUTH PASTORAL MINISTRY
These percentages vary, and can rise positively up to 10%

POSITIVE SUPPORT	15%
SOME SUPPORT	40%
NO SUPPORT	45%

Only 15% of all the religious felt that their community effectively supports the youth pastoral ministry. About 40% of the religious recognised that their communities support this pastoral ministry "somewhat", but they also said that they could be more welcoming to young people. As many as 45% felt that young people were distant from the religious life, as they understand it and live in their communities, and that in fact they do not support the pastoral ministry of young people.

These figures show that it is necessary to accompany adolescents and young people with a vocation to the religious life by a formative process to enable them to mature in the faith, while the religious life itself must try to draw close to and open up "a new space" – obviously an evangelical space – within its communities in order to welcome in young people.

4.5. A testimony which calls out to us regarding vocations to the women's religious life

At this conference of religious we feel that it is important to quote the testimony of a young girl aged 22. We gave her a personal interview, forming part of the methodology for a survey of vocations. We are mentioning it because it is very eloquent and it is not an exception, but is fairly representative, and clearly expresses something which our findings constantly reiterate, and which is seriously affecting the religious life – including the male spheres of the Church. This young woman, who is about to complete her training in law, told us that she felt a vocation to the religious life, but she added, "In my professional life as a lawyer I shall be what I am and what I am worth in terms of my capacity and skills and professional work. But if I become a sister, I know that, because I am a woman, I shall always play second fiddle in the Church".

The male religious world, which in so many fields in life is defending justice and human rights, should reflect on this "factum", and as the twentieth century draws to a close ensure that one of the most evangelical and important parts of the Church (our sisters as consecrated persons) are not treated as "juniors" in the Church of God.

4.6. Vocations in the secularised Western world and in the East, and in the developing countries

The religious life, particularly in the secularised societies has lived in semi-clandestinity for many years, not wishing to be perceived for what it is, only trying to carry out an apostolic service, frequently with great commitment, as just one agent more within the ecclesial community. It moved away from being in a situation of prestige, with a certain "social" power, into this much more critical stage. Today, in many countries, the religious life has become more credible as a result of the efforts made to adapt, and to tailor its work and mission in order to respond to the new calls of mankind and of the most disadvantaged, and also because of the simpler life it now leads, bringing it closer to the people (without privileges).

The results that we have acquired on the religious life tell us that it must pull out of this situation and offer its prophetic life and evangelising project with clarity. This is a challenge to the religious life in every part of the world, but it is all the more urgent and necessary in the Christian countries of the first world, where ageing has taken place most acutely.

On the other hand, the situation of the religious life in the developing countries (Latin America, Africa, certain areas of Asia, etc.) is very different. In these countries there are more vocations to the religious life, where the religious work with young people or in the Christian community, etc. But these vocations need a long formative process to accompany them, and general discernment, both to discover whether the candidates have the necessary human basis to take on the commitments of the religious life, and also to find out if their motivations for their vocation are evangelical and solid.

We should mention the fact that many congregations (it would be wonderful if we could say this of all) are showing great sensitivity today to the vocations in these countries, by allowing persons entering the congregations to do so in their own country, and to spend the first stages of their formation there.

NOTES

1. Raymond Hostie, *Vida y muerte de las Ordenes Religiosas*, Desclée de Brouwer, Bilbao, 1973, pp. 281-286.
2. Julian Lopez y de Isusil. *Las religiosas en España*. Ed. Mensajero, Bilbao, 1968, 420 pages (pp. 63-69).

2.

The mission
of religious

I.

The religious in mission

Michael Amaladoss, SJ

Our task today is to look at the world, and reading the signs of the times, discern the challenges that face us religious, and ask ourselves how we are meeting them and how we can respond to them more effectively in the future. We will have two panels and sharing in groups to engage in this discernment. I would not like to pre-empt this exercise by presenting a list of challenges. However, our purpose in this Congress is not so much to draw up action plans, as to contribute to the renewal of our religious institutes by helping them to acquire a clearer consciousness of their mission in the Church and in the world. With this aim in mind I shall try to provide a framework within which to place our discernment by reflecting with you on the theme of mission in relation to the religious. I shall explore questions like: How do we understand mission today? What is the relationship between mission and the charisms of the consecrated life? Are there some general orientations that could help our discernment?[1]

As a first step in the preparation of this Congress, the Secretariat of the USG sent around a questionnaire to the religious institutes. This included a question about how religious respond to the missionary challenges of our time. The answers to this question are influenced and are limited by the meaning one gives to the term "mission". Some understand it only as mission *"ad gentes"* and as "foreign mission" looked at from the "North" and the "West". Others take the broader view of *Redemptoris Missio*, which includes mission *ad gentes*, pastoral work among the faithful and re-evangelization of dechristianized groups.[2] Then they go on to list the various challenges: first evangelization and the building up of the local Churches, inculturation and the dialogue with secular culture, the promotion of justice and human rights, the practice of inter-religious dialogue and ecumenism, work with the non-poor and the media, option for the poor and helping the formation and growth of basic communities, reaching out to people who are in greater need, like the refugees, people who suffer from AIDS or are addicted to drugs, etc. One could add to this list. One could discern priorities in a particular area or according to particular charisms. Besides, any list of tasks could seem overwhelming today, given the progressive reduction in numbers.

I suggest that our reflection will be better helped if we move our focus away from the *tasks* of mission to ask ourselves: "What is mission?" The idea of mission has been developing very much since the Council. This development is best realized if we can explore our own *images of mission*. These images need not be exclusive: there may be more than one that compositely guide our thinking. The images I evoke are typological. Each may have a certain validity, which could be exaggerated by an one-sided emphasis. When we think of mission what is the image that we have in our awareness?

Images of mission

Mission as *crusade* looks at the world as divided between good and evil, true and false, saved and in need of salvation. There is an atmosphere of conquest, primarily spiritual, but some times mixed up with economic, political and cultural power. One thinks of the Church as an institution that has to be planted often, as a matter of fact, transplanted – in ever new areas.

Mission as *teaching* focuses on faith as a creed or a body of truths that has to be communicated. One speaks of revelation as communication of knowledge. One develops the media – written, oral, electronic – to communicate the revealed truth. As will follows reason, conversion will follow knowledge. The Church is the Teacher.

Mission as *conversion* stresses the personal dimension. Each individual is called to a change of heart – to be "born again" – in response to a moral challenge. It is a charismatic experience. The Church is the Noah's ark of the saved in a wicked world.

Mission as *liberation* presents salvation as the transformation of life starting here and now, though it is not limited to the present, promoting healing, development and justice.

Mission as *witness* refers to Christian life as a silent but active presence in the midst of a hostile world. One builds up model communities of service and fellowship.

Mission as *inculturation* evokes the need of the missionary and of Christianity to become incarnate in a particular culture. One tends to think of it still as the translation in local cultural categories of an unchanging tradition: maintaining unity of meaning in a plurality of expressions.

Mission as *dialogue* recognizes the other religions as positive elements in the salvific plan of God. Some see them as the hidden or the preparatory activity of the Spirit. The Church then is seen in relation to them as an exploitation or fulfilment.

In contrast to these and other such images,[3] I would like to propose three mutually complementary images: mission as *pilgrimage*, as *prophecy*, and as *peoples' movement*. These are best evoked as part of an emerging, integral view of mission in the period after the Second Vatican Council.[4]

Mission today

Our mission has its origin in the "mission of God". As the document on mission of the Second Vatican Council has said:

The Church on earth is by its very nature missionary since, according to the plan of the Father, it has its origin in the mission of the Son and the Holy Spirit. This plan flows from the "fountain-like love", the love of God the Father... He generously pours out, and never ceases to pour out, his divine goodness, so that he who is creator of all things might at last become "all in all" (1 Cor 15:28), thus simultaneously assuring his own glory and our happiness. It pleased God to call men to share in his life and not merely singly, without any bond between them, but he formed them into a people, in which his children, who had been scattered, were gathered together (cf Jn 11:52).[5]

The mission of the Son and of the Holy Spirit, through which God communicates God's life to us, has a two-fold aspect. While it is true that the Son becomes human in Jesus and the Spirit is sent by Jesus Christ at Pentecost, the Word of God is present at creation and enlightens every human person coming into the world (Jn 1: 1-3,9) and the Spirit of God is present and active too in the world from the beginning (Gen 1:2).[6] While proclaiming the Good News of Jesus therefore we have to take account of the ongoing action of the Word and the Spirit in humanity and in history. We have to respect peoples' cultural and religious traditions and consciences. Our mission therefore starts with the contemplation of the mystery of God in history (Eph. 1:3-10). Since God's action is mixed up with human imperfection and also sinfulness, our contemplation needs to be discerning. This effort to walk with God and with others in the fulfilment of God's plan for the universe makes our mission a *pilgrimage*.[7]

The process of reflection after the Council has also made us aware of the multiple dimensions of mission. The Synod of Bishops in 1971 declared that the *promotion of justice* is an integral aspect of evangelization. This has been repeated by the various social encyclicals of Pope John Paul II.[8] The Synod of Bishops on Evangelization in 1974 highlighted the dialogue between Gospel and culture so that *inculturation* became a dimension of mission.[9] Declarations of the Pontifical Council for inter-religious dialogue as well as the Pope's gestures and statements in Assisi in 1986 and the recent encyclical *Redemptoris Missio*[10] show how *inter-religious dialogue* is an integral dimension of evangelization. Further reflection however shows us that inculturation, dialogue and liberation become evangelization when the Word of God becomes a prophetic presence that seeks to transform culture, to be critical of the easy legitimations of religion and to challenge the oppressive economico-political and socio-cultural structures. Mission then is *prophecy* that radicalizes the evangelizing dialogue of the Good News with human cultures, religions and oppressive structures.[11]

The focus of mission is the *Reign of God*, which Jesus himself proclaimed (Mk 1:15) and the *Church* as its sacrament and servant.[12] The Church is for the world and is called to animate a *movement of peoples* towards the realization of God's Reign which is both historical and eschatological.[13] The way of the Church is the way of Jesus Christ himself. It is a way of love that gives itself even unto death (Phil 2:6-11). It is an incarnational way that is oriented to the total transformation of the resurrection (Rev 21:1-5). It is a task of reconciliation and unification of all things (2 Cor 5:19; Eph 1:10; Col 1:20).[14] Mission therefore can be seen as a *movement of peoples* animated by the Church.[15] George Soares-Prabhu describes this well.

> The Kingdom of God proclaimed by Jesus is ultimately his revelation of God's unconditional love... When the revelation of God's love (the Kingdom) meets its appropriate response

in man's trusting acceptance of this love (repentance), there begins a mighty movement of personal and social liberation which sweeps through human history. The movement brings *freedom* inasmuch as it liberates each individual from the inadequacies and obsessions that shackle him. It fosters *fellowship*, because it empowers free individuals to exercise their concern for each other in genuine community. And it leads on to justice, because it impels every true community to adopt the just societal structures which alone make freedom and fellowship possible.[16]

The Church in mission

In the context of this broad vision of mission I would like to point to and stress, for our purpose today, three points. First of all, mission is not merely an activity of the Church; it is its very being.[17] It flows from the mission of God, in Christ and in the Spirit. It is a community called and sent – *missioned* – by God, in continuity with God's own mission. That is why I prefer to use the term "mission", and not "evangelization". The sacrament of Baptism is not merely a gift of salvation, but a call to mission.[18] The acknowledgement by the Second Vatican Council that "the Holy Spirit offers to all the possibility of being made partners, in a way known to God, in the Paschal Mystery"[19] has made us rediscover the missionary dimensions of Baptism, analogous to the baptism of Jesus in the Jordan that launches his public ministry. All the members of the Church, with the variety of their charisms and responsibilities, share this mission. This mission may manifest itself in a variety of tasks according to circumstances and needs.[20] But underlying these tasks is its very identity of being missioned sent – to proclaim and build up the Reign of God in the world.

Secondly, the characteristic of this mission is prophecy. A prophet is someone called and sent to recall to people God's saving interventions in the past, to challenge them to conversion from their disloyalty to God in the present and to urge them to build up a new humanity that is God's promise to peoples. It is a call to active hope based on experience and memory.[21] The Church and every Christian, each in his/her own way, share in the prophetic priesthood of Christ. The Church, not merely points to a future Reign of God, but should provide a symbol of this Reign in its life and community. Its life itself is, or should be, a prophetic proclamation and an invitation to action. It is called to be a counter-culture, not merely being critical and negative, but proposing an alternative way of being and living community.

The horizon of the prophetic mission of the Church is the Reign of God, as a community of freedom and fellowship, justice and love. The Reign of God and the Church are intimately related. They should neither be identified, nor separated.[22] The Reign of God is a reality much wider than the visible, institutional Church. The Church is a pilgrim, sinful and limited in its expressions, but moving towards the fullness of the Reign of God, which it proclaims and seeks to realize as its symbol and servant, while being aware that it does not monopolize the action of God in the world through Christ and the Spirit.[23]

When we speak about mission we easily fall into a dichotomy of Church-world. In a single number of its document on the *Church in the Modern World*,[24] the Second Vatican Council speaks of the Church as "leaven" and "soul" of the world, as a "visible organization and spiritual community" and as the "heavenly city" opposed to the earthly one. The Church and the world are involved in the same human history. Whatever the formal differentiation between the Church as a visible organization and the world, the Church as people and as institution is as much affected by the deeper cultural and moral currents of the world as the world itself. Therefore while we speak of the mission of the Church and of the religious we should not forget that we are also under the judgement of the Word that we proclaim.

The religious and mission

If to be religious is to be disciples of Christ, then it is to be, like Christ, on mission in the world. We participate in the mission which is the Church. If Baptism is not a passport to salvation, but a call to mission, then the religious who live their baptismal commitment in a radical manner also share this mission in a radical way. Their consecration can be seen as a missioning or sending, because the Spirit calls and "anoints" them or sets them apart for a particular task or function in the Church and in the world. Mission then becomes an element of the self-understanding of the religious, though how they live and what they do is determined by the specific way in which they share the mission of the Church.

Within the Church, the religious are the radicalization of the Church as mission or movement towards the Reign of God.[25] There is a tradition that relates religious life as a special option in view of the Reign of God. In a Church that became a mass institution, the religious were among those who commit themselves to embody the values of the Gospel and build up communities that are symbols and beginnings of the Reign. In the Church, they are a prophetic pole, not only counter-cultural, but creatively prospective.[26] Their prophecy is directed not only to the world, but also to the Church community. By radically living and/or promoting through their apostolic action some of the values of the Reign of God they are reminders of and invitations to a possible new world for all the People of God. They are also the cutting edge of the Church's mission to the world, in so far as they symbolize in a specially visible way the radicalism of the Reign of God which is being proclaimed. The subtitle of the Congress, "Charisms in the Church for the World", seems to limit the prophetic role of the religious to the world and pass over their prophetic relevance also within the Church community.

In an address to the Union of Superiors General, Sr Joan Chittister underlined powerfully the prophetic role of religious. She said:

> It is not the loss of institutions that religious must fear; it is the loss of the fire/heat of the charism itself. It is the potential loss of prophetic presence that strikes at the root of religious life today. Religious life is to remind the world of what it can be, of what it must be, of what it most wants to be: deep down, at its best, at its most human core. Religious life lives at the edge of society to critique it, at the bottom of society to comfort it, at the epicentre of society to challenge it. Religious life is a reminder of the will of God for the world. The charism is fire in the eye of God that focuses in our own. Who will ask the whys of life in every period, if not the religious of the Church? Who can possibly be called "religious" unless they do?[27]

Unfortunately, there is always a gap between institutional or professed radicalism in the following of Christ and actual personal commitment and transformation. Here there is reason for humility, but not for inactivity, because we are only servants of a mystery that transcends us.

Mission and the charisms

The various charisms in the Church are only functional differentiations within a group with a common mission. So there is no question of seeing this differentiation in terms of more or less, superior or inferior. Such valuations depend on the depth of life and commitment of each person and not on structural function. But what I would like to point out here is that the differences between the functions in the Church – clerical, lay, religious – should not be seen only in themselves or in their mutual relationship within the Church, but also in relation to the mission of the Church. The whole community, the People of God, are the bearers of the mission. The clergy have a role of leadership, that is, service. The religious are the symbolic, prophetic pole in the Church and in the world in view of the Reign. They respond to a special call of the Spirit. A call comes with a special gift or charism. Every vocation involves a mission.

If mission is simply identified with a list of apostolic challenges, then the contemplative religious may have difficulty in seeing themselves as being on mission. But if the whole Church is seen as being on mission, then the contemplative religious also are on mission. They are on mission precisely as witnesses, by their very lives and community, of an alternate way of life, based on the values of the Reign of God. They do not have to get involved in activity of some sort in order to become missionary. Looking at the other side of the spectrum, simply engaging in various apostolic works does not make the active religious missionaries. They are on mission when their life and action prophetically point to and promote the Reign of God.

In the global project of the mission of God in the world, as radical, liminal groups, the religious are in fellowship with similar liminal groups or persons in other religions.[28] The Buddhists have their monks, the Hindus their sannyasis and the Muslim their Sufi holy men. In relation to the world as a whole one can see these groups as having a prophetic fellowship. Even if their experiences and objectives may be very different, they have a certain structural similarity in religion and society. This has not yet been sufficiently exploited in the service of the Reign of God. There have been occasional dialogues between such groups in inter-monastic encounters or living together. Such coming together could be an antidote to a certain divisive fundamentalism in religion. It can also make present the Transcendent in life in creative ways, especially in a multi-religious society.

Religious in the contemporary world

Keeping in mind that there are going to be two panels, which will speak about concrete challenges of mission today, I would like to reflect in a general way on what I see as the challenges that the contemporary world is addressing particularly to religious.

An option for the poor

In a world that is divided between the rich and the poor, the oppressors and the oppressed, the proclamation of the Reign of God as a community of justice and fellowship calls for a preferential option for the poor.[29] This is not done out of compassion. Neither is it the consequence of following the ideology of the class struggle. It is a spiritual choice made in imitation of Jesus who identified himself with the poor and the suffering (Phil 2:5-8). It is not only a choice *for* the poor, but also to *be* poor and to struggle *with* the poor. It is not a political or a strategical choice, but follows the experience of Mary who felt that she was chosen to confound the strong in her lowliness and powerlessness (Lk 1:46-55). It is the wisdom of God of which Paul became aware in his own ministry (1 Cor 1:27). It is the basic principle that violence is not overcome by counter-violence, but by the force of truth and love. Mahatma Gandhi called it *satvagraha* – clinging to Truth.[30] It is an option to be counter-cultural.

The power of love will transform every one, the poor as well as the rich. But it is most effective when it emerges out of the oppressed, committing them to struggle for their liberation in truth and love.[31] It liberates them from fear and hatred, giving them a sense of dignity and vision and enabling them to experience the transforming power of the Spirit active in history. Material and spiritual poverty here merge in a prophetic force.

I think that today the real focus of mission in such a situation are the non-poor. The option for the poor is not against the non-poor, but a challenge to them, in the perspective of human solidarity.[32] To be with the poor and to care for their needs is necessary, but may become an easy way out of a challenging mission situation. If the goal of mission is transformation of society into the Reign of God, then challenging the non-poor is even a priority. Challenging the non-poor in this manner is a concrete and relevant way of living the option for the poor. The challenge can manifest itself as much in a counter-cultural way of life as in the participation in the struggles of the poor.

Though every one in the community of the disciples of Christ – that is, the Church – is called to opt for the poor, I think that it is a particular challenge for the religious today. Dom Luciano Mendes de Almeida, addressing the Union of Superiors General, identified option for the poor as the typical mission of religious life in the Church, after the example of the dynamism of the incarnation of Jesus, who identified with the poor and the suffering... Then the poor become the necessary mediation to reveal the figure of Jesus. In the suffering faces of the poor, we can discover the face of the Lord.[33]

This option for the poor may take different forms in the First and in the Third World. In the First World, it needs to take the form of being counter-cultural and of challenging the non-poor to do justice in love, not only locally, but also globally. In the Third World, it certainly questions the frequent counter-witness of the comfortable way of life and rich institutions of the religious and their easy dependence on economic, political and media power in their proclamation of the Good News.

Towards the transformation of culture

The proclamation of the Reign of God is a call to conversion. One used to think of conversion as a personal spiritual process. But reflection in the context of social injustice and oppression made us realize that in order to promote the Reign of God we need also to change sinful social structures that are unjust and oppressive. Ongoing reflection today shows us that, underlying the sinful social structures, there are cultural ones like world views, attitudes and value systems. They can become ideological if adhered to fanatically. Therefore to change society we must change also these cultural structures.

The Good News does not offer us economic and political blueprints for a new world. What it proposes are new ways of looking at God, people and the world, new attitudes to life and to community and a new system of values to guide our choices and relationships. This is an alternate culture based on a spirituality of the Reign of God. Therefore the Good News calls for a cultural transformation. John Paul II has said in his encyclical *Centesimus Annus*:

> These criticisms are directed not so much against an economic system as against an ethical and *cultural* system...[34] Evangelization plays a role in the *culture* of the various nations, sustaining culture in its progress towards the truth, and assisting in the work of its purification and enrichment.[35]

I think that cultural transformation is an area on which the religious are called today to concentrate their efforts and zeal. Their way of life in community and relationships, as well as their apostolic action, whether apart from the world in contemplative communities or involved with the poor or fully inserted in the midst of cultural forces like education, the arts and the media can be a witness, a challenge and an encouragement for cultural change. Though the whole Church is called to be a counter-cultural community as we see in the Acts of the Apostles (Acts 2:42-47; 4:32-35), the religious are called to concretize this dimension of the Church in a special symbolic way.

The culture of *modernity* is an affirmation of the human and the release of human creativity and potentiality, especially through science and technology, that can lead us to a new world. But these positive and creative forces are abused by materialistic and individualistic consumerism, fragmentation of community and exploitation of creation and of the woman. Could communities of religious witness to the proper use of creation, to the growth of free and integrated persons, to the experience of fellowship and solidarity and to the sense of transcendence in the modern world? These are values of the Reign of God.

Creativity and freedom

New groups of religious have often risen in response to new needs and challenges. The religious, not belonging to the institutional dimension of the Church, structured by the ministerial leadership and the laity, should have a certain freedom to be at the frontiers of the Church and be available and mobile to go where the Spirit leads them. This freedom of initiative and movement is particularly relevant in the modern world characterized by rapidity of movement and change. Two factors, however, may restrict this freedom. One is the over-institutionalization of the religious group itself, in terms both of internal structures and of institutional commitments. The quest for internal and external freedom may not be easy, precisely because it is tied to objective structures that are not changed just by willing it, especially in a period of reducing numbers, unless appropriate and bold strategies are devised.

The second factor is the articulation in the Church between the charism of leadership and the various charisms of the religious. I think that it is not proper, in our context, to oppose charism to institution, as sociologists tend to do. But there are different charisms in the Church. The religious do not have the monopoly of charisms. But they do have a special call – vocation – from the Spirit and the appropriate gifts to follow that call in life and work. The leadership in the community has the responsibility of discernment and coordination. But discernment is different from domestication and coordination, from control. The spirit of discernment supposes openness to the newness of the Spirit, unfamiliar, unforeseen, unplanned for, "blowing where it wills" (cf Jn 3:8). There could be situations involving a certain risk, even danger. The Spirit leads us into uncharted territories where precedents, past experiences and the safe legal frameworks may not always help. Loyalty to the "mission of God", in Christ and in the Spirit, and to their own "liminal" function within the Church community, would create for the religious the space of freedom necessary to respond with initiative and imagination to the call of the Spirit.

Conclusion

In concluding, I would like to recall again some of the main points that I have tried to make. Mission is not primarily a list of challenges and tasks that face us in the "missions", but a Trinitarian and cosmic movement leading to the realization of the Reign of God. The religious, both contemplative and active, manifest in a special way the prophetic character of mission, in view of the Reign of God, in their life and apostolic involvements, in freedom and creativity. Option for the poor, cultural transformation and reaching out to other believers in the Transcendent even beyond the usual institutional frameworks seem to me to be the special challenges that the religious are called to face today. Revitalization of religious life demands that we rediscover not only our charisms, but also their dynamism in mission in the Church and in the world.

NOTES

1. In this paper I have used material from three earlier ones on the same theme.
2. Cf No. 33.
3. Stephen Bevans lists various images of the missionary as treasure hunter, teach, guest, stranger, partner, migrant work, ghost, etc. Cf "Seeing Mission through Images", *Missiology* 19 (1991) 45-57.
4. Cf David J. Bosc, *Transforming Mission*. Paradigm Shifts in Theology of Mission. (Maryknoll, Orbis, 1991); Mary Motte and Joseph R. Lang (eds), *Mission in Dialogue* (Maryknoll, Orbis, 1982); William Jenkinson and Helene O'Sullivan (eds), *Trends in Mission. Toward the 3rd Millennium.* (Maryknoll, Orbis, 1991); *For all the Peoples of Asia.* Vols. 1 and 2 (Manila, IMC, 1984 and 1987).
5. *Ad Gentes*, 2.
6. Cf *Redemptoris Missio* (hereafter RM) 20.
7. Cf RM, 20: "The Church contributes to mankind's pilgrimage of conversion to God's plan..."
8. Cf for example, *Sollicitudo Rei Socialis*, 41.
9. *Evangelii Nuntiandi*, 20.
10. Cf Nos. 55-57.
11. Cf M. Amaladoss, "La mission comme prophétie", *Spiritus* 128 (1992) 263-275.
12. Cf RM, 18: "The Church is not an end unto herself, since she is ordered towards the Kingdom of God of which she is the seed, sign and instrument."

13. Cf RM, 14-15.
14. Cf RM, 13; 16.
15. Cf RM, 20.
16. "The Kingdom of God: Jesus' Vision of a New Society", in D.S. Amalorpavadass (ed.), *The Indian Church in the Struggle for a New Society* (Bangalore, NBCLC, 1981) 599, 601.
17. Cf Severino Dianich, *Chiesa in missione* (Milano, Edizioni Paoline, 1985).
18. Cf M. Amaladoss, *Making All Things New* (Maryknoll, Orbis, 1990) p. 58.
19. *Gaudium et Spes*, 22.
20. Cf RM, 41-60.
21. Cf Walter Brueggemann, *The Prophetic Imagination* (Philadelphia, Fortress, 1978); Idem., *Hopeful Imagination* (Philadelphia, Fortress, 1986).
22. Cf RM, 17-20.
23. Cf RM, 28-29.
24. Cf No. 40.
25. Cf Thomas P. Rausch, *Radical Christian Communities* (Collegeville, The Liturgical Press, 1990).
26. Cf Diarmuid O'Murchu, *Religious Life: A Prophetic Vision* (Notre Dame, Ave Maria, 1991).
27. Cf *Religious in the Evangelizing Mission of the Church* (Rome, USG, 1993, pp. 28-29).
28. Cf Swami Abhishiktananda, *The Further Shore* (Delhi, ISPCK, 1984).
29. Cf *Sollicitudo Rei Socialis*, 42.
30. Cf Ignatius Jesudasan, *A Gandhian Theology of Liberation* (Maryknoll, Orbis, 1984).
31. Cf Leonardo Boff, *New Evangelization. Good News to the Poor.* (Maryknoll, Orbis, 1991). Gustavo Gutierrez, *The Power of the Poor in History* (Maryknoll, Orbis, 1983).
32. Cf *Sollicitudo Rei Socialis*, 38-40.
33. Cf *Religious in the Evangelizing Mission of the Church* (Rome, USG, 1993), p. 40,39.
34. No. 39.
35. No. 50. The underlinings in these two quotations are mine.

II.

Round Table on "The mission today"

"THE MISSION TODAY" BY GEOGRAPHICAL AND CULTURAL REGIONS

Fr Leonard Kasanda, CICM: Africa

Fr Kasanda, Scheut missionary, answered the question: "As a consecrated person, how do you see the challenges for the mission of consecrated life in the African context (society, culture, etc.)?" He listed seven challenges. The first is that of avoiding the confusion between "mission of consecrated life" and "mission and consecrated life"; the second is not to think of consecrated life solely in relation to pastoral urgencies; the third concerns the categorical position of consecrated life in the Church and in society; the challenge is to make consecrated life become African; the fifth is that consecrated life has the mission to witness to the love of God, thus helping many people, men and women, to discover the presence of the living God who journeys with his people toward liberation; the sixth challenge is that it must form people so impassioned for man that they be ready to give their life for him, and to offer examples of fraternal life in communion, of gratuity and forgiveness; the seventh challenge is commitment for the whole person.

Fr Paul Tan Chee Ing, SJ: Asia-Pacific

Taking as point of departure two characteristics of consecrated life: its radical witness to the love of God for his creation, and its prophetic dimension to bring the world back to God, for Fr Tan (a Chinese Jesuit who was born and lived in Malaysia), the first challenge for consecrated life in Asia-Pacific is that of dialogue with other faiths, recalling that this excludes the desire to make conversions. Thus, consecrated life wants to highlight what it has in common with the consecrated life of other faiths.

The second challenge is linked to the first because the religious traditions of Asia are part of the Asian culture and therefore if we speak of dialogue with people of other faiths we must also speak of dialogue with what is different in the cultures that we have inherited as Christians.

The third challenge for us in Asia and the Pacific is to live a radical and simple religious life, similar to the true spirit of St Francis of Assisi.

The fourth challenge consists in highlighting the fact that the prophetic role of religious should shine forth forcefully because, in spite of the increasing well-being, there are problems of justice in all its dimension; there is discrimination in Asia and the Pacific. There are still millions of people who are very poor; if we do not do it, who will speak up in favour of the "oppressed" and defend their rights, when the hierarchical Church must be "prudent" in order not to compromise the good of "the whole Church"?

Fr Juan Vecchi, SDB: Latin America

After Vatican II, consecrated life in Latin America proposed a reflection on its mission. This reflection, confronted with the present situation of the continent and with recent orientations of the Church, highlights the following elements of challenges:

A. In urgencies heard: evangelizatio; human promotion; education and culture; the spiritual life of believers.
B. In certain significant subjects: the poor; the young.
C. In prophetic messages: the sense of God; the efficacy of charity; hope.

Urgencies, subjects, prophetic message are in fact but one challenge: to give birth to a kind of life, presence and action that truly express, and immediately in the Latin American context, what we wish to witness to, proclaim and achieve.

Written intervention sent by a Latin American study group

In the context of the Congress, a group of Latin Americans reflect expressly on the topic of "Challenges for religious", and on "Mission today" proper to Latin America. Their conclusions on these two topics were presented.

1. "The progress made": it is "marked" by the following key words: there is a Latin American way of religious life; listening to the cry of the poor has suggested a life option often expressed by insertion; there has been a new experience of God and the following of Christ and therefore a new spirituality, community life and insertion in the local Church. Tensions, conflicts and martyrdom were not lacking. Inculturation with the poor and the marginalized is an important acquisition.

New forms of religious life are developing as well as new inter-congregational relationships. The importance of women is highlighted. All this has opened up on a rediscovery of the identity of religious life, of its prophetic image and the charism of the founders.

2. "The challenges today": the growing poverty and extreme misery; inculturation of the Gospel and consecrated life; conscientization and liberation of women; commitment to build communion within the Church and a true integration in Latin America; commitment for life and human rights; to live fraternity with the local Church and the basic ecclesial communities; live the experience of God following Christ by nourishing prayer with the Word of God to whom we must refer to seek and follow the will of God with his people.

Fr Timothy Radcliffe, OP: Europe and North America

With just ten minutes to speak, I have not the time to develop an analysis, just share with you a picture, an image that represents some of the challenge in our mission in the West. What image symbolizes the challenges of our culture? What is its most typical story? And I would say that one could take the story of "Jurassic Park". If you have not yet seen it, do so. It will be, by now, the most popular film ever made. It has been declared a threat to the French

143

national identity by the French Minister of culture, and it is showing in one in three Italian cinemas. In England the children even eat Tyrannosaurus Rex biscuits! This is our world!

The story is simple. A millionaire uses experiments on DNA to bring the dinosaurs back to life. He creates a great Park on an island where they can run free. They go around killing the visitors, and finally it is all too much, and the humans desert the island and fly away. This is the narrative of our times, and it is fruitful to ask how it can be contrasted with the typical story of Christianity, the Last Supper. I might just add that if the picture I will present is rather gloomy it is not because I am pessimistic about modern culture. I am not. I think that it incarnates some wonderful values – a cherishing of the individual, human rights, a tolerance of those who are different etc. But in the time I have I can just focus on the challenges.

A violent world

The World of Jurassic Park is a world ruled by violence. The dinosaurs kill each other and the human beings, and the human beings kill the dinosaurs. The other day I asked a group of Dominican brothers and sisters from the United States, who work together as itinerant preachers, what they considered to be the principal challenge to our preaching, and without a hesitation the answer was "violence". It is not just the violence of the wars that afflict much of the world, as in Bosnia or Georgia; it is the daily violence of our cities, the ordinary routine violence that women and children especially suffer; the racist violence against immigrants; it is the verbal violence of daily life; the environmental violence of the modern city.

In contrast to Jurassic Park, our founding story is of a man who endured violence, but did not pass it on, of a man who let himself be a victim so that the violence would stop there, on the cross, "like a sheep that is led to the slaughter, he did not open his mouth" (Is 53:7). Perhaps the first challenge that we face as religious is to be people who live non-violently. I do not mean only that one might hope that the brethren might refrain, usually, from attacking each other with hatchets or pistols, though that is good. One thinks of the battle between Irish and English Franciscans in 1221 that led to 16 of the friars being slaughtered!

More profoundly we are called to live as people of peace, who face and root out the seeds of violence and anger in our lives, who have the courage to find ourselves with the victims. At the heart of religious life is an option for vulnerability.

The jungle

It is worth noting that this is a story about a jungle, a jungle in which dinosaurs and humans compete to survive. It is a picture of the Darwinian world of the survival of the fittest. The weak fall by the wayside and become extinct. This was the fate of the dinosaurs. What I wish to stress is that this has been one of the dominant images of Western culture for almost two hundred years. It is not only at the basis of a scientific understanding of evolution, but also of contemporary economics and politics. Economics have adopted a Darwinian theory of competition, and politics is just a function of economics. It is only with the growth of ecology that there has been a shift of our perception of "the jungle" from competition to complementarity, with consequences we cannot yet see.

In this competitive consumerist jungle that is Western culture, we religious surely have the mission to live out an alternative vision of reality, and to embody another narrative. This is not the competitive jungle of the market place but a world of gift. In Darwin's and Keynes' jungles there are no gifts. And it is my belief that it is impossible for us to have any perception of God, the giver all good things, unless we are able to see and feel the world and ourselves as gift and grace. Our story climaxes with a man who says "This is my Body, which is given to you." I believe that we cannot really see the world as grace and gift unless we radically distance ourselves from the dominant consumerist culture. And that means becoming poor, really and visibly poor. We talk much about the "option for the poor" but we tend to live a far more middle class form of life.

A world of silence

One of the reasons why "Jurassic Park" is so popular all over the world is that it is a story which hardly depends upon words.

Even without translation a Russian could get almost as much from it as an English speaker. It is a world within which words hardly matter. And it is alas true that we belong to a society which has largely lost confidence in language as a tool to build society, to seek truth, to achieve understanding. As Vaclav Havel once said, "You in the West have largely forgotten the power of the word." It is a world which is deeply suspicious of any claims to truth. This makes Christianity, which depends upon the proclamations of truths, hard to understand for many people.

One of the fundamental challenges for us religious is to create communities in which people learn to love words, to delight in the power of truthful language to build community, to overcome division, to make a human home. The first question I always put to any community that I must visit is: Is this a community in which people speak to each other? Do the brothers share truthful words? Does our formation encourage our students to love language and to delight in truth. In our society debate is seen as a version of the jungle; the victor is the one who crushes his opponent. We do have, in the Church, a different tradition, represented by people like Thomas Aquinas. As a Dominican I must mention Aquinas at least once! And for Aquinas disputation was always a process by which one learns from the other person, discovers the sense in which the other is always, in a sense, right. Disputation is always part of the building of human community. Alas, within the Church itself there is often a fear of debate and a reluctance to learn from the other. Often, in the name of the defence of orthodoxy, we have adopted an intolerance of difference and a fear of debate that is contrary to our deepest traditions.

Our society is afflicted by a crisis of meaninglessness, indifference, which is linked to this retreat from language. There is little popular culture, as in Central America, for example. A deep fear haunts our cities, that nothing has meaning at all. Hence the temptation of fundamentalist religions which give you a meaning on a plate. Our role is surely to work with people in the recovery of their dignity as those who can make sense of the world, and so draw near to the God who is the source of all meaning.

Fate

Finally, I would point out that the world of "Jurassic Park" is one of fatalism. The dinosaurs were doomed to extinction. And

146

in the face of this failed experiment the humans can do nothing except to run away. Of course this is convenient since it means that we can see "Jurassic Park II", but it is also symbolical of a deep fatalism of our society.

Faced with growing economic and social problems there is often a fatalism, a belief that we can do nothing. Galbraith, the American economist, has argued that this passivity is central to our civilization. If you believe in the laws of the market then they will provide the answer. There is nothing that we can or need do.

In our contrasting story of the Last Supper we see a man who is doomed, fated to death. And in the face of disaster, he makes a gesture of extraordinary freedom. He takes bread and offers it to his disciples saying, "Take and eat, this is my body." Faced with the collapse of community, he was free to make a future. He believed that these mediocre bunch of disciples could build the Kingdom. Do we live such a freedom? Many of us find ourselves trapped by diminishing vocations and commitments we can no longer honour. Are we doomed to have no freedom, to be prisoners? Do we dare to be free to make something new? Do we dare trust the young to make something new and unexpected? If not we will join the dinosaurs in Jurassic Park!

Our world thinks of itself as "the free world", but it is often just the freedom to choose in the market place. We need to embody a new and more radical freedom in religious life, which is the freedom of the Last Supper, the freedom to give our lives away, saying to our brothers, "This is my life and I give it to you, I dispose of it." This is not obedience as a flight from responsibility but God's own freedom and vulnerability.

Questions

1. How far are we called to live a "counter-culture", to distance ourselves from the society in which we live? Pros and Cons?

2. How do we live out the glorious freedom of God?

Fr Armand Veilleux, ocso: Contemplatives

The religious who commit themselves in contemplative life seek to centre their life on seeking a personal experience of God.

That is why they have a particular contribution too offer in the area of *inculturation*, because inculturation is essentially the meeting of the Christian *experience* with the particular human experience proper to a specific culture.

For the same reason, they have something special to accomplish in the area of inter-religious dialogue, since dialogue is much more fruitful at the level of experience than that of conceptual systems or exterior religious practice.

Don Riccardo Ezzati, sdb: Apostolic religious

The religious of apostolic life feels challenged by the many situation to which he strives to bring an answer. In particular, he faces the following challenges:

1. The challenge of the "meaning" of his own vocation-mission, either in relation with the world and culture that surrounds him, or with the ability to be, for men and women of today, a sign and instrument of hope. An adequate initial and ongoing formation enables him to better express his identity because it conforms him more fully to Christ and enables him to respond creatively and with apostolic thrust to the ever new demands of the times.

2. The challenge of "organic ministry" in the local Church. This challenge underlines the need for religious to be present, but with their identity, in the pastoral projects and plans of the local Churches, and that the pastors really give a place to these charisms in their dioceses. There is need for greater sharing of pastoral plans, more efficacious structures of dialogue and more sharing of pastoral experiences with the various components of the local Church.

3. The challenge of "creativity" and "apostolic boldness". The new problems of today's society and the new conditions of religious communities themselves, stimulate the duty to re-think the apostolic presence in new forms and fields.

Fr Raymond Rossignol, MEP: Missionary institutes

As John Paul II points out in *Redemptoris Missio*: "If it is destined to all, salvation must be brought concretely to all" (RM 10). That is the challenge to the mission expressed globally. But the Church feels particularly ill prepared when it considers the more than two billion Muslims, Hindus and Buddhists who are convinced that they already know "the way to salvation". We may wonder if the great challenge to the mission, in this end of the twentieth century, does not consist in rethinking the great religious traditions in relation to Christianity, and Christianity in relation to these religious traditions – which cannot be done without risks, calling into question certain attitudes, certain cultural syntheses, etc.

Missionary institutes are "at the service of the mission in and with the local Churches". By their specific commitment at the service of the mission *ad gentes*, but also by their simple presence, the missionaries "from outside" commit themselves to help all the particular Churches and "strive to proclaim the Gospel to all men" (AG 1).

Fr Pierre Drouin, CJM: Societies of apostolic life

The Societies of apostolic life, as their name indicates, pursue an apostolic end. They live the missionary challenges of the Church within the particular Churches with whom they collaborate.

There have been three changes within the ecclesial community: 1. a change in evangelizers; 2. the eruption of the laity; 3. openness to the missionary dimension.

The missionary challenges to be faced are: 1. accompaniment and formation of priests; 2. the formation of the laity; 3. a renewed effort at inculturation.

3

The Communion of religious

I.

Fraternal life in common

Fr Fabio Ciardi, OMI

Through the present article we would like to consider an essential component of religious life: the communion expressed in fraternal life and common life, in the existential sharing of the ideal of life, of charismatic identity, and of the apostolic project which unites the members of a religious institute.

It is an aspect which must not be separated from the other components of the religious project, and hence must be considered in continuity with the aspects of mission and of identity.

To speak of religious life as communion implies first and foremost a reference to the Church as communion, and in consequence to the relationship with other vocations in the Church. Since this will be the object of the round table which will follow this presentation of mine, I limit myself to the dimension of the internal life of the religious community

After a glance at the recent evolution and present situation of the religious community (Part I), we shall dwell on its charismatic and theological dimension (Part II). Finally we shall suggest some lines along which to continue the process of renewal (Part III).

I. A GLANCE AT THE RECENT EVOLUTION
AND ON THE PRESENT SITUATION OF
THE RELIGIOUS COMMUNITY

In recent years the religious community has undergone profound changes, linked with the evolution of society, of the Church, and of religious life itself. Without pretending to be exhaustive we point out some elements that we think more important.[1]

1. A new kind of relationship with the outside

One of the factors which has had a greater influence on the change of community life is the new kind of relationship with society and the consequent evolution of evangelization.

The positive view of worldly reality offered by the Council, and the appeal to become ever closer to the people of today, implied courageous commitment options, which have become translated into closeness, solidarity, authentic communion and sharing with people, even to feeling and embracing "the joys and hopes, the grief and anguish of the people of our time, of the poor, especially of those who are suffering" (GS 1).

The evolution of the mission has led religious life to take seriously the choice made by the Churches for the preferential option for the poor. Those most abandoned, those suffering the most varied kinds of abuse, the aged, drug addicts, exiles, the lowest members of society, have become the focus of apostolic activity in an attentive and concrete service which has spoken out for those who cannot speak for themselves. This has given rise to new kinds of ministry, which have inevitably led to new experiences of community life. It is a case especially of working with the poor of every description, but also in new areas such as ministry for justice, peace and the ecology.

Hence the birth, especially in the southern hemisphere, of "small communities" inserted in poor and densely populated environments, with a true geographic and spiritual exodus towards the "periphery". This is a universal phenomenon, even though it has assumed a typical vein in Latin America. Already at Medellin the Bishops had written: "Congregations, which feel called to form from among their members small communities truly established in poor environments, receive our full encouragement" (no. 14,6). At Puebla such communities were already an accepted reality. To the bishops they appeared to be the result of the "desire to be involved in poor neighbourhoods or the countryside, or by the desire to undertake a specific mission of evangelization" (no. 731).

If the southern hemisphere has been galvanized principally around social problems, in the northern half of the world the major challenge has concerned the values of personal freedom and respect for human rights. In this case also increased sensitivity to the demands of the individual has led to notable consequences within the bounds of the community.

The re-evaluation of the individual contrasts with a certain standardization, anonymity and uniformity often found in communities in the past. It has led to a greater attention, esteem and respect for the individual. Due regard is given to the dignity of the person and emphasis is laid on human aspects and the contribution each one can make with his particular talents and personal charisms. The accent is now on personal responsibility, thus fostering the sense of freedom and responsibility. The increased desire for self-realization in some cases has led members to adopt an autonomous style of life, living by themselves while maintaining a more or less structured bond of communion with their community of origin to which they belong.

Just as the manner of relationship with society has changed, so too has changed that of relationship with the Church. From attention to the universal Church – which nevertheless remains valued and fundamental – the accent has moved to the particular. The ecclesiology of Vatican II has led religious to a more active presence and commitment within it. The religious community has become more open to the parish and diocesan community, with the abandonment of certain independent traits which could sometimes make it appear to be a Church within the Church. In daily practical contact with the ecclesial environment the community has acquired new sensitivities, changing both its own rhythms of prayer and the settings for its apostolate and ministry.

As a consequence of this new relationship of communion with other vocations in the Church, recent years have seen the maturing of a deep bond with the laity. There is an ever increasing number of those who ask to share in the spirituality and mission of the institute. It is a request that acquires new connotations and demands deeper relationships than those lived by members of the traditional third orders. Communities facing this kind of challenge feel themselves called to open themselves to new forms of broader community. This is another factor which is contributing to the giving of a new look to our communities.

2. New situations within religious life

The evolution of the religious community, especially in the northern hemisphere, has been conditioned also by factors internal to the religious life. I refer to the progressive decline in the number of members of the institutes, their ageing and the scarcity of new vocations, with the consequent redimensioning of the works.

Once specific activities had become no longer available, the big communities linked with works reached one or other of two opposite conclusions. On the one hand we have witnessed the concentration of old and sick members in large houses, and on the other, a fragmentation of younger personnel into smaller communities.[2]

For very many religious the new structural situation has meant the disappearance of frequent and deep rapport with companions and superiors, causing a sense of loneliness, even though they may be living in communities of ageing religious in large numbers. The places which used to guarantee the continuity of tradition, like the long-standing centres of apostolate and the novitiates, are either closed or gradually coming to an end. The properties of the communities to which they were sentimentally attached are being sold. Without those structures which gave them security, religious have often felt that they have been left exposed to an empty and chaotic world, which gives rise to anxiety and uncertainty or, as a reaction, patient resignation.

The closure of large works has occasioned (and to some extent has been occasioned by) the rise of small communities with particular characteristics, the so-called "elective communities". They are communities where persons with a common vision of the religious life unite to live a life that is more intense. In general they adopt a rigorous rhythm of common prayer and a simple life-style; they take up a particular community project with a flexible timetable and ample space for sharing. Leadership is collective or taken by rotation by the members of the community. The community lives in an apartment or in an ordinary house among the common people. Each member carries out his own work in different environments, not really ecclesial in nature. The accent is on the mission, even though they withdraw from work in educational or charitable works in favour of commitments for social justice with a greater political involvement.

Experiences of these kinds are frequently the result of reaction to the standardization and depersonalization of the large communities, and of the search for greater self-realization in more authentic relationships and in direct work with the people.

On the other hand, recent years have seen the birth of new kinds of communities of a monastic character, where the accent is markedly on life in common. They rediscover the classic elements of the religious life, even the most exterior ones like the habit. But they do so with a new freshness which derives from the newness of the charisma.

New forms of community, of which we can make here no more than a passing reference, are also those which arise within ecclesial movements of a lay nature, whose members feel a need to express themselves also in consecration. In this way is renewed the phenomenon, even though in an original way, of a lay life which reaches its goal of consecration and a manner of living in common.

3. The anxiety for unity and the ecclesiology of communion

A further determining factor in the evolution of the religious community has been the awareness and the widespread need for unity that has matured among mankind in recent decades. At an ecclesial level this corresponds to the discovery of the Church as the mystery of communion.

Our century is characterized by a strong tendency towards unity, a tendency that is relentlessly pursued despite recurrent failures. The signs of this are many. The acceptance met with by Marxism and the various kinds of socialism for so many years has been, in its own way, a response to the demands for a new social balance and unity of peoples. International organizations have come into being in an attempt to bring the world together. New opportunities for relationships are offered by the mass media, by cultural and commercial exchanges, travelling, sporting manifestations, etc. Political, economic and social structures seem ever more linked together by an organic interdependence. Everything seems to bear witness to an irrepressible thirst for unity.

The tensions in the search for freedom and autonomy through which we are living so dramatically at the present day seem to contradict the yearning for unity. The former Soviet Union is making painful progress towards a new ethnic equilibrium. Czechoslovakia has been divided into two states, reflecting two peoples differing in history and culture. Yugoslavia has been shattered by the explosion of conflicts between different ethnic groups. No less dramatic is the situation in many countries of Africa. The same kind of trouble, although in a manner perhaps less dramatic but no less urgent, afflicts other European countries, from Spain to Ireland, to Italy. Autonomy and unity are Europe's big problem.

This double orientation – freedom and solidarity, unity and distinction – which can apparently seem contradictory, expresses an identical demand: for relationships of a new quality. The thrust towards autonomy arises from the fact that frequently unity has been experienced in the distorted form of totalitarianism and suppression, just as independence has been understood as absolutism of the particular and exclusion of diversity. What is asked for at the present day is an identity which does not withdraw into selfish individualism, but is open to communion with other social, cultural and political realities. And a unity is asked for which does not reduce to standardization but can respect differences. Paradoxically the yearning for communion seems to be in direct proportion to the reality of the division experienced by humanity at the present day.

By a divine strategy, the same Spirit who has placed in the heart of man the desire for unity, has also inserted in the Church new dynamic elements of communion. The Church is discovering and living with a new intensity the mystery of the *koinonia* which constitutes its profound nature, so as to render it able to respond to today's human expectations. Theological thought has become progressively centred on ecclesiology, highlighting Christ's role in his Church, the union with him of the faithful, and in him, of the faithful among themselves in the strength of the Spirit. It is the rediscovery of the Church as the *Body of Christ, Temple of the Spirit, Communion, Sacrament,* and *People of God.* At a vital level the thrust towards communion is particularly vigorous in the basic ecclesial communities and in the various forms of group associations that animate the life of the Church. In more recent times a powerful thrust in this direction has been provided by the ecclesial Movements.

All this has made a notable contribution to the reawakening among men and women religious of the deep sense of communion, obliging them to the further analysis and development in a new way, of aspects already contained in their particular vocation even if not lived in a conscious way and thus delved deeply into. They have been impelled into enriching the horizons of the religious community with new values and sensitivities, opening it to the new horizons to which the Holy Spirit is calling the whole Church at the present day, such as ecumenical and inter-religious dialogue and with all men of good will, so as to realize the testament of Jesus "that they all may be one" (Jn 17:21).

In the face of a strong demand for communion like that of the present day, the religious community cannot be backward in its duty to provide an example and instrument of communion.

4. Acquisitions of the journey of conciliar renewal

Under the pressure of these multiple factors (and we have given only some examples, which could be further enriched and developed) the religious community, especially at the urging of the Council, has acquired some fundamental values and has made steps forward which cannot be reversed.

The deeper understanding of the Church as a mystery has fostered a new awareness of the mysteric dimension of the community and of fraternal life. The theological motivations of community life have been rediscovered, and they become ever more clearly recognized as an essential element of religious life.

In line with theological development, the experience of spiritual and community life and the rediscovery of the particular charism of each institute, new models of religious life have emerged. Recent years have seen the evolution from a prevalently monastic form, as it was described in the old code of Canon Law and of the Constitutions which were lined up with it, to a wide diversity of more authentic expressions, especially of an apostolic character. It is a process which has required courage in the revision of both life-style and structures. In this way it has been possible to bring about a renewal of the Constitutions in line with the charisma.

The maturing of the sense of the person is expressed in greater shared responsibility and subsidiarity in common decisions, in dialogue, in decentralization, in participation at lower levels. There is greater openness and transparency in relations, and less psychological dependence on superiors. This has led, among other things, to emphasis on the community dimension of discernment and planning.

The rediscovery of the Church as communion has helped the religious community to live a fraternal life in which relationships become simpler, more authentic and less formal. It has freed it from incrustations and withdrawal into itself. The religious community is understood as a place of welcome, sincerity, concord, familiarity, tolerance, care for the aged, mutual understanding, attention to human virtues and interpersonal relationships. Authority is understood to an ever greater extent as guidance, service and animation. In the renewed Constitutions and Regulations the structures have been notably reshaped in this direction.

In short there has been the passing from the community understood prevalently as "common life", based on structures which govern living together, to the community as "life in communion", "communion of life" expressed in new relationships. What makes the community are not primarily acts done in common, but rather the divine *koinonia* which is shared and becomes translated into authentic relationships of mutual love, fraternity and friendship. This allows the including in a real life of community those religious also who live in particular situations of separation for the ministry of the gospel and the service of their fellow men.

5. Problems that remain open

The process of renewal, as can well be imagined, has been neither easy nor straightforward. There have been therefore the inevitable discrepancies which constitute a challenge we are called to accept so as to bring about a further maturing in our process of growth.

Among the problems which remain open one of the most evident appears to be one which is in contrast with the very nature of the religious community: individualism, subjectiveness and independence. It is natural that for anyone called to a particular life of communion the prevailing temptation will be in the sense opposed to communion. The temptation to withdraw into one's own or to be concerned only with oneself and personal problems is an ever present trap. But there is often a fresh outbreak of individualism, subjectivism and independence.

The dependence model has been replaced by that of participation, but has sometimes resulted in independence. In turn the value of participation and democracy can bring about a crisis of authority, with the function of the superior little in evidence and leadership lacking. The role and function of the superior are seen in many different ways. Emphasis on the individual and on his personal charisms has often led to the giving of priority to the efficacy of the individual apostolate to the detriment of the community dimension of the life. Respect for pluralism risks providing an incentive to individualism.

These difficulties reveal the yearning for freedom which is inalienable in the human heart and which has to be harmonized with the equally strong longing for communion. The call to freedom and to solidarity belongs to the very nucleus of the Christian image of man. It is my belief that without reference to the Trinitarian model and to the Paschal Mystery – of which I will speak later – this double human need will never find a full response.

A further open question concerns the community models to which reference can be made. A charismatic identity which is not always clear, canonical uniformity, the accumulation of different historical experiences, raise the problem of the kind of community an institute is called upon to live: monastic, conventual or apostolic. Different ecclesiologies can also be detected.

This problem is made more acute by the practical tension frequently observed between community and mission. When the bipolarity between "being" and "doing" has not been resolved, there are repercussions on community life, a certain disharmony is created between fraternal relationships and apostolic activity, a conflict between apostolic commitments and the structures of consecrated community life. The ever greater diversity of forms of apostolate within the same community and the lack of common apostolic objectives seem to complicate the situation even further. Sometimes the problem is resolved in an over-simplistic manner by eliminating one of the two poles: maintaining that the religious community has no value in itself and exists only with a view to the functioning of the apostolate, or else by reverting to models of the monastic and conventional style.

More generally the religious community is threatened by the materialistic culture, by consumerism as a style of life, by secularism and the trend towards bourgeois ways, from the assumption of worldly values such as horizontalism, pragmatism, hedonism, and excessive concern about efficiency. But religious life has no monopoly of this problem. It is common to all vocations in the Church. The basic problem is what kind of relationship to build with society and modern times. How are we to exercise today the prophetic role to which we are called? What must religious life say to today's world? How can it bear witness to the mystery of which it is the custodian? How can it live in present-day conditions the charism deposited within it by the Holy Spirit? These are the fundamental questions the community asks itself in a secularized world.

An examination of the present situation would seem to disclose a further difficulty: split between the doctrinal understanding of the religious community and the actual manner in which it is lived. This leads to certain inconsistencies. Intuitions and aspirations do not always get carried over into life. The new normative texts have not yet been absorbed interiorly to an adequate extent and are slow in being put into practice. The process is going on for a full assimilation of the principles of evangelical, ecclesial and charismatic renewal, but it is not always clear how the renewal codified in the new Rules is to be given living expression. The present moment is felt to be one of evolution and perhaps of uncertainty. The past has disappeared, but the new has not yet fully appeared. Religious life is no longer what it was yesterday, but maybe it has not yet become what it should be. Many presuppositions have been put forward for a new religious life, but they have not yet reached fulfilment.

The open problems stimulate us to seek with courage and trust new ways to render our communities more adequate to their vocation and to respond to the expectations of the man of today.

Before formulating practical proposals for making progress in renewal and facing up to the obstacles we still find along the way, we must pause to recall briefly the constitutive elements of the community so that we may keep them in mind as inspirational factors.

II. CHARISMATIC DIVERSIFICATION AND THE THEOLOGICAL DIMENSION OF THE RELIGIOUS COMMUNITY

1. *Many communities, but a single* koinonia

The first question to ask is: Can we speak of religious communities in general? Are there not in fact so many forms of community? The same term of 'religious life' or of 'consecrated life' embraces different manners of expression which vary greatly among themselves, even though they are intimately linked together by a deep substratum which is common to all of them in some way.

Throughout its history consecrated life through the evangelical counsels has in fact found expression in original ways, either in the form of personal consecration by personal title, like the ascetics, the virgins and the widows, or in organized groups, such as the Monastic Orders, the Canons Regular, the Orders of Knighthood, the Mendicant Orders, the Regular Clerics, and clerical and lay Congregations. In more recent times the consecrated life has found a new form of expression in the Secular institutes. Finally, assimilated to the consecrated life are the Societies of Apostolic Life. Today too we are witnessing the birth of new experiences and realizations of consecrated life which do not fit into the previous juridical forms. Such a variety testifies to the vitality and creativity of the Church in its response to the demands of the Gospel and the needs of men.

The different ways of living the consecrated life appear even richer when we move inside their various forms. If, for instance, we examine the Mendicant Orders, which certainly have traits in common, we find a great variety of expressions. How different as regards inspiration and life experience do the Franciscans, Dominicans, Carmelites, Augustinians, Servites, Trinitarians, etc., appear to us.

Such multiplicity in the forms of religious life implies also a multiplicity of communities in which the religious life is lived. Rather than speak of a generic religious community, we should look at the concrete experience of the communities to which the founders or foundresses gave life. Communities have concrete features and settings. They differ from one another. It is a matter of experiences that can be forced to fit into preconstituted schemes only by a process of reduction. The Spirit is like the wind – you do not know whence it comes nor where it goes. Only by examining the experience of history can one manage to draw up a theology of the religious community, not vice versa.[3] It can be risky to build a theology *a priori* and then go on to verify it in its various historical expressions.

The very models of inspiration, for example, differ from one another. The community of the first Christians at Jerusalem became the prototype for the first cenobitic communities. The itinerant community of the disciples and apostles who followed Jesus became the source of inspiration for later religious communities, as also did the Old Testament style of prophetic communities or the family of Nazareth. The different sources of evangelical inspiration and the differing emphases placed on specific aspects of the Christian mystery have given life to further forms of community. In some the ascetic element is emphasized, in others the liturgical or fraternal aspect, in others the charitable and ministerial dimension, and in still others apostolic service.

A further determining factor for the different ways of understanding and expressing the religious community is found in the objectives the founders and foundresses had in mind in giving life to their work. A community with the *laus perennis* as its purpose will have a different way of life than another which takes on the service of the sick, or education, or the mission *ad gentes*. The differences between communities are also linked with sociological and cultural factors proper to the times and places of their l irth. No less determining also is the influence of the theologic ; and spiritualitys which the communities absorbed at their origins.

Fraternal life in common, therefore, acquires specific physiognomies according to the nature and mission of the individual institutes.

The Second Vatican Council contributed in a decisive manner to a new awareness of this specific charismatic quality of religious communities, inviting institutes to rediscover their identity in being and activity, and to rethink and renew their life and mission with the reference to the founder and his prophetic charism as the starting point.[4]

This is the line followed by the post-conciliar magisterium. Documents like *Evangelica Testificatio* and *Mutuae Relationes* have highlighted the charisma of the various institutes as a fundamental element for the identity of the religious life. In the document *Optiones Evangelicae* there occurs once again a reminder of the "dynamic fidelity to the intentions for which the Spirit brought institutes into existence in the Church" (no. 8), to the "specific identity of the institute" (no. 33), and a "fidelity capable of restoring to the present life and mission of each institute the ardour with which the founders were inflamed by the original inspirations of the Spirit" (no. 30).

There is therefore a constant and explicit invitation on the part of the magisterium to avoid any levelling down of religious communities. Rather is the intention the preservation of their "wonderful variety" (cf CJC can. 578). From the time of the Council onwards the conviction has been developing of an intrinsic linkage between fidelity to the charism, renewal, prophetic presence, and apostolic enterprise.

Despite the variety of its forms the fraternal life in common in every institute presents common traits in so far as it expresses and shares in the unique *koinonia* which is typical of the Church, to which every Christian as such is called. Perfectae Coritatis 15 has set out in a wonderful manner the physiognomy of every community in its theological roots: "Common life, in prayer and the sharing of the same spirit (Acts 2:42), should be constant, after the example of the early Church, in which the company of believers were of one heart and soul (cf Acts 4:32). It should be nourished by the teaching of the Gospel and by the sacred liturgy, especially by the Eucharist. Religious, as members of Christ, should live together as brothers and should give pride of place to one another in esteem (cf Rom 12:10), carrying one another's burdens (cf Gal 6:12). A community gathered together as a true family in the Lord's name enjoys his presence (cf Mt 18:20), through the love of God which is poured into their hearts by the Holy Spirit (cf Rom 5:5). For love sums up the law (cf Rom 13.10) and is the bond which makes us perfect (cf Col 3,14); by it we know that we have crossed over from death to life (cf 1 Jn 3.14). Indeed, the unity of the brethren is a symbol of the coming of Christ (cf Jn 13:35; 17:21) and is a source of great apostolic power."

In turn the Code of Canon Law has summed up with equal clarity the growing awareness of the value of the communion which has been maturing in the period following the Council: "The fraternal life proper to each institute unites all the members into, as it were, a special family in Christ. It is to be so defined so that it proves of mutual assistance for all to fulfil their vocation. The members, then, with their fraternal communion noted and based in charity, are to be an example of universal reconciliation in Christ (can. 602).

In their diversity all religious communities take their origin from the common evangelical *koinonia*. The specific charism and the consequent particular identity of each community are like the petals of a flower or the fruit of a tree which draw their vitality from the roots. If the flower is to blossom or the tree bear fruit work, is needed on the roots, and the latter embedded all of them in the common evangelical *humus*, whatever may be their specific charisma. For this reason Vatican II, taking up an image dear to tradition, describes consecrated life as being like a tree with many branches, rich in flowers and fruit (cf LG 43a). Starting from expressions of the life of the tree, in their wonderful variety, we can work backwards and follow the path of the lymph to reach the roots.

Religious communities are led back to that first criterion of renewal that the Council formulated in the following words: "Since the final norm of the religious life is the following of Christ as it is put before us in the Gospel, this must be taken by all institutes as the supreme rule" (PC 2).

These last reflections indicate that to understand in depth the sense of every religious community it must be placed in the widest context of Church communion.

2. *The religious community in the ecclesiology of communion*

The ecclesiology of communion is without doubt a mature fruit of Vatican II, which highlights one of the most genuine concepts of revelation with respect to the reality of the Church, as is shown also by the great patristic tradition.[5] Although the word "communion" does not appear clearly in the conciliar texts, its reality constitutes the horizon of the conciliar ecclesiology, as was well emphasized by the Extraordinary Synod of 1985 in its Final Report, where it is stated: "The ecclesiology of communion is the central and fundamental idea in the documents of the Council... much was done in the Vatican II Council that the Church would be more clearly understood and concretely translated in life"(II, C).[6]

In drawing up an ecclesiology of communion the Council maintained a constant reference to the original model: the Trinity. The ecclesiology of *Lumen Gentium* is profoundly Trinitarian.[7]

Developing the Council's teaching, experience and ecclesial awareness are characterized today by the rediscovery of the Trinity as the horizon of Christian life and indeed of Christian thought, and the most recent developments in ecclesiology follow precisely the line of a deeper understanding of the Trinitarian dimension and of the Paschal Mystery as a way for the unveiling and participation in the Trinitarian life. The reality of the Trinitarian *pericoresis*, which shows the divine Persons in reciprocal communion, the one with the other, the one through the other, the one in the other, becomes the original and ultimate model on the reality of the Church in the reciprocal and circular relationship of whatever exists in it: life, persons, communities, ministries, charismata, cultures.

In a Church which is rediscovering communion and is called to live within itself the Trinitarian dynamism, the religious community has a particular task to carry out. It appears in fact the visible and radical reproduction and at the same time the prophecy of the communion which the whole Church is called to live and to which it tends as its final goal. "As experts in communion – we read in a happy formulation of *Optiones Evangelicae* – religious are therefore called to be an ecclesial community in the Church and in the world, witnesses and architects of the plan for unity which is the crowning point of human history in God's design. (...) In fact, in a world very deeply divided and before their brethren in the faith, they give witness to the possibility of a community of goods, of fraternal love, of a programme of life and activity which is theirs because they have accepted the call to follow more closely and more freely Christ the Lord who was sent by the Father so that, firstborn among many brothers and sisters, he might establish a new fraternal fellowship in the gift of his Spirit" (no. 24).

This is true for all types of community, even for those institutes which, while setting before themselves objectives which are eminently apostolic, do not have a deep tradition of life in common. In fact, as we are reminded by *Mutuae Relationes*, the various charisms are not only to be preserved but continually developed in harmony with the Body of Christ continually in the process of growth (cf no. 11). Men and women religious, precisely because of the charismatic dimension of their life are the first who must be attentive in listening to what the Spirit is saying to the Church. If today the Spirit is guiding the Church to a deeper experience of communion, men and women religious, to whatever institute they may belong, through the very fact of being Christians at the present time cannot fail to study more deeply the dimension of communion and pulsate in unison with the charismatic stimulation which is animating today's Church. All religious, like all Christians, are called upon to respond to the new communal sensitivity. Our very life requires it. "The effectiveness of religious life – said John Paul II recently – depends on the quality of fraternal life in common. Even more so, the current renewal in the Church and in religious life is characterized by a search for communion and community. Therefore religious life will be all the more meaningful the more it succeeds in building "a community of brothers or sisters in Christ in which God is sought after and loved before all else" (can. 619), and will rather lose its *raison d'être* whenever one neglects this dimension of Christian love, which is the building of a small "family of God" with those who have received the same call'.[8]

It would be absurd if consecrated persons, called to be by vocation "experts in communion", should fall short in their prophetic mission, especially at the present day. It would be absurd if, now when the call for unity is greater than ever, men and women religious failed to implement the project of *koinonia* to which they are called, in this way leaving unfulfilled the hopes of so many people. They cannot abandon their task of being builders of communion, of living and spreading communion. And so rendering *koinonia* authentic and building living communities becomes one of the most urgent obligations of the religious life, a commitment from which religious cannot withdraw if they really want to fulfil the task entrusted to them by the Spirit of being an eschatological sign.

It is necessary to be able to distinguish between communion and community. We are all called upon to live a unique *communion*, but this takes place in different forms of *community*[9] according to the charism, as we have recalled earlier.

And so there are two paths to follow in connection with renewal: to live in depth the theological dimension of communion, going to the root from which the different forms of community develop and must be continually nourished; and to find once again the charismatic structures which express this communion and which adapt the community to the development of the task they have accepted.

Presupposing the rich Christian theology of communion, let us now highlight some of the lines along which we see it reflected in the religious community.

3. The community – place of the experience of God, of freedom and of self-realization

The life of fraternal communion within the community has a central role in the spiritual journey of men and women religious. It was so for the community of the apostles and for that of the Christians of the primitive community of Jerusalem, the principal models from which the different religious communities draw their inspiration. The Twelve followed Jesus in a precise historical and geographic itinerary which made the physical following of the Master the locale of their interior transformation. He introduced them to the mystery of the Kingdom and to an intimate relationship with the Father through unity among themselves. The first Christians, in their turn, lived united in the name of the Risen Lord and in the strength of the Spirit.

Today as then the religious community is called to become the setting of the experience of God. The document on *The Contemplative Dimension of Religious Life*, addressing all religious, recalls that "the religious community is itself a theological reality, an object of contemplation. As 'a family united in the Lord's name' (PC 15), it is of its nature the place where the experience of God should be able in a special way to come to its fullness and be communicated to others. Mutual fraternal acceptance helps "to create an atmosphere favourable to the spiritual progress of each one' (ET 39)" (no. 15).

The community is a theological reality in the sense that it is the place of the presence of the Risen Lord. In it he continues to bestow his Spirit and introduce into a filial rapport with the Father. As Igino Giordani wrote very effectively: "Just as sacramentally the words of the priest evoke Jesus as God in the Eucharistic species on the altar, so socially the union in love of two souls – their communion in Christ, in virtue of which they act as components of the royal priesthood, – evoke Jesus as God mystically in human relationships on earth."[10]

The brother is no longer an obstacle to union with God; indeed he becomes the sacrament of Christ and of meeting with God. He comes to be in fact the concrete possibility and, still more, the *sine qua non* for living the commandment of mutual love, which by definition demands reciprocity. The brother is the possibility of attaining the presence of Christ amongst us.

Living the commandment of mutual love is the condition for

becoming community and experiencing the presence of God amongst us. For the community to become like this therefore persons are needed who are disposed to love "in the way" that Christ loved, with the same measure of love: a love without any limit at all. It means complete self-giving even to the extent of sacrificing one's life. If Jesus has loved us even unto death, "we ought to lay down our lives for one another" (1 Jn 3:16). In fact, in the mystery of his abandonment on the cross and of his death, he has revealed the radical nature of love. There he dispossessed himself of everything, in a mystery which is at once one of annihilation and donation. His is a love of self-oblation, a complete and total gift. Jesus teaches us that love is self-giving. It means going out of oneself so as to enter into the other person. Love, as John would put it, is recognized by this offering of oneself to the person loved. "By this we know love, that (the Son) laid down his life for us" (1 Jn 3:16). Following this path of consummate donation, Christ created a new people, and hence became the model for all those who want to build unity with their brethren.

Following the path their Master trod, the members of a community cannot abstract from that elementary evangelical norm: "Whoever would save his life will lose it, and whoever loses his life for my sake will find it" (Mt 16:25). The building of a community so that it may be an authentic place for the experience of God demands of its members a love with the characteristics of the Christian agape: openness towards all without exclusions or preferences, and a capacity for service of a completely gratuitous and disinterested kind. It is also necessary that such love be reciprocal. This in fact is how disciples of Christ can be recognized, if they live in mutual love (cf Jn 13:35).

In fraternal life lived in mutual love, precisely because we find God we attain also to authentic self-realization: "If we love one another, God abides in us and his love is perfected in us" (1 Jn 4:12). The perfection of love, and with it our full identity with ourselves, is the fruit of mutual love, of giving life itself for one another. We know, even from the human sciences, that only in relationship with others does man become truly an individual, i.e. achieves self-realization as a man, attaining the full vocation which calls him to be the image and likeness of a God who by his very nature is a relationship of love. "Man – we read in *Gaudium et Spes* (no. 12) – is by his innermost nature a social being, and if he does not enter into relations with others he can neither live nor develop his gifts." In this context the Council roundly declares: "God desired that all men should form one family and deal with each other in a spirit of brotherhood" (GS 24), a vocation that finds its perfection and fulfilment in Jesus who willed to share in human fellowship (cf GS 32). The transition from individual to person is linked with openness and self-giving. "To say that man is created in the image and likeness of God means that man is called to exist 'for' others, to become a gift" (MD 7). Since God is Persons-in-communion, man is called to be a person and a person in communion. For this reason, unless he lives in a relationship of love man will never be what he is called to be. As the image of the triune God, who is in himself pure love, man is able to love and becomes truly man only when in fact he loves.

The new commandment of Jesus is not, therefore, something extrinsic to humanity, added or imposed from above, but the rendering extrinsic of what is already implicit in human nature. If the entire messianic people has as its law the new precept to love as Christ himself has loved us (cf LG 9), it is because this is the norm through which the whole of humanity can attain to its particular identity of origin. "The Word of God – says the Council again – reveals to us that 'God is love' (1 Jn 4:8) and at the same time teaches that the fundamental law of human perfection, and consequently of the transformation of the world, is the new commandment of love" (GS 38). Hence if we wish as religious to attain to full maturity, even from a human standpoint, we must learn ever more to love and give ourselves. It would seem to be contrary to an instinctive impulse were we in self-affirmation led to impose ourselves on others, instead of following the authentic evangelical way of freedom and self-realization.

4. Instrument and sign of evangelization

If the religious community lives with a constant effort to improve its aspect of self-donation, it will not withdraw into itself but spend itself in service to others, witness and proclamation. Just as within the community the members do not live for themselves alone, so the entire community does not live for itself alone. If through mutual love the Risen Christ lives in it, communicating to it his Spirit, he makes it a testimony to the resurrection. As the Holy Spirit, the bond of unity in the Trinity, is the element for the "opening up" of the divine Persons, or in other words disclosing creation and the work of the incarnation and redemption, so analogically the unity of the community, which is the fruit of the same Spirit, becomes the authentic possibility for the "opening up" of the community towards the world. Just as the Risen Christ sent the community of the Twelve into the whole world, and as the Spirit sent forth the first Christian community from the cenacle to proclaim the kerigma, so every religious community, made an authentic pneumatic community by the Risen Christ, is projected towards the world and appears of its very nature apostolic.

True communion, far from being narcissistic and withdrawing into itself for the pleasurable enjoyment of its own intimacy, is open to the giving of itself and to the service of others for the broadening of communion. John Paul II has expressed this conviction in deeply effective words when he wrote in *Christifideles Laici*: "Communion begets communion: essentially it is likened to a mission on behalf of communion... Communion and mission are profoundly connected with each other, they interpenetrate and mutually imply each other, to the point that communion represents both the source and the fruit of mission: communion gives rise to mission and mission is accomplished in communion" (no. 32).

The religious community in the diversity of its ministerial activities, which extend from contemplation to the service of the least of mankind in a diaspora ordered by charity, puts itself at the service of God's plan for humanity, which is that of uniting all men in the family of the children of God and forming them into a single people. And this at a threefold level: that of mysteric presence, of exemplifying sign, and of charismatic ministerial activity.

– Mysteric presence. The community as such is already an evangelizing factor before being a means to that end. It proclaims Christ by its very presence, even before doing so by word. If, as we have already pointed out, it is the abode of a mystery (in its unity it contains the Risen Lord), Christ living in it radiates light; he touches hearts and converts those who come into contact with the community or with its members who, even individually, are always and everywhere its expression. He himself, through the mediation of the community, makes himself newly present among men to communicate to them his own life. The more the community is what it should be, the more will the presence of Christ in it be alive and radiate light. Valid for all Christians, and hence also for us religious whatever be the kind of our community, is the missionary dynamic enunciated in the Gospel of John, where Jesus asks the Father: "That they may be in us, so that the world may believe that thou hast sent me" (17:21); "That they may be perfectly one so that the world may know that thou hast sent me" (17:23). "We are missionaries above all because of what we are as a Church whose innermost life is unity in love, even before we become missionaries in word or deed" (RM 23).

The community as such is the subject best suited to evangelization. If the Kingdom of God is the gathering into one of his children around the one Father, the constitution of the new People of God brought about in the blood of Christ through the work of the Spirit, then it can be proclaimed only by a community, or at least by someone expressive of the community. How can the message of the Kingdom, which is of its nature communion, be credible unless it be proclaimed by a community? "Proclamation is never a merely personal act" (RM 45). If one is to communicate what one has seen and known, one must have had practical experience of the life of unity, or in other words of both the Trinitarian *koinonia* and the ecclesial *koinonia*.

– Exemplifying sign. To manifest community with the practical travail of overcoming tensions, divisions, and egoism, is to show in prophetic fashion how man should be in his relationships, to display human society and the Church itself. The religious community, after drinking at the fountain of unity, can indicate the path for providing a response to present-day needs in respect of the sense of the person, and the desire for authentic relationships of communion and unity. "It is not only the Church, explains John Paul II, but our society too which can draw great benefit from fraternal communities which are called to be shining reference points for those who must overcome difficulties stemming from a diversity of interest, age, race or culture. Thus the religious community can be a living witness in a world desiring peace and seeking to resolve its conflicts."[11]

– Charismatic ministerial activity. The religious community is called to contribute to the mission of the Church as the sacrament of unity of the human race not only through its mysteric and iconic existence, but also through the typical mission of the institute. Whatever be the kind of ministry the communitarian component remains a determining factor even at this level. If founders gathered around themselves a community of brothers it was because they knew that the efficacy of every apostolate depends on the strength of unity. When Christ makes himself efficaciously present in his community through mutual love, this is not only the place where God is experienced but also the subject of evangelization. The specific ministry will acquire a new and unhoped for efficacy and fruitfulness, because Christ himself will be the active agent, through the community; it will be he, through the community he informs, who proclaims the Kingdom of God, who heals the sick, who converts sinners, who carries out every good work. In this way religious life proclaims God by the way it is lived.

Furthermore the charism, if it is to be alive and relevant at the present day, must be constantly given new life by the same Holy Spirit that gave it its origin. It will always be Christ in the community united in his name who bestows his own Spirit, which of its very nature is always creative. The founders were able to be creative because they were docile to the guidance of the Spirit and were thus able to respond to the needs of their times and the expectations of their contemporaries. Equally it will be under the guidance of the same Spirit, given to the community that lives in unity, that today's men and women religious will rediscover the charismatic dynamism of their own vocation, the ability to decipher the signs of the times and the way to respond to them. The charismatic renewal of the institute will be born of the life of the community.

In this way the community becomes the place of discernment, where are perceived what is needed for the salvation of men and, at the same time, the place in which adequate responses can be planned.

5. A Trinitarian and Christological model

These reflections converge towards the ultimate foundation of the communitarian reality: the Trinitarian and Christological mystery. I am sure that we are not tempted to say, with Kant, that from the mystery of the Trinity nothing useful can be deduced! Where else can we look to understand something of our dynamic of life?

The pericoresis of the Persons in the Trinity, stemming from reciprocal donation and acceptance, is the archetype of our unity. It would seem an unattainable ideal because we, as human beings, cannot penetrate one another as do the divine Persons. But participation in the divine life means that God can penetrate us and make us one in him.

Here we immediately recall the word (subsequently translated into the institute's rule) which builds the community and the Eucharist which makes it one. If in this address I place so much stress on the contribution of the members to the building of the community, especially through the practice of mutual love, it is because I want to emphasize that the building of the community is a task and commitment of us religious. But that does not mean that we can fail to have always in mind that the community is a gift of God and a participation in his own communion. Before being a model of unity, the Trinity is its origin and constant source.

Participation in his life of *agape* makes possible the reciprocal nature of mutual love which makes us in a mysterious way to be one in each other. To love one another in Christ, and to the same extent, is to live the Trinitarian life on this earth, engrafted individually and communally in the life of love of God himself. Mutual love is therefore the life of Trinitarian *pericoresis* shared with men. The new commandment can be considered as the translation in human terms of the inter-Trinitarian *pericoresis* and *koinonia*.

The religious community should be in the vanguard in this process of adaptation of the Church to its Trinitarian model. It is called upon to show that unity in no way belittles the individuals but rather strengthens them and makes the most of their personality; and that the emergence of individual personality does not destroy unity in a flight towards individualism, but enriches it — just as in the Trinity, where there is the maximum realization of Personalization in Unity.

This is where the Christological reference comes in. Contemporary theology has found in the paschal event the privileged place for the understanding of the Trinitarian mystery and the way for its full participation. To revive within itself the Trinitarian dynamic, the community must penetrate into the Paschal Mystery.

As we have already indicated, Christ's death on the cross opens the intelligence to the mystery of God as a relationship of love, showing at the same time the dynamism of such love. Jesus has revealed on the cross the manner and extent of love – the one love that he can live, Trinitarian love, at the moment when he was fully "emptied" (Phil 2:7). He lived the experience of kenosis, even to the extent of feeling in his human nature abandonment by the Father, expressed in his cry: "My God, my God, why have you forsaken me?" (Mk 15:34). It implies the separation of Jesus from the Father, as though in a translation into the human situation of the living relationship within the Trinity between the Son and the Father. The separation from the Father which Jesus felt on the cross takes us back to the eternal generation of the Son which the Father brings about within himself. The Father renders the Son different from himself in an infinitely joyful generation of love which is the Holy Spirit. The reverberation on earth of the "other" aspect of the generation was suffered by Jesus in his human nature as a painful abandonment which re-echoes, assumes and accomplishes the abandonment and remoteness from God in which man has been placed by sin. "He discloses the intelligibility of the Trinitarian mystery in the divine *Agape*: it is by giving himself and pushing this self-donation to the abyss of abandonment and death, that the person of the Word incarnate fulfils his specific identity in the unity with the Father."[12]

Jesus shows us therefore that the true dynamism of love in which man finds the fulfilment of his own personal being, is traversed in its constitution by a moment of "death", of "self-giving", of "loss of one's life". In its deep dynamism the Paschal Mystery reveals to us that love has a moment of "non-being", a prelude to a new fullness of "being" which is transcendent.

If the kenosis of Christ reveals the reality of a relative and constitutive "non-being" of the "other" within the Trinity and allows for the relationship of pericoresis in the freedom of the Three which is the foundation of unity and distinction, kenosis is a necessary law of the community which is born of the paschal event. The tensions, difficulties, misunderstandings and disunity which we often notice in our communities are not symptoms of lack of generosity and commitment. They form part of the Christian project of communion. They tell us that the path towards unity passes of necessity through the sharing in the passion and death of Christ. In the communitarian dynamic, Christ in his Paschal Mystery remains always the model of how unity is generated.

III. SOME PATHS ALONG WHICH TO CONTINUE THE PROCESS OF RENEWAL

After considering the present situation of the religious community and emphasizing certain fundamental aspects of its identity and theological dynamism, we ought now to suggest some paths for continuing the process of renewal and tackling the problems that remain open. These are only guidelines for launching the work of this assembly, which is called upon to make a creative statement, especially in an environment of this kind.

1. Believing in the value of community

I think that a first and important point for the future is that of believing in the value of the community as such.

Despite the difficulties expressed, the replies to the questionnaire sent out by the USG reveal that emphasis on the community continues to be a determining element for the renewal of religious life. It is an important factor in the eyes of the young, has something to say to people in general and is a sign of hope for the future. Religious communities can become places of prayer and experience of God, where the Kingdom is realized in a concrete manner and the evangelical *diakonia* can be seen in action. There are many paths that lead in this direction:

- promoting theological life in the community; discovering new forms of community life and encouraging the creation of new communities more coherent with the sensitivities and needs of today's world;
- defining more precisely the missionary community;
- avoiding the fragmentation of religious communities into residences that are too small;
- increasing the extent to which the lower ranks take part in community decisions;
- defining the role of the superior.

There is a great variety among the suggestions put forward. Especially in the Anglo-Saxon world, where a great deal is said about "refounding" religious life, the restructuring of the religious community is a determining factor. Maybe as a reaction against the tendency to individualism and isolation the combined assembly of the major superiors of men and women religious of the USA, in their programme for the transformation of religious life, propose for example that communities of the future be characterized by "inclusiveness and internationality". The inclusive aspect is described as follows: "Our communities can include persons of different age, kind, culture, race and sexual orientation. They can include lay people and clerics, married and celibate, and also members with vows or without them... Our communities will be ecumenical, with people of different faiths if possible: faith-sharing will be a constituent element of the quality of life in this context of membership. An inclusiveness of this nature will require a new understanding of membership and appropriate terminology."[13] We are facing a true reinterpretation of the community and with it of the whole of religious life, with clear suggestions for refoundation.

According to some writers, especially those working in the field of sociology, religious life is called to leave the models of the "intentional community" or of "bureaucratic organization", as the classical communities are described, in favour of new "associative models".[14]

Every hypothesis is possible, even if one cannot agree with all of them. What is needed is an authentic "creativity" to "reinvent" or "refound" the religious community. The only thing necessary is to be certain that each plan is guided by the Spirit. Religious life is not born of flesh or blood desires, nor from any human planning, but of the will of God. Only the Spirit who created different communities can refound them. Let me emphasize once again that the primary strategic objective for the renewal of religious life is that of giving welcome acceptance to the Spirit, and following his inspirations with docility. And I repeat that to have the Spirit what are needed, at the present time more than ever, are not charismatic individuals but a community of persons united in the name of Jesus who ensure his presence in mutual love. The first experience of the Spirit, at Pentecost, was in fact the experience of an entire community. It will be the Risen Christ present in his community – in the midst of those who live a reciprocal love and are willing to die for each other – who will communicate his creative Spirit.

2. *Order community life in conformity with the charisma*

In this search for new paths for the religious community, I think it is important to find models that correspond to the charism. Founders and foundresses were able to give concrete structures to their communities. In the updating period that has followed the Council such structures have been abandoned because they no longer responded to the new times. But they have not always been adequately replaced by others more suitable.

Dominic, for example, founded his community on the pillars of study, prayer and preaching, all well defined with regard to time and manner. My own founder, Blessed Eugene de Mazenod, had set up community life in two phases: six months in the religious community, recollected in prayer, study and fraternal communion, and six months outside in tours of preaching. Founders too had given precise instructions and norms for the exercise of government, fraternal correction, reciprocal exhortation, communion, discernment, etc. In short, they were able to give rise in their own way a communal style of life that was well balanced and harmonious. It is true that they were ways of life that can become outdated, but in them there was an element that is always valid: there must be order in life.

It is not a question of allowing ourselves to be ensnared once again by structures, but rather of ordering life in such a way as to guarantee harmony between work, study, prayer, rest, apostolic ministry, etc. The rejection of structures so as to let ourselves be guided by spontaneity or by freely expressed creativity may be necessary, but only as a step to a more adequate arrangement.

The criterion for this new arrangement is the charismatic criterion. Starting from its charism every religious community must find the way of arranging its own life with rhythms corresponding to its particular kind of fraternal life in common. It will be necessary therefore to seek constantly the unity of the community by common reference to its own charism, as it has been transmitted by the founder and preserved and developed throughout the life of the institute. The possession of a common legacy and spiritual patrimony, before being a sociological factor for cohesion, is a component instilled by the Spirit. It is easy to understand why the conciliar and postconciliar magisterium has entrusted so large a part of the renewal of religious life to the commitment to highlight the authentic nature and richness of the particular charism, so as to "cause your own sources of energy to spring up with renewed vigour and freshness", as Paul VI asked (ET 51).

The rediscovery of one's own charisma proceeds *pari passu* with the setting up of relationships of authentic communion with other charismata. Every charism is, in fact, a word of the Gospel which becomes incarnate, an interpretation of the mystery of Christ. Its "particular" nature demands communion and unity with all other charisms. The whole Christ is like a magnet drawing all the fragments into unity. In Trinitarian logic, there can be no identification with one's own reality except in the communion which allows a better evaluation to be made of reciprocal relationships on the basis of God's unique design, to which he has called us and for which he has raised us up in the Church. It is the moment of unity of religious families, of the mutual love in which we are prompted to seek the best charisms, in growth in faith and in service to the Church.

3. Refine the instruments of communion

A further path to renewal lies in the direction of exploiting and reinventing the practical means which foster communion at the level of life between the members of the community. The life of unity has its own dynamic and needs specific "communal spiritual exercises", analogous to the spiritual exercises we are accustomed to make for the personal spiritual life.[13]

Is it not time to develop a spirituality "of the Mystical Body" so as to go to God together? Clearly such a proposal does not exclude the individual path. The two styles of spiritual growth are complementary: without personal prayer, for instance, one does not get very far. But it would be necessary to follow a way of life in which personal and communal commitment interpenetrate, harking back to the life of the Trinity where distinctions come together in unity and this strengthens the distinction.

We urgently need to discover means for: the communal discernment of the will of God, especially in regard of the apostolic options of the community; a real participation in the concrete life of the community in all its aspects; full economic sharing; accountability for one's own way of life; the practice of revision of life, both personally and in respect of the communal project. Furthermore it is necessary to find new rhythms for liturgical and community prayer, suited to the times and the type of community. I would like to emphasize some aspects in particular.

– *The communion of experiences of life in mutual openness.* First of all I think we have to find ways for the explicit sharing of our will and intention to walk together in the following of Christ. Often we take this for granted because of the fact that we are together in the same community, but it is not sufficient to live together to have the guarantee of an authentic fraternal life. The true and deeper realities run the risk of not circulating among us. A certain timidity or reserve with regard to the supernatural, human respect, education to a reticence in what concerns the interior life, often prevent us from speaking amongst ourselves of God, of the things of God and of our living together. We need to find ways of speaking with each other about the common project that has been communicated to each and all of us by the Spirit, so as to understand more deeply the reason for which we are together. For this purpose we can take advantage especially of particular times like retreats, community meetings and times of prayer. But it may be too that specific times of relaxation lived together can provide an occasion for speaking of our ideals. In this fraternal communion we can share together whatever God is doing in and around each one of us: the progress made, the fruits of the apostolate, as also doubts and difficulties. None of it is kept to ourselves and all is communicated so that it becomes known to all. Such a practice fosters a spirit of collaboration and initiative, helps us to share and give each other mutual support, and to take care of each other.

In effect there is no true fraternity if we are unwilling to enter the life of our brother, and do not allow him to enter ours. Without this communion of life, fraternity remains nothing more than a physical aggregation or a working partnership. It will be important therefore to understand the other person fully in depth, becoming aware of his interior thinking processes, of the motivations that cause him to act in a particular way. And this is something that can be reached only through a deep mutual openness.

– *Personal contact.* Personal contact, in the form of conversation, guidance, spiritual direction or advice, a sincere friendly relationship, continues to be of the utmost importance. In fact in a personal contact, as distinct from communion among all the members of the community, it is possible to share specific difficulties or particular moments of a spiritual process that it may be inopportune to communicate to all. At this level it is easier to solve problems, check up on interior progress, and take a good look at the state of one's spiritual life.[15]

– *Fraternal correction and mutual support.* A further means of which the need is ever more noticeable is fraternal correction and mutual encouragement in the following of Christ, a path on which we have set out together. It is a means for common growth, solid with each other, living in the frankness and truth of a mutual openness. This is another case in which we need to find new forms suited to new needs.

– *"Community spiritual direction".* In recent years there has been a new discovery in the field of spiritual direction. Community spiritual direction has been found more difficult, though it had been a component of religious life from the days of the first monastic communities; one need only recall the *collatio*. The community needs to find its "direction" because it is called to make a journey of growth in unity. It demands therefore, especially on the part of superiors, the ability to offer a service of discernment and guidance. Hence there is an urgent need to prepare a leadership that believes in the evangelical values of community, and has the ability to foster unity among its members in dialogue, welcoming acceptance, listening, involvement, etc.

4. *Qualify apostolic work by fostering greater communion*

As men and women religious decrease in number, it is clear that they are having to work harder, and in consequence they frequently run the risk of a dizzy missing of the mark. Apostolic needs (with which can be linked also tendencies to protagonism or possible difficulties in collaboration) lead to dispersion and the tendency to work autonomously.

With due respect to the nature of the different communities I think that, bearing in mind the signs of the times, the new ecclesiology, and the needs of the religious themselves, it is best to foster to the maximum the formation of communities avoiding the fragmentation of personnel, even at the cost of sacrificing works. Geographical extension will be cut back and the quantity of work reduced, but there will certainly be a gain in depth. We must not forget that our kind of work has a theological grading. If in our works the Lord Jesus, who lives in the midst of those who love each other, is not active and the breath of the Spirit is missing, we are labouring in vain.

5. *Form the new generations of religious to a community sense*

A final fundamental path for the renewal of the religious community is to form the new generations to a community sense. If it is true that religious, as experts in communion, "are called to be witnesses and architects of the plan for unity which is the crowning point of human history in God's design" (OE 24), we must have a sound knowledge of the dynamisms of the life of unity. How can we inculcate communion if we do not live it ourselves? It is a matter therefore of introducing young candidates into the practical dynamic of the life of unity. They will not be able to create Christian communities if they have not learned the laws of communion by living them in the concrete situation of their relationships.

Inter-congregational meetings between young religious should be encouraged, and even planned, for a broader sense of communion, as also institutions which foster collaboration between novitiates and theological institutes. It is even more important to form a sincere rapport with all the components of the People of God: the laity, families, various Catholic aggregations, the diocesan clergy. In this way the ever present temptation to withdraw into themselves, emphasize their own institute, and assume clerical attitudes, can be forestalled. Formation is called to educate to esteem and deep respect for other vocations, for the value of women in general, for women religious, for the family, by launching a real collaboration with all of them.

In this way it will be possible, also with the contribution of men and women religious themselves, to achieve a proper ordering of all the ecclesial components in dependence on and following the model of the Trinitarian relationships. It will then be "on earth, as it is in heaven". The Church, become communion, will be the efficacious "sacrament or sign and instrument of communion with God and of unity among all men" (LG 1).

NOTES

1. I use in part the summary of the replies to the questionnaire sent by the USG to General Curias and national conferences of religious. Cf F. CIARDI, *Identità e comunione: a che punto è oggi la vita religiosa*, "Vita consacrata" (29) (1993) 16-42.
2. The closure of large houses and works, however, is not due only to the drop in personnel, but also to a new vision of the community and mission.
3. This is what I tried to do in the study: *Koinonia. Itinerario teologico-spirituale della comunità religiosa*, Città Nuova, Rome 1993, 2nd edtn. To this I refer the reader for a fuller historical and theological presentation.
4. *Perfectae Caritatis* emphasizes in the first place the "wonderful variety of religious communities" that came into existence through the centuries and the great "variety of gifts" with which the Church is enriched (PC 1), and which "vary according to the grace that is given" (PC 8), the "primitive inspiration of the institutes and their "proper character and functions" (PC 2), the "spirit and native genius" of the institutes and the "specific nature of each" (PC 20). Other conciliar documents speak of the "form of the proper vocation" (LG 44), the "special character of each religious institute" (CD 33). *Perfectae Caritatis*, along with a continual return to the sources of all Christian life, indicated the return to the "primitive inspiration of the institutes", the "spirit and aims of each founder" and the institute's "sound traditions", as one of the essential criteria for an adequate understanding of its particular identity and mission in the Church and for its "up-to-date renewal" (cf PC 2).
5. Cf J. CASTELLANO, *Il carisma della vita religiosa nella chiesa comunione. Nuove prospettive e criteri operativi*, in VV.AA., *I religiosi nella chiesa italiana*, Rogate, Rome 1993, pp. 17-76.
6. The same document also offers a valuable synthesis of the concept of communion: "What does 'communion' mean here? Fundamentally it is a matter of our communion with God through Jesus Christ in the Holy Spirit. This communion exists through the word of God and the sacraments. Baptism is the door to the Church's communion and is its foundation. The Eucharist is the source of the entire christian life and is its summit (cf LG 11). Communion with the Body of Christ in the Eucharist signifies and accomplishes, or builds up, the intimate union of all the faithful in the Body of Christ, which is the Church (cf 1 Cor 10:16 ff)." Also the recent document of the Congregation for the Doctrine of the Faith *Letter to the Bishops of the Catholic Church on some aspects of the*

Church understood as communion (28.05.1992), opens with a solemn declaration of principles: "The concept of communion (*koinonia*), already highlighted in the texts of Vatican II, is very suitable for expressing the profound nucleus of the Mystery of the Church and can provide a key to the understanding of a renewed Catholic ecclesiology" (no. 1). The document recalls some of the essential elements of communion: its Trinitarian root and ecclesial expression, the dimension of the communion of Saints, the relationship between the universal Church and particular Churches in which reference to the former is the foundation of the reality of the latter, the bond of communion through faith and the sacraments, especially the Eucharist, and the communion with Peter and under Peter.

7. Already in its first chapter it enunciates the theme *Ecclesia de Trinitate*, using Cyprian's famous expression: "The universal Church is seen to be a people brought into unity from the unity of the father, the Son and the Holy Spirit" (LG 4). The conciliar documents come back frequently on the relationship Church-Trinity as a constitutive element of the Church's very being. It is Trinitarian in its source = *Ecclesia de Trinitate* (cf GS 40), Trinitarian in its image and destination towards humanity with a mission of universal salvation = *Ecclesia in Trinitate* (cf UR 2), Trinitarian in the result of its journey in history and its full realization = *Ecclesia in Trinitatem* (cf LG 17).

8. *Address to the participants in the plenary assembly of the Congregation for institutes of consecrated life and Societies of apostolic life*, "Oss.Rom.", English edtn., 2.12.1992.

9. In this connection the Italian Episcopal Conference has given a crystal-clear description of these two realities which are different but intrinsically related: "When we say 'communion', we think of the gift of the Spirit in virtue of which man is no longer alone nor far from God, but called to be part of the same communion that binds together the Father, the Son and the Holy Spirit, and rejoices to find everywhere, especially among believers in Christ, brothers and sisters with whom he shares the deep mystery of his rapport with God. (...) When we speak of 'ecclesial communion' we think of a concrete form of aggregation which is born of communion: in it believers receive, live and pass on the gift of communion". The community, as an expression of communion, "has at its disposal structures and equally visible instruments, through which are transmitted to men the message and grace of Jesus, the incarnate Son of God. With its concrete determinations and its limitations the community does not downgrade the breadth and depth of communion but neither does it exhaust it; it is as its sacrament, i.e. the manifestation and instrument which reveals its presence in human history' " (*Comunione e comunità*, Pastoral plan of the Italian Episcopal Conference for the eighties, no. 14-15).

10. *La divina avventura*, Città Nuova, Rome 1993, 7th edtn., p. 36.

11. *Address to the participants in the plenary assembly of the Congregation for institutes of consecrated life and Societies of apostolic life*, "Oss.Rom." Eng. edtn., 2.12.1992.

12. P. Coda, *Per una ontologia trinitaria della carità. Una riflessione di carattere introduttivo*, "Lateranum" n.s., 51 (1985), p. 73.

13. Typewritten text, taken in part from B. FIAND, *Where two or three are gathered: Community life for the contemporary religious*, Crossroad, New York 1992, pp. 15-16.
14. Cf P. WITTBERG, *Creating a Future for Religious Life: a Sociological Perspective*, Paulist Press, New York/Mahwah, N.J. 1991.
15. For further explanation I refer the reader to what I have written in greater length: *Gli strumenti concreti per la vita di unità*, in *Il coraggio della comunione, Vie nuove per la vita religiosa*, edited by F. Ciardi, Città Nuova, Rome 1993.

II.

Round Table on "Religious and ecclesial communion today"

Fr Gianfranco Ghirlanda, SJ

The moderator of the round table, Fr Ghirlanda, a well-known expert on Canon Law, offered the summary of the answers to the questionnaire sent by USG before the Congress. He made a series of observations of a general nature ("in general, we find a greater awareness of ecclesiality in religious life", but "some difficulties crop up in the relations among the various ecclesial components"). He then looked at the relations between religious and other realities in the Church, in particular, relations with the Bishops and the diocesan clergy, with the laity and among religious institutes. Finally, he proposed "lines to be studied in the future": develop a sense of the Church as organic communion; the hierarchical structure is not the whole life of the Church, but it too must be awakened to its charismatic origins; we must respect and valorize the plurality of charisms, trust and dialogue; increase the insertion of religious institutes in the local Church without losing the particularity and the note of universality; diocesan seminarians should have a better knowledge of the theology of religious life; religious should know better and respect the lay vocation in the Church; intensify the collaboration among institutes while avoiding a levelling off and the loss of identity.

Msgr Wilhelm E. Egger, OFM, Cap. Bishop

Called upon at the last minute to replace Msgr Luciano Mendez de Almeida, Msgr Egger, Bishop of Bressanone and president of the episcopal commission for religious in the Italian Episcopal Conference and of the joint Bishops/Religious/Secular institutes commission, spoke of "reshaping communion", that is to say that in the Church-communion everyone (laity, ordained ministers, consecrated persons) must be more aware of the charism they have received and live it with great fidelity. Then there can and must be a true "exchange of gifts", as the recent Italian Bishops' letter recommended. The letter was the fruit of the Italian Episcopal Conference assembly of October 25-28, which says that "none of the three forms of life can live without the contribution of the others". Finally, consecrated life can truly be "an alternate proposal" because it is "called to be in the forefront of a prophetico-alternative movement".

Fr Tadeusz Bargiel, OFM, CAP: Conventual

The particular situation in which the Church in Eastern Europe, emerging from the catacombs, finds itself demands a lot of attention and discretion in the application of formulas and solutions to the problems of communion drawn up in another context. The particularity of the situation of the Church in Eastern Europe, in what concerns ecclesial communion, lies mainly in the following facts:

– in some countries, religious life is not yet recognized
– the great majority of the clergy are religious
– the dioceses have very few priests of their own; the great majority are foreigners
– many religious families are coming to install or re-install themselves in the Eastern countries
– there is a lack of structures; there is need for a patient and respectful Christian formation, given that they are not mission countries
– religious and priests enjoy a great esteem and respect from the people who also expect much of them
– the people make great sacrifices to defend the faith, the Church, the priests and the Churches.

Fr Georges Darlix, CSSR: Apostolic institute

My reflections are based on the experience of my relations with a local Church, especially with the Bishop, as provincial for seven years and as general councillor for two years. These relations were lived in France, in West Africa and in other parts of the world.

I note:
- positive aspects
  - missionary projects built together
  - regular meetings between bishops and major superiors
  - collaboration during an itinerant mission
  - ceding of a parish to the local clergy.

- some difficulties
  - as religious, are we perhaps marginated
  - difficulty in facing the "urgencies" of a particular region
  - being able to leave parishes to "go farther"
  - accepting indigenous vocations

Bro Alvaro Rodrígez, FSC: Religious brother

Communion is an evangelical imperative which is achieved when the Church and religious life are attentive to respond to the needs of the world and are not so folded upon their own internal problems. Participating in the toils of our brothers enables us to discover the essential and to relativize certain secondary aspects which very often are precisely what divide us. Communion is the "sacrament" of the possibility for a new model of society in which we can all live as brothers. Faced with the inevitable conflicts for the Kingdom, we must first of all purify our often ambiguous motives, not close ourselves off from the dialogue that is always possible in faith; not renounce the prophetic character of religious life; participate courageously in the Cross of the Lord, with the certainty that the last word will be that of the God of life and of history.

Sr Doris Gottemoeller, RSM: Religious woman

Sr Doris started by noting that "during the past 30 years, there has been a paradoxical development within religious congregations that has had an impact on our relations with other groups. Specifically, religious are both better organized and our presence is more widespread. This dual process has influenced critically our relations with the hierarchy, the clergy and the laity."

In particular, the participation of religious in their "organizations" "has promoted a greater awareness on the part of religious and strengthened our capacity to develop and share programs and to speak publicly of our common concerns". This has "promoted a legitimate autonomy, competence in the decision making process and strengthened our public presence (at least in some places). At the same time, this has increased the possibility of public disagreement among religious and other groups in the Church." Even, "the relations among organizations has underlined the gap that exists between life styles and behaviours, specifically in the style of participation in organizations of religious life and the hierarchical style of the episcopal conferences. Individually or in groups, the bishops often admit to some confusion before certain public stances of religious organizations, especially in matters of politics or on questions concerning women."

"Relations between religious and clergy, as well as between religious and lay people, depend on individual contacts, without there being a great understanding of the charism of religious life as gift of the Spirit to the Church" and "the majority of lay people have no or very few occasions to meet a religious in a meaningful way or to have a just perception of religious life today."

In spite of that, "mutual trust and apostolic solidarity among religious and other groups in the Church are still a goal to be reached, but also realities to be celebrated."

Roswitha Cooper, Consecrated lay person

Since 1992, Roswitha Cooper has been secretary general of the Communities of Christian Life (CVX), after having been business manager in Germany and Hong Kong. She referred especially to her personal "experience" of "organic communion", which could be a model for our relations with each other in the Church. Nine religious women, four religious men, five diocesan priests and six lay persons began a journey together to review their human maturity, their faith and personal vocation. Each one experienced very deeply that this could enrich and strengthen their own vocation.

Among us there developed relations of friendship which were fully oriented to the strengthening of our own vocation, and that has already produced evident fruits; there could be others in the future for the service of the world. In mutual exchanges and challenges, prejudices fell, mutual understanding and trust were strengthened and especially each one became more aware of his/her identity and was strengthened in it.

"You religious, you must help us to assume our responsibility and the role that belong to us in the Church for the world, which Vatican II and the post-conciliar documents, especially *Christifideles Laici* defined so clearly... But you too need lay people, who confirm you and challenge you seriously on your specific vocation and your authenticity. It is not renewal alone that can really help us, but the conversion of all to the simplicity and the radicalism of the Gospel and fidelity to each person's vocation. From this dynamics can develop a closer and more lasting collaboration based on full confidence and mutual complementarity."

4.

The identity
of the religious

I.
How to understand and present religious life today in the Church and in the world

José Maria Arnaiz, SM
J.C.R. García Parades, CMF
Camilo Maccise, OCD

Introduction

1. In reaching this fourth day of the Congress, we have glanced at the present day situation of consecrated life in the Church and in the world. We examined the panorama brought to us by sociological and historical research on institutes of consecrated life in the world: our numbers, where we are to be found, how we feel about ourselves, what we long for, what afflicts us, in what direction our institutions are going. We questioned ourselves about our involvement in the great missionary urgencies challenging the Church. Next we turned our attention to the great mystery of ecclesial communion to rediscover in that context our manner of living it out and bringing it into effect.

It falls to us today to take the final step, summed up in the following question: What is our identity living a consecrated life in the Church? What is our understanding of it, in what manner do we describe and present it to others? How ought we to do it? This year, our reflection group worked on this question. We met regularly to air our reflections and to draw up this text we now present.

2. By way of introduction, we want to explain what field of vision we set for ourselves:

a. *Who are we now speaking?* We are male members of the religious life of the Catholic Church. We speak from our own knowledge of the tradition of religious life,[1] of humanity, of Christianity and the Catholic Church. We speak from our own experience and that of our institutes, religious Conferences and the Union of Superiors General. We speak also from the reflection on consecrated life carried out by theologians in special depth, particularly in recent years. This reflection came from the practice of religious life and gave religious a new way of looking at things.

b. *To whom do we address ourselves?* We are speaking to our Pastors, particularly those taking part in the Synod on religious life; to the secular Christian laity and ordained ministers. We also want to present consecrated life to the members of other religions and other religious confessions.

c. *How do we want to speak about consecrated life?* We want to avoid an "essentialist" language. We prefer a theological and narrative language which takes into account that consecrated life is *life and history*, and arising from that, *a theological reality*. The forms of consecrated life are passing, as they have passed, through the lapse of time: they are situated and find form in times and places, cultures and historical events. They take different forms according to the human groups that found them and continue their work, and according to the places in which they are situated. Along with this it is evident that there is a guiding thread passing through the historical reality of religious life: in it and through it God achieves his Kingdom and the Lordship of his Son, Jesus Christ in an original and often unexpected way.

3. Thus, our work answers the question: How to understand and present consecrated life in the Church and in the world today? We will divide our answer into four parts:

    a. contested identity: a new historical and cultural era;
    b. religious and anthropological identity: a form of religious life;
    c. ecclesiological identity: amid the People of God;
    d. spiritual identity: interior dynamism of charismatic following (of Christ).

I. CONTESTED IDENTITY
A NEW HISTORICAL AND CULTURAL ERA

4. It is the person of Jesus and his Gospel that have been and still are the great inspiration giving birth to the various forms of

consecrated life. That is where it gets its unique originality and its permanent characteristics. However, there are historical and cultural conditionings that also define the different forms of consecrated life and render it comparable to other human phenomena. This obliges us to think of the theological identity of consecrated life from a serious consideration of its history and cultural limitations. In other words, the phenomenological and theological study of consecrated life must go hand in hand if we wish to express adequately what are its permanent values and those that have importance for a certain time only.

5. The historical phenomenon of consecrated life in the Church belongs primarily to the Western culture and northern hemisphere. Its inspiration and moulding came from the monastic model. Since the Second Vatican Council, we are conscious of standing on the threshold of a new historical era. Already we are able to catch a glimpse of the dawning of a new form of consecrated life because a strong crisis of cultural identity is exerting its influence on the traditional model of consecrated life. Its symbolic universe finds itself at odds with the new emerging culture and the foreign cultures into which it is inserted. The traditional model of consecrated life and its theological explanation are rendered culturally anachronistic by the cultural phenomena of our times such as post-modernity, new forms of religiosity, the dominant neo-liberalism, the growing predominance of the scientific and technological apparatus thanks to reporting and the means of communication, the rise of nationalism, the phenomenon of migration, the chaotic situations into which whole nations and ethnic groups are plunged because of poverty and subjection.

6. Consecrated life is at a decisive crossroads. It seems that the historical figure it took for granted till now, is out of date and declining. The symbols which for so long gave it body, soul and spirit (the habit, forms of prayer, distinctive traditions, iconography, theological explanations, etc.) are questioned. There occur instances of disintegration and disorientation, enormous loss of collective charismatic energies and a lack of spiritual leadership. It seems that the renewal begun by Vatican II is turning into such an excessively slow sunrise, that the day never manages to break. Many things are guessed at, but the pervading gloom prevents seeing their outlines.

There is something objective and structural, almost diabolical, that continues making our situation paradoxical: it gives the impression of being what we want yet we are incapable of it and so we fall, depressed and disoriented, into an acute crisis. For us this is a decisive moment for questioning ourselves once more about our identity. The theological answers of the past are no longer valid for us. What is needed is a new theological outlook, in harmony with the theology of our time and culture. And it is just as indispensable to return, in a fresh way to the fundamental statements in order to rid theology of the dragging weight which has encumbered it during the course of history.

7. It is necessary to adopt or create a new model, which is not yet available, even though it is perceived. Once again, the Holy Spirit will have to be the great protagonist in this time of revitalization. We sense that this new emerging model of religious life offers a new vital synthesis between "contemplation" and "mission", between the spirit which gives life and the body which expresses it, between the founding experience and historical reality. Reflection on the new identity must know how to integrate the different dimensions which appear in this form of life: anthropological and religious, Christological, ecclesial, ecumenical, eschatological, cultural and historical. This time demands of us fidelity to the founding aspects of our identity, and creativity in adapting to the new cultural and symbolical model that is emerging in the world or that already exists in the places where we are.

II. RELIGIOUS AND ANTHROPOLOGICAL IDENTITY: A FORM OF RELIGIOUS LIFE

1. A religious and anthropological phenomenon

8. In questioning ourselves about the theological identity of consecrated life, we cannot avoid a fundamental fact: consecrated life is not an exclusively Christian or Catholic phenomenon, rather it is anthropological and religious. In the Church, this phenomenon is a minority – consecrated life forms only 0.12% of the baptized. Of this 0.12%, most are women (3 out of 4) – and

therefore non-cleric. Ordained ministers, who are religious, form a tiny minority. There are centuries of history behind this phenomenon which found form in well-defined groups and life styles: the original itinerant missionaries, ascetics and celibates, virgins, monks (hermits as well as cenobites), canons regular, mendicants, clerics regular, apostolic institutes, societies of life in common without vows and secular institutes. All these forms exist today and new forms continue to appear.

However, this minority phenomenon is not exclusively Catholic or Christian. Forms of religious life – also proportionally a showy minority – exist in other Christian confessions and other religions.[2] That is why we ask: What is the fundamental inspiration and aspiration shared by these forms of life? What reason for existing do these minority groups have within the lay and secular majorities of their religions? What are the trans-cultural and trans-historic values they share and that gave them life?

9. The existence of religious life shows that what is most profound and most authentic is common to all men and women; that basically every human person, of whatever race, culture, religion, people or nation, tends irresistibly towards what is "holy" what is "mystery", an impassioned search for God. The authenticity of the human person passes through the founding religious experience. The persons who live this experience in an original and outstanding manner act as initiators and models for the rest. Their religious experience and social role makes them clear witnesses, if necessary in contrasting situations, of precise human values such as simplicity and austerity, the centrality of relationship and the encounter with the "holy", mercy and non violence, moderation and self-centering, harmony with the cosmos and community life. They also show an admirable freedom with regard to external structures which they regard as relative, sometimes notably so.

This phenomenon of religious life in the religions also highlights the fact that every society creates – unconsciously in most cases – its own minority and marginal groups so that they exercise over it a role that is symbolic, critical and transforming: one that is liminal.[3] These groups have to give an outward radical form to the most profoundly prized values, especially sacred values, even if it is at the cost of social marginalization and isolation. It is in these groups that society projects its most secret hopes, dreams and aspirations.

10. The role of religious life is evident. Understood in this way, it is a legitimate human form of total personal fulfilment and an original manner of being before God in society and the cosmos. This group of men and women transmit a communal message: without reference to the "holy", there is no humanity nor dignity for the human person. This can be achieved only through adoration, reference to the sacred, contemplation, recollection and service. In its varied forms and throughout the different religions, consecrated life is one of the most important and most authentic expressions of the symbolic-transforming role played by small groups within the whole body. In this manner, consecrated life offers an alternative scale of values, critical of the *status quo*, and becomes a model of inspiration for society.

2. Taken up by Christianity

11. The religious-anthropological phenomenon of religious life has also risen up, and strongly so, in Christianity. That is not surprising since Christianity is the measure of what is most authentically human, the fullness of which was given us in Christ (Eph 1:23). Through him human wisdom is transformed into Christian faith. But in Christianity this phenomenon acquires new characteristics: the Christian lives his vocation and mission of person in the world in an original and specific manner. After the example of Jesus Christ, he highlights the values of truth, freedom, love, mercy, largesse and justice. Since Christ became man, man can be born and die, suffer and take delight, work and enjoy the fruit of his labour in an original manner, because of the light and grace that reaches him from the one who died and rose again. The first principle of human radicality is the following of Christ. Christ became one of us so that we might arrive at the plenitude of being persons. Through the action of the Spirit, he sowed the seeds of the Kingdom in peoples and religions. Christ places in the believing religious the need and novelty which come from the triple perspective of proclamation and encounter, denunciation and flight, renunciation and autonomy.

12. Religious men and women in the various Christian confessions, as in all religions, form a tiny group. But our search for what is "holy" and our life style are characterized by an original

manner of belonging to Christ and following in his footsteps. Using the example of Jesus, we know with certitude that maximum incarnation and inculturation correspond to maximum universality, whereas what is most mundane and superficial is the least able to be made universal. In this regard, being Catholic is for us an original way of living what is Christian and what is human. Like Jesus, we try to place ourselves at the unconditional service of the Kingdom of God in this world. This we do with the intention of being transparent signs, living parables, messianic anticipations of the full realization of this Kingdom. We attempt to re-present existentially the poor, obedient, chaste and merciful Christ in the world. In this way our "religious life", which is in deep communion with the other forms religious life in the non-Christian world, contributes its inescapable Christological quality.

3. To be born and re-born

13. The fact of being born, growing and dying or being re-born is also one of the components of the groups of religious life. They are born through the perception of a call from God, or of the Transcendent, and fidelity to this perception (vocation). They are born likewise as a symbolic, critical and transforming response (liminality) to the true demands of the human person – which constantly seek re-birth and re-forming – and to answer to the need felt by different human groups for messages and archetypes that show them the way to re-live their origins, anticipate their destiny, and radicalize their originality (prophetic mission). Religious life was born gradually by means of some persons or groups gifted with the charism of foundation. Disciples followed them. They were all deter mined to take on a way of life that totally involved the whole person. The consequence – but not the condition – of this total commitment is the renunciation of precise, real goods. The fruit of this totality is adoration, gratitude and profound adherence to God, mercy and solidarity with human beings. That is how they find the pearl of great price which the Gospel identifies with the Kingdom of God.

14. Consecrated life is a phenomenon that sometimes rises from its own ashes. It is constantly being renewed: its internal vitality

is impressive. As times change it takes on different aspects. Its vital energy brings about the diversity of expression it assumes and prevents it in turn from exhausting its modes of expression. But groups of religious life also die. There is a curve of life that affects them. In periods of cultural change there have been groups that have succumbed or disappeared through lack of adaptation and creativity.

III. ECCLESIOLOGICAL IDENTITY: AMID THE PEOPLE OF GOD

1. Statement: identity in correlation

15. The theological identity of consecrated life in the Church responds on the one hand to the anthropological and religious phenomenon that we have just finished analyzing and on the other to the framework of charismatic and ministerial relationships which has been established between various groups within the People of God.

a. The language we use has left its imprint on these relationships. In the Church the laity are so called because they do not belong to the ordained ministry, and vice versa. A secular is one who does not belong to an institute of consecrated life and vice versa. That is why those who belong to lay institutes of consecrated life are called lay to distinguish them from ordained ministers – be they secular or religious – and *religious* or *consecrated* to distinguish them from the secular laity and the secular ordained ministers. Those of us who have received the ordained ministry within an institute of consecrated life are – it goes without saying – *ordained ministers* distinct from all the ecclesial laity – secular or consecrated – and we are *consecrated religious* distinct from the secular ordained minister. While this language may be useful to distinguish one from the other, it remains very imprecise: it uses theological categories that belong to the general (consecration, secularity) to describe those things proper to a way of life. It has not always been used in this way.

b. It is certain that each form of life, independently of language, gradually acquired its identity and specific characteristics in correlation with the rest. Since all forms of life are in constant evolution, the correlation has obviously been and is fluid. It depends on the self-configuration and self-comprehension of each form of life in a given historical era and culture. Thus, for example, Vatican II obliged us to reformulate, with other categories, the theological identity of consecrated life, and to restore to seculars people concepts such as vocation, consecration, charism, mission. If seculars are also the recipients of a particular call from God (particular vocation), if they receive a charismatic enabling to carry it out (passive consecration), if they are sent into the world as witnesses of the Gospel and agents for the restoration of the Kingdom, how can we reserve exclusively to the consecrated life such theological categories as "vocation", "consecration", and "mission"? If we as religious also live in "Christian secularity", how can we reserve to non-religious the theological category of "secularity"?

c. Likewise, the theological understanding of the Church as People of God, ministerial and charismatic community – Vatican II insisted strongly on this – has helped us understand the ordained ministry from within the whole ministerial and charismatic context of the People of God and its members. This has made us retrieve a theology of the ordained ministry that strongly reaffirms the identity of the laity as fully-fledged subjects of the life and mission of the Church.

16. The particular identity of each one of the forms of life is connected because all of them come together in one fundamental identity: to be *Christian faithful*. That is what we have been affirming since Vatican II and that is what we find in the Code of Canon Law (CIC nn. 208-293). *"Christian faithful"* is our noun and *"lay"*, *"secular"*, *"ordained minister"* are our adjectives. Our identity is described on both levels: the substantive level – that which is fundamental and common, and on the adjectival level – that which is particular to each in our common being of *Christian faithful*. The two levels are interwoven and one is not found without the other. It becomes evident, as a result, that the first thing necessary to grasp the identity of consecrated life, is to reflect upon our identity as *Christian faithful* within the one People of God. This is our deepest identity; coming before, existing alongside and subsequent to whatever other form of participation.

2. Our original and final identity: To be Christian faithful

17. We have been called to faith, to divine filiation, to follow Jesus. To this end we have been anointed-consecrated by the Spirit in baptism-confirmation and the other sacraments. We form the holy People of God, the eucharistic and missionary community in the world. With all our brothers and sisters we are a royal people, a holy assembly, a priestly people. We all enjoy the same dignity. We are all brothers and sisters having but one Father: Abba. The Holy Spirit has graced each one of us with different charisms and various ministries, contributing to the fruitfulness of *Mother Church* and to the dynamism of her evangelizing mission. We are all co-responsible for the life and the mission of the Church: it goes with our filial and royal condition. By the anointing that comes from the Holy One we, the whole body of the faithful, cannot err in matters of belief (LG 12) and are made ready to be prophets of God.

18. This identity is not fully realized, it is found "along the way". We are a pilgrim People of God. What we will become has not yet been revealed. We journey towards the fullness of our identity. The lack of Christian coherency of those baptized without sufficient discernment, without authentic means of initiation and without subsequent serious spiritual direction has been the cause that communal elements of Christian existence have become considered the exclusive preserve of consecrated life. When we return to a Church born by means of authentic initiation and reborn by means of penitential re-initiation – in response to God's call to faith and conversion – then the experience of what it means to be *Christian faithful* together, offers the building blocks to put together a description of the identity of each form of the life. We who belong to consecrated life are first of all *Christian faithful*, trying always to become more so until there comes about the fullness of time in Christ Jesus. The origin and the goal of consecrated life, to which we have felt particularly called, is solely to be *Christian faithful*.

3. Structural and ministerial identity: between lay Christian faithful or Christian faithful who are ordained ministers

a. Ordained ministers and laity in a ministerial Church

19. Although we form a ministerial Church and we have all received from the Spirit charisms that imply a ministry, we recognize that the *charismatic-founding ministry* of the "apostolic root", which is a way of saying the ordained ministry, was instituted by the Lord and maintained in the Church by the Spirit. It is an indispensable ministry which succeeds the ministry of the Twelve to keep the Church united in the same apostolic faith. It is the principle of communion between all the communities and persons and it renders the Lord sacramentally present among his own. The Church ordains to this ministry, with an irrevocable character, those in whom she recognizes a special call and gifting from the Lord to exercise the apostolic ministerial functions in their different orders. To be an ordained minister is not only to exercise a function, it is an authentic state of life characterized by an unreserved love and pastoral commitment and preoccupation for all the Churches with undivided heart.

20. The ordained ministry is exercised especially in the *interior mission* of the Church: feeding the Lord's sheep and making it possible at every moment that the Church be a royal, prophetic and priestly people, a people that everywhere glorifies God and evangelizes. In this sense, it is the responsibility of the ordained ministers to keep the People of God available and prepared to launch out into the *exterior mission* of evangelizing the world.

21. The ordained ministry has not always been understood and lived in the same way. On occasions ordained ministers have forgotten the shared ministerial condition of the whole People of God, and have segregated and separated themselves from it, placing themselves on a superior, hierarchal level. This forgetfulness began when the word *lay* was resorted to for the first time in the Church. In the Roman world, the word *lay* applied to the ordinary people. In the Jewish world, it referred to the profane, the non-consecrated. The Church began to use the word to refer to all those who were not ordained ministers. The lay person was the non-minister. When the Church of North Africa (third

century) began to call the bishops "priests", the word *lay* then began to mean "non-priest". Even if at that time the *Christian faithful* were greatly esteemed and valued by their pastors, there appears a tiny cracking that would become enormous with the passage of the centuries, reaching the Renaissance opinion of the Church as a *societas inæqualis* formed of superiors and subordinates. Forgotten was the fundamental unity within which diversity should, of necessity, be placed.

22. Vatican II opposed this mentality and demanded a mutual relationship (= charismatic mutual ministering and deference) which has as its background Christian fraternity (LG 32). Moreover, the Council spoke of the lay state as the subject of charisms and ministries in the Church. The ordained ministry is charism and ministry *par excellence* but not to the exclusion of others. The *lay Christian faithful* are also ministers according to the various gifts they have received. Ordained ministers and lay people are subjects of charism and ministry, both have the same dignity, but they interrelate from the charismatic difference that makes up the Church. The ordained ministers exist for the laity and not "above the laity" (*pro laicis, non super laicos*). They must not usurp the place of Jesus Christ nor that of the Spirit, nor that of the Church. Between the ordained minister and the laity there has to be a "balanced relationship". The great majority in the Church are *lay Christian faithful*. Ordained ministers are the tiniest minority. The "mutual relationship" must be balanced. For all that, there will be times in which the ordained minister has to assume a role of intense leadership. On other occasions it may also happen that the Christian community is sufficiently mature to not require a strong leadership. What is important is that both feel they are People of God, Christian faithful, together forming a large fraternity; that mutually they recognize the gifts or charisms received and that they permit each other to exercise them as ministries.

23. The laity with all their charisms and ministries are by vocation the agents of the *exterior mission* of the Church. It belongs to the laity to be in the forefront of the Church in the transformation of society, in proclaiming the Gospel and in the struggle against structures that favour injustice, sin and oppression. They have to carry the Church beyond its borders, for they

are the principal protagonists of the "missio ad gentes" and of the "new evan-gelization".

b. Consecrated persons as "lay Christian faithful"

24. A great number of the men and women leading a consecrated life form part of the laity in the Church. They have a place in this priestly, prophetic and royal People of God that has to be served by its ministers and has to be accompanied, in Christian freedom, in its vital and missionary initiatives. While the great raison d'ètre of the ministry is "interior", the raison d'ètre of the consecrated laity is "exterior", towards the world. With lay *Christian faithful*, men and women, lay consecrated life is sent to all nations and cultures, until the end of time. With them, lay consecrated life must reach all the deserts, outskirts and frontiers of the world to make present the Gospel of the Kingdom of God. The secular laity normally carries out its mission in the structure of the particular Churches to which it belongs. The laity in consecrated life shares in the supra-diocesan structure of their institutes of Pontifical Right. This is historically so in order to allow the religious laity, masculine or feminine, a greater missionary mobility as well as the ability to carry on their exterior mission with greater audacity, availability and creativity.

c. Consecrated persons as "Christian faithful who are ordained ministers"

25. A minority of men belonging to consecrated life are ordained ministers of the Church: priests or deacons. Ordained ministry and consecrated life are not two separate vocations for them, nor is one subordinate to the other. They are two aspects of the one vocation. The ordained ministry is carried out in the charismatic identity of those who are consecrated, and this charismatic identity is lived out in the ministerial status of priests or deacons. Nevertheless, in consecrated life, the ordained ministry is not so closely bound to the diocese as it is for secular priests or deacons. Moreover, the ordained ministry is carried on according to the demands proper to community life or the congregation and the spirituality and charismatic mission proper to the

institute. The ordained ministry emerges in consecrated life characterized by a certain freedom and charismatic mobility. An excessive "parochialization" or "diocesanization" does not agree with the nature of consecrated life, neither does a consecrated life which involves the religious priest to such an extent that he is prevented from serving his Christian community generously.

4. Charismatic Identity: "Consecrated Christian faithful"

26. Among the *Christian faithful* those belonging to consecrated life are the tiniest minority. Given this phenomenon of consecrated life, it is indispensable to restore a sense of proportion. We are dealing with a state and form of life that is out of the ordinary and in the minority. In the Church, it does not exceed more than 0.12% of the People of God. The universalization of this form of life would lead to the death of humanity. Therefore, its identity must be explained from the place it occupies in the selection of forms of life in the People of God.

a. Charismatic origins

27. The institutes of consecrated life arose from among the Christian faithful as a movement of the Spirit and a gift for the whole Church. They have kept on appearing at various moments in history through charismatic men and women founders and founding communities. They were graced with creative and contagious capacity. They felt the Spirit of Jesus possessing them and, like him, they identified with the Father's plan. From there, they were able to sense the great spiritual and missionary needs of the Church and society of their time and place. They responded with minority and significant forms of life and works of service. By their style of life and activity they were able to convey their enthusiasm to others, sharing everything with them.[4] In spite of the limited scope of their projects, they felt the need to insert themselves into the social framework of the Church, seeking its approbation, because they knew that they were raised up by the Spirit to influence the Church as a whole. Through hierarchical authorization, the various institutes belong publicly to the life

and holiness of the Church. They rise up from her and it is towards her that they tend, avoiding any semblance of sectarianism.

28. The initial charismatic enthusiasm is usually followed by institutionalization and universalization which allow the charism to grow and settle down in other places and times. Every institute has it own life curve, ascendent in the beginning, which reaches an apex or zenith, then becomes descendent. The ascendent period is buoyed up by charismatic enthusiasm; the time of descent is marked by routine, disenchantment and doubt. Charismatic institutes lose their identity and prophetic force, to the same extent that they move away from their initial charism, because of routine and necessary institutionalization.[5] A return to their origins and suitable adaptation to the times has made possible the ongoing renewal of not a few institutes. Since Vatican II, this has been the criterion of a proper renewal. Nevertheless, institutes of charismatic life can also die, once they fulfil their reason for existence. That explains the different phases in which the institutes of consecrated life may find themselves in the Church.

29. Although we cannot say that consecrated life was instituted by Jesus, it must be positively stated that the various forms of consecrated life saw their vocation reflected in embryo in the tiny group of men and women who closely followed Jesus. In Jesus' public life, we find two groups of people who have a distinct form of relationship with him. The first, numerically greater, the disciples, were from the ordinary people, the masses who followed him. In the forefront of these were the apostles, selected from among the disciples: "He summoned his disciples and picked out twelve of them; he called them apostles" (Lk 6:13); "and some women also followed him." Each group had its own diverse mode of following Jesus. The first, the most numerous, is centrifugal: ("go", "he sent them"; the second is centripetal: ("come", "they remained with him", "they followed him"). The call to form part of the tiny group is meant to symbolize how the whole People of God is welcomed into the Kingdom through fellowship with Jesus. The intense experience of the Kingdom being the great treasure, so monopolizes the life of the one favoured thus that everything is left behind (nets, father, family,

job, property). The person goes to wide open spaces far from the securities of this world, to a place not foreseen by creation, *outside the camp* (Heb 13:12-13), to the place of the Cross as the final consequence of service to others. The answer to this call unfolds when fear is vanquished, all concerns and earthly security are left aside and one trusts. Well then, not only the ordained ministry, but consecrated life has found its fundamental inspiration right to the point of understanding it as *vita apostolica* in this very group, representative of all the people. In this sense, the ordained ministers and the *religious lay Christian faithful* feel called to a common life style: the *vita apostolica*. This explains why, right from the very beginning of institutionalized monasticism and throughout the long history of consecrated life, groups of priests have opted and continue to opt for this life.

c. Imbalances in defining the identity of the forms of life in the Church

30. The emergence of the minority charism of consecrated life in each of its principal forms has obliged the thinkers in the Church to resituate the remaining ecclesial group in relation to it. For example, that is what the Fathers of the Church did with regard to monasticism (John Chrysostom, Basil, Augustine), or the great theologians of the Middle Ages with regard to monasticism and the mendicant orders (Thomas Aquinas, Bonaventure), or the theologians of the Renaissance with regard to all forms of religious life, including those springing up in their time (Francisco Suárez, Bellarmine). When it came to defining the distinctive traits of consecrated life, an adequate balance was not always struck. When secular lay life was understood and lived as an inferior form of Christian life, consecrated life was considered as a superior and more perfect form. The rediscovery of the grandeur of the vocation and specific mission of the secular laity in the Church and the secular forms of Christian life render necessary a new theological redefinition of consecrated life; or better still, a new theological redefinition of the two forms of life understood in "mutual relationship". It is unjust, and even odious, to explain the identity of the different forms of ecclesial life by comparisons wanting to place consecrated life always above the others: it is more perfect, follows more closely, more totally

committed, etc. Only by an adequate evaluation of all the forms of ecclesial life and their correlation is it possible to explain their identity adequately.

31. This new awareness of the lay-secular vocation and its spiritual and missionary possibilities also obliges us to modify our theological understanding of consecrated life. It demonstrates how the definition of the identity of consecrated life becomes associated with the identity of the ordinary and secular Christian life in all its forms, while at the same time being interdependent upon it. In fact, what each form may be existentially, will redefine the other. The forms of Christian existence are being identified progressively in the extent they relate through debate and dialogue. So much so that each form of life interacts with the other forms of life and as such defines itself.

d. "Christian secularity"

32. Consecrated life is but one of the forms of Christian life occurring in the Church. These are the particular ways in which, under the action of the Spirit and guided by the Church, each individual puts a personal stamp on his or her vocation which is essentially to be "faithful to Christ". It is God the Father who sends a specific call-vocation to each one, and it is the Spirit who gives a particular charism to every one of the believers rendering them capable of carrying it out, gracing each one with a particular mode of being and doing. It has become accepted to speak of "secularity" when expressing the theological identity of secular Christian life and "consecration" when expressing that of consecrated life. Well understood, these can be valid expressions. That is what we will now consider.

33. *Secularity* belongs to all the members of the human community, hence to the members of institutes of consecrated life. The concept of secularity is determined by the process of secularization proper to modernity. The latter appeared as a force during the Renaissance and reached its apex during the Enlightenment. Secularization made us rediscover and assume important values: freedom, autonomy, man's creative and organizational ability, and in consequence, the image of a God creator of autonomy,

freedom, respectful to the extreme with his creation. Certainly, the process did take on anti-religious and anti-ecclesiastical traits. It called for emancipation from dogmas, established morality, authoritarian tradition. It took pride in the capacity of instrumental reason. The results were the de-clericalization, de-confessionalization, de-sacralization, de-axiologization of society and the unrestrained march toward progress. Vatican II recognized the fundamental validity of modernity's process of secularization in as much as it is a process of liberty-liberation. Consequently, it accepted this manner of being Christian in secularity and exercising ones Christian mission in secularity, without clerical tutelage and the strict surveillance of religion.

34. However, modernity's process of secularization is running into not a few logical difficulties presenting speculative problems, that make many people crave after an era of post-modernity. Secularity – understood in the terms of modernity – has clipped away excessively the world's representations (emptying human experience of its religious content), its concept of time (stripping history of its protology, its eschatology and utopias). It has preferred the robot to the human person and nature (ecological devastation and reduction of the human person to a secondary factor in the process of production). Today we postulate a post-modern secularity, dynamic and open to transcendence. That is the secularity that the religions postulate: a secularity determined above all by faith in God. The spiritual and moral consequences are remarkable: they lead to the rejection of these or those values forming part of a normal and ordinary human fulfilment. It is this secularity that Christianity postulates.

35. Christian secularity understands itself as autonomous but not independent of God. It is a secularity determined above all by faith in Jesus Christ. It is the secularity of those who have made a covenant with him by faith sealed in baptism. It is the secularity of his followers and those consecrated by his Spirit. It is influenced by awareness of the redemption and its reality. Which is to say it is not ingenuous concerning the possibilities of nature and history, since it is aware of the ravages caused by sin and the need for redemption. This secularity is proper to all believers. It is the ambience in which we unfold our lives, whether we be lay-seculars, consecrated or ordained ministers.

36. Nevertheless, the sole misgiving seculars have in living "complete secularity" presuppose not making the process of secularization absolute and not understanding modernity in a mode closed to transcendence. This complete secularity shows that the radical following of Jesus is not at odds with vital commitment to the service of culture, science, economy, politics, art, work, society. It shows that the Gospel of the Kingdom is perfectly compatible with being authors of a dynamic and creative modernity. To the contrary, the Gospel of the Kingdom impels believers to introduce into the humanization process the characteristics of peace, justice, love, truth, defense of life and human dignity, fraternity, safeguarding nature. Jesus does not ask his disciples to renounce property, marriage or liberty. On the contrary, he asks them to conform to the original plan of God the Father: "In the beginning it was not like this..." Secularity is a state of life in constant movement. It demands the taking of decisions constantly: in family, economic and professional areas.

d. "Christian secularity": total and limited

37. While the forms of secular Christian life incarnate the normal creational modes of the historical faith experience, the forms of consecrated life – as was particularly evident in their monastic origins – try to be the memory of God's original plan expressed in the first pages of Genesis and prophecy of the eschatological fullness. Given that the integrity and cosmic unity into which God planned the human being were marred and made unrealizable by sin, consecrated life led by the Spirit feels called to present to this fallen world – like Jesus – the aspects of God's original plan that sin has obscured. That is why it renounces those goods that have been perverted. Celibacy-virginity, poverty and the service of obedience are thus transformed into prophetic reminders of a creating-eschatological plan which has been, and still is, so often contradicted throughout human history. Thus the prophetic forms of consecrated life attempt to harmonize the historic existence of believing seculars with the memory of their origins and ultimate end.

38. The charism of consecrated life is characterized by consecrating and captivating the whole existence of those who received it,

putting them in a socially abnormal condition through an evangelical missionary life of celibacy, poverty, obedience, community. This charism places the "Christian faithful" in a "limited secularity". The Church itself protects and requires this secularity to allow it to exercise its prophetic and symbolic role within it. The *consecrated lay Christian faithful* are called to the same mission as the secular *lay Christian faithful* ("because in the Church there is unity of mission", AA 2), but not in the same way. The seculars get to be present in the mission of the Kingdom of God and of the Church by incarnating human values, while those who belong to consecrated life do so by a form of life that is prophetic by its contrast and abnormality: their vocation is lay Christian, but not fully secular. Therefore, lay religious life cannot be placed in a context of total secularity. But what does this affirmation imply? It implies that, in the Church, religious life forms a liminal group. That is, an alternative group, separated by its life style and ministry from the normal structures of society. It forms a liminal group by its life style of community celibacy, the option for the poor and permanent discernment in search of the will of God the Father. To live this way in all its radicality is to be in society in a manner distinct and somewhat distant from it. As religious this is our prophecy. It is our way of being symbols of the Kingdom.

e.   An existential parable within the People of God

39. Within the life and mission of the Church, consecrated life functions as symbol, as the Council acknowledged (LG 44). Symbol within a Church which is itself totally a symbol with regards to the world. This form of life is most necessary where Christian existence is most affected by the disintegration and corruption that sin brings about, where grave deviations in following Jesus take root. Some Fathers of the Church even saw monastic life as a "holy deviation" leading the Church to enter into God's straight path. Consecrated life makes sense then where there is most need of the exaggerated signs of the originating or of the eschatological order. It is only because of sin that poverty, virginity-celibacy and obedience have become renunciations.

40. Consecrated life appears as an existential parable told by the Holy Spirit in the age of the Church. By means of it the Spirit

recalls some of the existential gestures of Jesus (his mercy for sinners, his closeness to the least and the marginalized, his continuous prayer, his evangelizing activity, his miracles worked for the sick and the possessed), evoke some of his teachings (charity, hospitality, forgiveness), express some of his mysteries (birth, life in Nazareth, passion, death, resurrection). Each institute of consecrated life makes prominent, over-states in a charismatic manner, some aspect of the Mystery of the Lord, thus converting it into a living memory of him in the Church. All the forms of consecrated life re-enact in a special manner the celibacy of Jesus for the Kingdom, his option for the poor, his total dependence on the will of God the Father, his style of community. So much so that the members of consecrated life are symbol-memorial of the Lord more so through their lifestyle than their activities or undertakings. Nevertheless the activities and institutions of consecrated life are under the primacy of the symbol. They must be meaningful: activities and institutions through which are realized the little miracles of the Kingdom which are significant transforming actions. Consecrated life does not have to renounce efficiency, rather symbolic efficiency belongs to it.

41. The symbolic role of consecrated life means neither particular privilege nor superior status; being sensational is not typical of consecrated life. It is better to say that one is dealing with a role noted for "minority" and "subsidiarity". The Church does not exist for consecrated life, rather it exists for the Church. Just as the accounts of the parables and miracles are secondary and subsidiary within the Gospel text, so too is consecrated life within the Church. Consecrated life does not exist for the purpose of giving vigour to the instrumentality of the Church, nor to stand in for all the secular *Christian faithful* in their contributions to secularity. Its secularity is limited, branded by the utopia that does not yet exist. The most profound intent that gives rise to consecrated life is not that alone of solving problems of one type or another. Consecrated life did not emerge as an efficacious instrument for this. It sprang up as a symbol that inspires and stimulates society and the Church to solve their own problems, to answer their own needs for salvation, concerning the Kingdom of God. The verbs that characterize the mission of the *consecrated Christian faithful* are not so much verbs of instrumentality (do, educate, take care of) as the symbolic verbs (to signify, inspire, refer to, stimulate, transcend).

To fulfil a symbolic role within the People of God and society in the educative environment is a fascinating and relatively easy task for those who have received that charism.

42. To exercise a symbolic role in the present world, with its imbalances, conflicts and perspectives is a complex task that demands discernment and boldness. Discernment to know where, when and how. Boldness to go beyond the historical conditionings that weigh down heavily upon us as persons as well as institutions. Exercising a symbolic role is not a matter of numbers but rather of quality. By intuition, the religious institutes know that the presence of the Kingdom of God is most evident where there is poverty, marginalization, dehumanization. It is the option for the poor, for the least, that gives meaning to the role of consecrated life.

IV. INTERIOR DYNAMISM OF THE LIFE OF CHARISMATIC FOLLOWING OF CHRIST

43. The theological identity of consecrated life within the common Christian vocation is not a reality given once and for all. It is a process, a journey, which enjoys an interior dynamism whose principal agent is the Holy Spirit. But it is not a journey in the exclusive sense. Those who belong to consecrated life journey with the People of God. Within them and with them we journey together toward the Kingdom of God already present, but still incomplete. We draw near to the Kingdom in the measure that we follow Jesus and identify with him under the pluriform power of the Spirit. It is the Spirit who grants to the various forms of religious life the ability to insert themselves into the spiritual journey of the People of God with a particular style and outlook. Proper to consecrated life is to place itself in those areas of the People of God where it can best exercise its symbolic role of attraction and guidance: the desert, the periphery, the frontier and even in the heart of the People of God.

44. Within the one and only great spiritual journey of the People of God, consecrated life brings into prominence some fundamental aspects that give it identity and make it an attractive and stimulating symbol:

1. conversion and exodus,
2. ...in an alternative-prophetic style community of life and prayer,
3 ...under the primacy of the Word of God,
4. ...and creative fidelity to the charismatic gift received,
5. ...near to the people and inserted into their culture and human condition,
6. ...Mary, inspiration, presence and stimulus for a prophetic spirituality,
7. ...living in the Spirit within the spiritual journey of the People of God.

1. Conversion and exodus

45. The charism of consecrated life demands living in a permanent condition of exodus and conversion. It cannot exercise its symbolic function without adapting itself to the present-day's profound socio-cultural and ecclesial changes and through them expressing the most fundamental aspects of its Christian and charismatic identity. The conversion that this adaptation demands is on a grand scale: it extends to attitudes, structures and traditions. Consecrated life discovers the need to accompany the People of God, particularly where it is most wounded and impoverished; where it is on a laborious exodus toward the homeland of liberation. Consecrated life wants to be the pioneer in this exodus, generously accompanying its brothers and sisters. For consecrated life this means not only renouncing the protagonism of other times, but living intent on poverty, simplicity and minority, placing itself "liminally" wherever its presence proves to be more symbolic and compelling. The conversion and re-conversion of institutions and persons who form part of them is one of the most arduous tasks that this new spiritual look in consecrated life requires. Conversion and exodus are today the two fundamental attitudes of the spirituality of consecrated life.

46. What conversion really means is serious and renewed commitment to following Jesus under the unpredictable inspiration of the Spirit. To be converted to following Jesus, to the Gospel, is to be converted to love, to justice, to our neighbour. The Spirit makes conversion and exodus possible so that these attitudes are

not confused with voluntaristic undertaking, a destiny which consists in vigilantly accepting each one of the *kairos* that the Spirit offers in which everything is possible for those who stay open. Likewise, the Spirit revivifies and re-actualizes his charism at each historical moment. To follow Jesus, to live in the Spirit then becomes a journey in creative fidelity to the charism – trying to respond to the challenges of each era and to receive and extend the Kingdom of God.

2. *In an alternative life style of community and prayer that announces the final parousia*

47. Consecrated life's reason for existing is to belong to the People of God who follow Jesus, at the same time impressing on this following traits that re-present Jesus' historical life. That is why consecrated life attempts to follow Jesus who was born and lived in poverty, consecrated his life and energies to service of his brothers and sisters, in a life that was celibate and obedient to the will of the Father. Consecrated life gives a particular approach to the three fundamental demands of following Jesus (cf Lk 14:25-35): the relativization of family ties expressed by consecrated chastity; the relativization of goods expressed by poverty; the relativization of ones own plans for an autonomous life which is symbolized by carrying the cross, seeking and fulfilling the will of God in obedience. The life and teachings of Jesus also stir us to overcome the desire for goods by poverty, the thirst for power by obedience, and to live free for the service of the Kingdom by celibacy. Chastity, poverty and obedience are thus converted into pointers towards an alternative style of life. The alternative comes from the Parousia, that is, from the future of the Kingdom. It thus accents the pilgrim character of the Church. Consecrated life becomes ardent longing for the Lord who comes, a depending on his unexpected coming.

48. The basic structure of this alternative way of life is a living together to some extent exaggerated by that Christian fraternity that Jesus sought from all his followers. To be a living parable of the apostolic community has been the great objective of consecrated life since its monastic origins, from Pachomius who marks the transition from anchorites to cenobites, down to the most

recent religious institutes.[6] Since the Council there has been a desire to emphasize the fraternal aspect of consecrated life. In this experience of radical fraternity lies one of the principal testimonies of consecrated life: it makes present the Kingdom preached by Jesus and highlights the reconciling power of the Spirit of Jesus who gathers everybody into a new family. Celibacy, sharing of goods, community discernment of God's ways, commitment to the mission they live together in and from a community, which with its common dwelling place and organization helps to overcome individualism. Openness to the wider communities, provincial or general, broadens the community horizons. Contact with other ecclesial communities helps to discover ones specific identity. The role of the coordinator in community life is to be the animator and builder of a fraternity which allows the transition from life in common to life in communion.

49. Communion in prayer stands out among the components of a community of consecrated life. The community, being a family gathered in the name of the Lord, needs to live continuously glorifying God the Father in his welcomed and nurtured presence. Thus the evangelical fraternity tries to live the experience of love of the Father, fraternity in Jesus and discernment in the Spirit of the ways of the Kingdom. To be a praying community means to live giving first place to listening to the Word of God – believing in it and committing oneself to live it in love. It means to live sacramentally, liturgically making life a worship pleasing to God expressing it in the liturgy of the Hours, the celebration of the sacrament of reconciliation, and especially in the Eucharist celebrated as a journey of faith, hope and charity throughout each liturgical cycle.

3. Giving priority to the Word of God

50. The vocation to consecrated life is nourished especially by listening to the Word of God. It is wonderful to discover how, in the beginning of monastic life, the reading, meditation and contemplation of Sacred Scripture in its entirety constituted the monks' principal occupation. They discovered in it their primary and fundamental norm of life. Following Jesus implies knowing his whole mystery and translating it vital and experientially to

our present day. The Council itself asked religious to have "the Sacred Scriptures at hand daily, so that they might learn the *surpassing worth of knowing Christ Jesus* (Phil 3:8)" (PC 6). Within the People of God, consecrated life tries to turn itself into a permanent memory of the Word of God by uniting the Word of God in Scripture to the Word of God in life. The practice of community reading goes with the community origin of Scripture. From reading and meditation on the Word of God we go on discovering the true face of Jesus and what following him demands, as well as the community dimension of the history of salvation and the dignity of the human person. This type of reading has taken on a technical name in the Church: *lectio divina*. This causes the People of God to see that the Bible is not a book of history nor of doctrine, but a book through which the Holy Spirit reveals, in concrete existence, the will of God the Father and his mystery. We read doctrine and history to find a meaning to life in them.

4. *Creative fidelity to the charismatic gift received*

51. The particular way consecrated life is situated amidst the People of God has been brought about by the Spirit through charismatic men and women: founders and foundresses and their initial communities. They were given their own particular way of understand and moulding the following of Jesus in the People of God. That is the origin of the special and proper characteristics within the spirituality held in common with the People of God. Through them, the Church continues to be graced, enriched and stimulated to follow Christ more radically. The loss of contact with the charism of the founders weakens unity of life, the identity of the institutes and congregational cohesion. The constant return to the charismatic source and its re-translation into the new historical circumstances makes personal and congregational identity as well service to grow. Charism forms an atmosphere of enthusiasm that creates unity in pluralism and boldness in enterprise for the Kingdom.

52. The Rules and Constitutions, which are the norms of life, ministry and organization, must seek to translate the original charismatic inspiration. However, the inspirational and legislative

texts of the various institutes have been frequently conditioned by the models of Church and by the theology of consecrated life of each era. After a very long period during which the juridical aspect of these texts prevailed over the spiritual, the legislative renewal of consecrated life required by the Council and directed by the Motu Proprio *Ecclesiæ Sanctæ* has allowed institutes to return to their original sources and origins in order to adapt and give form to them in our times. The institutes who have drawn closer to this ideal can show in their Rules and Constitution their authentic style of spirituality within the People of God and the traits that characterize their charismatic identity. The spiritual itinerary they define is called to integrate itself into the various socio-cultural and ecclesial contexts in such a way that, while preserving unity, it opens itself out to a legitimate pluralism. In this sense, Rules and Constitutions are a great sign and instrument of charismatic renewal. In times of cultural change, or in new cultural contexts, the revitalization of identity and its primary and fundamental aspects becomes absolutely necessary. It is only from this spiritual disposition that we can overcome those moments of disintegration, doubt and going astray.

5. *Close to the people, inserted into their culture and human condition*

53. The flight from the world (*fuga mundi*) does not separate us from the world that God loved so much and to which he handed over his Son. It separates us from the world ruled over by the Evil One and his diabolical powers. It is an apocalyptical flight, wrestling against evil and in unequivocal commitment to God's plan. It is flight from what Babylon, mother of prostitutes, symbolized in order to enter the world governed by nearness of the Samaritan, by the martyrs' commitment to justice, by God's presence confessed within the human fraternity. In the various eras of history, consecrated life drew near to the people, trying to serve especially the poor and the marginalized. It has poured itself out in the cause of human rights and justice. At the present time, it is very sensitive before two challenges that have emerged with particular force in a Church predominantly in the Third World: the one of giving attention to the poor, inserting itself in their midst, the other of inculturation.

54. *Insertion* is not the only way to serve the poor, to opt for them. It is, however, a privileged way of doing so because it leads to putting down roots, locally and physically, among them and to an active commitment in solidarity with marginalized people. This insertion, although it occurs in a minor way, questions the whole of consecrated life, because it jolts the conventional manner of understanding it and the historical forms of making it present in the Church and society. Starting from a social place, which is the departure point of a spiritual experience, consecrated life, that is so inserted, moves on to opening a path toward the totality of the Gospel. This also leads to recovering the originality of their charism beginning with the experience and commitment of their founders. At the same time it assists in discovering and overcoming the extraneous elements that had been introduced into the overall framework.

55. This discernment of essential values permits us to take on the task of *inculturation,* a profoundly felt necessity of evangelization in today's world. What is wanted is a consecrated life in which free rein is being given to the conviction that the charism itself can and ought to be re-read according to the particular circumstances. The traditional mode of consecrated life lived in Europe and transplanted everywhere else and accepted as most normal, is now being questioned. A legitimate pluralism in the form of life and expressing all this becomes indispensable to preserving unity in what is fundamental to religious consecration and what is essential to the individual charism. In every circumstance, it is necessary to listen to and discern the demands of the Spirit. This is how we enter into the historical dynamism of the spirituality. That is how we live the experience of God as Lord of history, someone who is next to us, in action, bringing about new things, who promises and opens out perspectives for the future. In a word, he is a God present in history, guiding it from within.

56. Inculturation and insertion form part of the specific traits of the spirituality of consecrated life. They are characteristics that make it particularly close to *apocalyptic spirituality* revealed in Scripture, and particularly vulnerable to the diabolical forces of the world. Because of this it is not at all strange that consecrated life in these circumstances leads to martyrdom and that is shared with the other members of the People of God, recalling in this way its origins.

6. Mary: Inspiration, presence and stimulus for a prophetic spirituality

57. In the interior dynamism of following Jesus, the Church contemplates Mary "the perfect model of the Lord's disciple" (MC 37). We who follow Jesus in consecrated-charismatic life know ourselves called to be prophets of a different world and because of this we discover in Mary our inspiration and receive a mysterious spiritual strength from her. The Virgin of the *Magnificat* proclaimed the end of the old corrupt world and announced the advent of a new history in which God puts down the mighty from their thrones and raises up the poor. Mary placed herself on the side of the Kingdom of God as the Woman of the Apocalypse (Rev 12), and against the Women, the City, mother of all prostitutes (Rev 17) and the empire she served. We feel consecrated by the Spirit to be part of the progeny of the Woman. Our fraternal and filial relationship with Mary is not to be reduced to a mere devotional attitude, rather it is a trait outlining our spirituality.

58. Consecrated life has always seen Mary as a model of total self-lessness towards the Kingdom of God. Seeking to take the Word of God as its kernel, it discovered in Mary an incarnated ideal of what it means to listen to the Word in Scripture and in life, and to believe in it in every circumstance in order to live all its demands, and doing this without understanding many things, pondering everything in the heart (Lk 2:19,50-51) until light comes. Consecrated life has seen in the Virgin its ideal and inspiration for its service to others. Together with openness to God, it lives close to the needs of its brethren and is concerned with satisfying them (Lk 1:39-45; Jn 2:1-12; Acts 14). In Mary it contemplates "the most perfect image of liberty and liberation of humanity and the cosmos" (RM 37), and this helps in understanding the sense of its mission.

7. Living in the Spirit, within the spiritual journey of the People of God

59. We have asserted that there is a correlation between consecrated life and the other forms of following Jesus in the Church. In every Christian life, the essential thing is to live faith, hope and love within the ecclesial community. That is, to live *in*

Christ, placing ourselves under the guidance of the Spirit. The charismatic forms of living the one spirituality are not hermetically sealed compartments, they communicate among each other. Each one of the states of life realizes in a determined form and with particular accent, selected evangelical values that belong to all and are for all. We cannot distinguish spiritualities on the basis of an out of tune model of the Church as a perfect society. Many things once considered exclusive to one state of life are common to all. What is important is the fact of maintaining one own identity so that, in it and through it, the values and dynamisms present more intensely in other spiritualities can be adopted.

60. The forms of living the one spirituality within consecrated life, have to know how to adapt to the condition of each one of their members: whether they be lay or ordained minister, woman or man. They must know how to correlate what is lay with what is hierarchic and what is feminine with what is masculine. Only thus each form of spiritual life will be able to manifest its specific traits within the fundamental unity.

61. With regards to dealing with the spirituality of ecclesial movements there exists a double danger: that of radical rejection and that of loss of the sense of belonging to one's proper identity or community on coming in contact with this spirituality. Relating with these ecclesial movements can help discover and live ones own specific charism with the spirituality that flows from it. Equally, the youth and dynamism of these new currents can assist reinterpreting the spirituality of founders to the present day. In a word, the relationship among the members of the People of God can help everyone know and live in a better way their own identity.

Conclusion

62. In these reflections, we tried to mould our response to the question encapsulated in the title of this presentation: How to understand and present today consecrated life in the Church and the world? Our answer could be summarized as follows:

a. *Consecrated life is a style of life assumed by a minority group of men and women:* Those who have begun and those who have taken up this form of life have always been a minority in the different religions. But the presence of these symbols of human and Christian radicality are indispensable for humanity.

b. *Religious life is an ancient and universal phenomenon.* We find these minority groups of religious life in diverse regions: in Asia, America, Africa and Europe and in the different confessions of the Church. In all of them, the broad intuitions are very similar. By intuition, we can hold that religious life assumes and gives strength to the human and religious value of the different religions.

c. *What is proper to these human groups is not exclusive to them.* Proper to them are asceticism, copious prayer, silence and solitude, concern and service to the poor and needy, community life. But there are other human groups who also live those values. The originality comes from the manner in which religious live them. For this reason the testimonial, counter-cultural and prophetic dimension are decisive. These human groups attempt to be a shaping of the fundamental dimensions of the human spirit and of the archetypal dimension of the religious perspective.

d. *Religious life has held out to society the offer of an alternative scale of values:* Its mode of being has presupposed a criticism of the *status quo,* and has converted this into a proposal for renewal of society. The religious man or woman represents the presence of the divine on earth.

e. *The identity of consecrated life,* as that of the other forms of life in the Church, is interactive because all come together in one fundamental identity: to be *Christian faithful.* "Christian faithful" is the noun designating consecrated persons, while "lay", "secular", "ordained minister", are the adjectives.

f. *A great number of men and women* who form part of consecrated life *belong to the laity* in the Church. A *minority of men* belonging to consecrated life *are ordained ministers of the Church:* priests and deacons who exercise their ministry from the charismatic identity of consecrated persons living this charismatic identity in the ministerial condition of priest and deacon.

g. *The theological understanding* of consecrated life has been conditioned by the model of the Church and the theology of each era.

h. While the lay Christian faithful are called to live total secularity, the consecrated lay Christian faithful are called to live a *limited secularity* as a liminal group, forming a prophetic contrast, to exercise a symbolic role.

i. *The theological identity of consecrated life*, within the common Christian vocation, is a process, a journey, having an interior dynamism whose principal agent is the Holy Spirit, the author of charisms.

j. Within the one great spiritual journey of the People of God, consecrated life brings to the fore *some of the fundamental aspects* which give it its identity and can convert it into an attractive and stimulating symbol: conversion and exodus in an alternative prophetic style of community life and prayer, under the primacy of the Word of God and the creative fidelity to the charismatic gift received, searching to live it near to the people and inserted into their culture and their human condition.

NOTES

1. We always use the expression "Consecrated Life" to designate the forms of life that the CIC puts under those two words. We are well aware that this expression is not theologically exclusive to those forms of life. However, when we use the expression "Religious Life" we refer to the similar forms of life that we find in other religions (Buddhist monasticism, for example); in this sense, we consider the call to "consecrated life" as a call to "religious life".

2. Chamanes; *sannyasi and sannayasini* in Hinduism; monks in Buddhism, healers, essenes, rechabites, and nazarenes in Judaism, Sufis and Tariquah in Islam; the Iskon group in the "new religions" of our times.

3. Liminality is an anthropological concept very much in vogue today. The anthropologist Arnold Van Gennep invented the term "liminality" to indicate a person's periodical withdrawal from the family, as happens for example in rites of passage. Recently, Edith Turner used this term and giving it a totally new significance to describe the characteristics of small groups and communities and their relationship and interaction with the bulk of society. "Liminality may be described as an ambiguous, sacred, social state in which a person or group of persons is separated for a time from the normal structures of society..." Diarmuid O'Murchu, *Religious Life: a Prophetic Vision*, Ave Maria Press, Notre Dame, Indiana, 1991, p. 36. That is a perspective that we need to study more deeply in order to understand our identity adequately: cf. Victor-Edith Turner, *The ritual process: structure and anti-structure*, Aldine 1969; Id., *Liminality, Kabbalah and the Media*, in "Religion" 15 (1985), 205-217; D. O'Murchu, *Religious Life: a prophetic vision*, Ave Maria Press, Notre Dame, 1991, pp. 36-41; R. Endress, *The Monastery as a liminal Community*, in *American Benedictine Review* 26 (1975), 142-158; R. Panikkar, *Blessed Simplicity: the Monk as universal archetype*, Seabury Press, New York, 1982.

4. Cf the monographic issue: "Los Fundadores, una llama carismatica", in "Vida Religiosa" 74 (1993), 1-80; and in the same, my article *Lideres carismaticos de la vida consagrada. Perfil antropologico-teologico*, pp. 31-40.

5. Cf. Lawrence Cada, *Shaping the coming age of religious life*, Seabury Press, New York 1979; Dairmuid O'Murchu, *Religious Life: a prophetic vision*, Ave Maria Press, Notre Dame, Indiana, 1991, pp. 88-101.

6. The appearance of Pachomian monasticism was hailed by Abbot Anthony as the revival of apostolic life. The birth of the mendicant friars (*fratres* = brothers) made explicit other characteristics of the evangelical fraternity of the apostolic life, adapting it to the new social circumstances: the fraternity within the group as a significant experience manifest of the evangelical poverty and fraternity in a middle-class and materialistic world; the fraternity outside the group as an apostolic projection that stimulated them to take fraternal care of the Christians in a period of apostolic neglect. While the reforms of the XVI century insisted on a greater austerity and evangelical abnegation, at the same time they attempted to restore fraternal equality, by renouncing class differences that had been introduced into the monasteries. Modern institutes deal with being apostolic fraternities.

REACTIONS TO
FR MACCISE'S CONFERENCE

Fr Heinrich Heekeren, SVD

He proposed to comment on a statement in the fourth part of the conference: "The vocation to consecrated life is nourished especially by listening to the Word of God." After the example of Jesus, the Church and the first monastic communities live by the Word of God. For its part, the Vatican Council II strongly recommended to religious the daily reading and meditation of Sacred Scripture. Thus we should give the example to the People of God, but very often it is the opposite that happens. On the contrary, biblical sharing, a biblical attitude of welcome, of "exodus" and conversion, an observance of the vows inspired from Scripture, fraternal relations among clergy and laity, the renewed Constitutions in the spirit of Scripture and finally a Marian devotion based on the Bible, can become a precious help to better understand ourselves and present to the outside a more attractive image of our life ideal.

Abbot Jerome Theisen, OSB

In commenting Fr Maccise's conference, Abbot Theisen proposed to highlight two points. First, to study the origin of the monastic movement to understand religious life today and, secondly, to show how, in general, religious and lay people are closely associated today. In fact, the monastic movement in the Christian Church can shed light on the understanding of religious life in general, because the first monks were Christians believers who wanted to live the radical demands of Jesus. Secondly, in the light of Vatican II ecclesiology, religious found and defined themselves in a way that brought them closer to Christian believers.

So he concludes: "It seems to me that we can rejoice in the fact that, in general, religious and Christians have again come closer , as they were during the first centuries of the Church. Religious are not a separate branch of Christianity, but they are Christians marked in a special way to follow Christ".

II.

Historical perspective

Bro Lawrence Cada, SM

History gives us an important perspective from which to assess the present situation of religious life and its future.

Several years ago, I had the good fortune to be part of a team of men and women religious in the US who made an extensive historical study of religious life.[1] The team was seeking a better understanding of the changes sweeping across religious life in the wake of Vatican II.

The eras of the history of religious life

The study distinguished 5 main eras in the history of religious life according to the following schema:

300-500	Era of the Desert Fathers and Mothers
500-1200	Era of Monasticism
1200-1500	Era of the Mendicants
1500-1800	Era of the apostolic orders
1800-2000	Era of the Teaching Congregations

Each of the above eras was characterized by a dominant image of religious life which prevailed during that period of history. I am using the term dominant *image of religious life* here to name a many-sided reality that includes how men and women religious view the life they lead and how they understand its function and role within the Church and the world at a given time. How do people, both the religious and the members of society at large, picture this way of life? What do they consider to be its most salient features? Whom do they hold up as the ideal or model religious?

Historical phases of a dominant image of religious life

There has been a succession of shifts in the dominant image of religious life through the centuries. Each shift follows a repeated sequence of phases:

Emergence: Major changes in society and the Church stir new movements and the founding of new religious communities. Certain aspects of these new communities gain prominence and fuse into a new image of religious life. The new image differs from religious life as it has been known. Some even say that the new image is not "true" religious life. However, many find the new image striking and give it wider acceptance.

Growth and success: The new communities expand and older religious communities find success in adopting features of the new image. The image inspires many and attracts ever larger numbers. As its implications are worked out and take hold, the image matures and becomes dominant. Its ascendancy lasts across generations, sometimes even centuries.

Decline: A period of crisis in which the dominant image of religious life comes under strong question. Religious life no longer seems suited to the aspirations of the age. Religious communities lose their sense of purpose, drift into laxity, and disintegrate. Some communities die out completely, and the number of religious men and women drops.

Turning point: A comparatively short period of revitalization in which new movements and new communities arise and respond to new needs in the Church and the world. Variations of the dominant image of religious life emerge, and one of these is gradually selected as the new dominant image.

Growth and success of the new image: Once the new image emerges, its influence grows until it matures into the new dominant image of religious life. The cycle repeats itself to the next turning point and shift in the dominant image.

The present position of religious life

In terms of this model, the study drew the following principal conclusions:

1. Religious life has reached the end of an era – the Era of the Teaching Congregations.

2. It is now passing through one of the turning points in its history.
3. This turning point is major. It appears to be the kind which leads to a new dominant image of religious life – the kind which has occurred perhaps only four times in the past.
4. A new era in the long history of religious life will emerge during the twentyfirst century.

In this short paper, I will not repeat the reasoning which led to the above conclusions. Neither will I present a full examination of the successive dominant images of religious life which typified the five Eras in the above schema.

I want to emphasize one point about the study. It did not describe the next dominant image of religious life. At the time of the study, the team thought it was too soon to predict what the new dominant image of religious life will be. Today, more than 15 years later, I still believe it is too early to do so. We wait with interest for the inspirations of the Holy Spirit to become manifest in the years ahead.

The trend of increasing involvement in the world

However, there is one long-range trend in the history of religious life which I do want to discuss. This trend has grown steadily across the centuries, and there are no indications it will not continue to grow. It thus sheds light on the future of religious life and provides a basis for the main thesis of this paper.

Throughout its history, religious life has been steadily moving away from a stance of separation from the world toward one of involvement in the world. This trend will continue and offers us a key to discern the future of religious life. Religious life is becoming more incarnational. It will disclose the mystery of the Incarnation explicitly more than it has in the past.

Religious were most removed from the world in the earliest era, the Era of the Desert Mothers and Fathers. These first religious were caught up in the great *fuga saeculi* which followed the age of persecution and martyrs. They literally left the world of cities and fled to the desert where they lived in ascetical isolation as solitaries or as members of hermit settlements.

231

During the Era of Monasticism, renunciation of the world was less total. Life in a monastery became the new ideal. It attempted to regularize religious life as "a life with God in separation from the world". However, this separation was not so complete as to exclude salvaging the treasures of classical civilization in refugee cloisters and eventually pursuing the love of learning that came to illumine monastic life in the early Middle Ages.

In the Era of the Mendicants, religious returned to the city. The trend toward involvement in the world grew stronger. Dominicans and Franciscans saw no need to remove themselves to monasteries out in the countryside, far from the worldly pursuits of urban life. They begged for their keep and flocked to medieval towns where they preached, served the poor, plunged into the intellectual ferment of the universities, and ministered to the needs of society in the name of the Church. They knew, like the masons who travelled from city to city building marvellous cathedrals, that *Stadtluft macht frei*.

The return to the world advanced with giant strides in the Era of the apostolic orders. Religious became an elite of highly educated and militant servants, filled with zeal to defend the Church on any front and ready to win new expansion for Christianity to the very ends of the earth. They fought the heresies of the Reformation and came to terms with the secularizing trends of the scientific revolution, modern philosophy, and the rise of nationalism in Europe. All this intense involvement in the world was integrated with the high ideals of holiness and union with God that had fired religious life form its origins.

With the dawning of the Era of Teaching Congregations in the 19th century, the trend of religious becoming more involved in the world took a new turn. Specific congregations were founded to specialize in particular ministries. Men and women religious in a flood of new communities dedicated themselves to the salvation of souls – others' souls as well as their own – in schools, hospitals, and other apostolic institutions. Other communities specialized in a particular work such as the foreign missions. For almost two centuries, this form of religious life expanded and prospered. By the time of Vatican II, membership in religious communities reached its highest point in the history of the Church.

As I said above, I believe that the Era of Teaching Congregations has ended and that a new era will emerge in the next century. I do not know what the next dominant image of religious life will be. However, because the trend toward ever greater involvement in the world is such a strong and steadily expanding current running through the history of religious life, it is possible to make some conjectures about the future.

Implications of the trend for the future of religious life

Let me devote the last section of this paper to a quick examination of some implications of this trend.

First, this trend means that the way of understanding and explaining religious life is moving away from the dualism that has both blessed and plagued Western civilization since classical antiquity. Matter and spirit, body and soul, manual work and mental work, earth and heaven, this world and the next, lay life and religious life, the human and the divine – these are all typical examples of our cultural habit of dividing realities into pairs. Distinctions such as these have made possible some of our greatest intellectual achievements. Our culture also inclines us to value or rank the second member of each of these pairs as somehow "above" the first. Before Vatican II, when the distinction between lay life and religious life was made, the latter was called "the life of perfection".

The long-standing trend of religious becoming more involved in the world runs counter to this habit of mind. Even though the world to come was thought "better" than this world, and even though religious were thought "better" than lay people because they had their eyes fixed on the world to come, religious have nevertheless constantly found ways out of the cloister and into the streets, where they perceive God to be calling them to do good. In the future, religious will probably be less inclined to think of themselves as "better" than lay people, and they will hesitate to view the sacred as "better" than the profane.

More profoundly, the trend of religious becoming more involved in the world means that there will be a deeper living out of the mystery of the Incarnation in religious life. Just as the divine is embodied in the human in the person of Jesus Christ, so religious will incarnate their world-transcending spirit in a world embracing life. The identity of religious will become incarnate in mission. Who religious are will be embodied in what they do. Religious will embody and disclose the mystery of the Incarnation even more than they have in the past.

In the next century, we will have to forge a new theology of religious life. The concept of renunciation will no longer be seen as lying at the essence of religious life. Since the Middle Ages, the theology of religious life has held up the evangelical counsels as the distinguishing mark of religious. The counsels were explained as various renunciations of the goods of this world for the sake of the Kingdom.

In the future, I believe attention will shift away from the counsels taken individually as renunciation. Instead attention will move to the counsels taken together as religious profession. That profession in turn will be explained as a choice made in freedom and in response to God's grace. The focus will be not on renunciation but on freedom. Recently, a person I respect said he thinks the future theology of religious life will be a theology of option – the Christian notion of option. This intuition seems on target. It suggest the idea of Gospel freedom and the free choice of a way of life for the sake of the Kingdom. The Word was made flesh to announce and disclose that Kingdom to this world. The way of life we know as religious life shares in that announcement and disclosure.

In this short paper, I will not explore other implications of the trend of religious becoming more involved in the world in the next era of religious life. However, I hope these brief considerations help us understand better the directions in which the Holy Spirit is leading religious life.

o o o

Fr Sidbe Sempore, OP: The point of view of different cultures

Unfortunately, because of problems in obtaining a visa, Fr Sempore was unable to participate personally in the Congress. His "testimony" was read by the Secretary of the Conference of Major Superiors of Zaire.

Consecrated life, like Christianity as a whole, emerged and evolved in symbiosis and rupture with precise cultural contexts. From the relation between the historical forms of consecrated life and the cultures that determined it there flows a dual movement of acceptance and reserve, of alliance and rupture. On the one hand, even if the various forms of consecrated life that appeared in the course of the centuries cannot be considered simply as cultural products of a Christian society, we cannot deny the impact, sometimes the imprint, that the mother culture has had on the Rules and Constitutions, on the organization of the structures and on the manner of government, on the codification of customs and traditions transmitted from age to age.

But in spite of all that, consecrated life is not identified by a culture that bore it and expresses it. On the contrary, the evangelical and prophetic vein that inspires the founders and institutes leads the latter to relativize, to question and even to refuse certain aspects of the cultures, at the cost of giving the impression of going against the current of history. "Whoever closes himself in a society cannot help adopting its prejudices, especially of these flatter his pride", said the French philosopher Helvetius. The temptation that threatens consecrated life is to let itself be imprisoned in intellectual frameworks and to forget to build bridges between cultures and exercise a prophetic discernment with regard to growing civilizations.

Today we are more aware of the need for a more differentiated and more authentic cultural radicalism in the forms of consecrated life. Nevertheless there are questions that crop up for the Western as well as for the non-Western Churches. In particular, are these Churches ready to accept and help the birth of new forms of indigenous consecrated life, rooted in the evangelical values and in the cultural and religious traditions of their own people? For example, could the Church in Africa be open to the experience and the religious and monastic traditions of the Egyptian and Ethiopian Churches, in order to enrich and consolidate its own experience? Attention to the behavior of the "independent African Churches" with regard to African cultures would also be a help in facing better the challenge of inculturation.

Sr Mary John Mananzan, OSB: The feminine perspective

1. Vatican II provoked the following changes in religious life in the Philippines:
   - personalization of religious life
   - social orientation
   - raising consciousness to sex discrimination.

2. Commitment in the peoples' struggle for justice produced the following reflections:
   - re-think the faith and theological concepts, that is, integral evangelization, etc.
   - re-thinking religious life: rules, spirituality, life-style.

3. Women's involvement in the struggle to get full recognition has obtained:
   - a theology that takes into account the feminine perspective in Asia
   - an integral, liberating, creative and inculturated spirituality.

4. Conclusion: Religious today must be open to all that is new and that God may ask of them in the evolving situation in their life and society. Today that means: commitment for justice and the transformation of society and aiming at full humanity for women, and conservation and renewal of the environment.

Sr Noëlle Hausmann, SCM: The feminine perspective

The steering committee of the Congress had asked for another testimony on the feminine perspective, but it was not possible to present it at the Congress. However, the entire text is available at the USG office.

After noting that the majority of the members of consecrated life are women, Sr Noëlle asks: if there is an identity of feminine consecrated life, what can consecrated persons do, before the present difficulties and challenges concerning women, and what conversion will the Synod allow us to perceive with regard to the identity of religious women?

She answered mainly by pointing out that, in the Church, all are called to be the "spouses" of Christ, because in Christ there is neither male or female, but we are all one in Christ and the feminine becomes the symbol of all the human. Thus we can say that, before God, there is a feminine identity of the whole Church, and especially of all humanity. But, on the other hand, Genesis recalls the distinction between the masculine and feminine roles. And this is where the difficult question of the priesthood, especially the religious priesthood, comes in; either because of the culture that exalts the equality of the masculine and feminine roles, or because it seems that the masculine role has been lessened, especially the role of paternity. "Thus it is very important for masculine religious life that feminine religious life remain or become itself, without that evasion of ordained ministries that for years has overshadowed the reasoning of both."

Moreover, all the states of life recognized by the Council are explicitly involved in the spousal mystery of Ephesians 5; the originating mystery of the Church is precisely that of the *koinonia* that has its source in the Trinity and culminates in the communion of saints. Therefore, religious life must give to the world the testimony of communion of all the ecclesial vocations and at the same time, the uniqueness of each one.

In conclusion, Sr Noëlle sends an appeal to the Synod, so that it does not let itself be absorbed by the question of ministerial priesthood, but rather that religious life may be reaffirmed in its value of sign, testimony and gift. And the answer of masculine religious life rests perhaps on the ability of feminine religious life to also reach the source of its identity in the Lord.

Cettina Militello: The perspective of a lay person

After having recalled that religious life is basically a lay phenomenon and wondering if there is opposition between secularity and consecration, synergy or polarity, she states that the consecrated and lay states have the same charismatic and ministerial root. "Ecclesiologically speaking, it is expressive-charismatic; expressing the Christian initiation and therefore the common royal-prophetic-priesthood, and as such linked to the building of the whole community. This ties the call to faith of all people to the charismatic call of a founder that remains in time and constitutes his identity and service in the Church for those who discover it similar to their own vocation." With religious life we cannot not discover the common value that is at the origin of the same baptismal consecration, and in particular the theological values of all who belong to the People of God. The question of identity can thus be solved in respect of differences without in any way sacrificing the common ecclesial root.

Finally, she formulates seven provocations relative to the "relational and community nature" of religious life: its "contextual nature", the present "crisis", the need to inscribe its charism in the context of service and to witness to the "service of otherness", in the context that really presents religious life as "anticipation and participation in the Trinitarian mystery".

Fr André Louf, osco: The perspective of a contemplative

The contemplative perpetuates the Exodus in the Church, always back up to the desert, listening to her Spouse; a listening that is transformed into praise and thanksgiving.

It also continues the Church being subjected to the temptations of the desert that reveal its frailty and radical need for salvation: asceticism is the continuous miracle of grace.

Moreover, it is a Church purified in its own faith and its desire to know God – the contemplative is an "expert in atheism" – before becoming the Church who has a foretaste of the joys of the hereafter.

In thus deepening its contemplative research, it gives "the best part" its true role in the Church: "in the back of the Church" but also "at the heart" because "in the depth".

At the same time it feels in solidarity with all the poor in spirit of our times, with sinners, those who suffer and who have no hope of ever believing in God.

NOTE

1. Results of the study were published in several places. Raymond L. Fitz, SM, and Lawrence J. Cada, SM, "The Recovery of Religious Life", *Review for Religious* 34 (September 1975) 690-718. This article was incorporated into the following book: Lawrence Cada, SM et all., *Shaping the Coming Age of Religious Life* (New York: Seabury Press, 1979; 2nd edition, Whitinsville, Mass.: Affirmation Books, 1985. Portuguese translation: *Em busca de um futuro para vida religiosa* (São Paolo: Ediçoes Paulinas, 1985).

5.

Audience with
John Paul II

The Holy Father's Address to the participants in the International Congress

1. With joy, I welcome you, dear Brothers and Sisters, on the occasion of the International Congress promoted by the Union of Superiors General. I greet each and every one of you. In particular, I address an affectionate greeting to Cardinal Eduardo Martinez-Somalo, Prefect of the Congregation for institutes of Consecrated life and Societies of apostolic life and I thank him for the kind words he expressed. I also thank Father Flavio Roberto Carraro, President of the Union of Superiors General, for the sentiments of devotion that he expressed in the name of all the participants. Then I greet the bishops here presents, and the numerous Superiors General of Religious institutes, the delegates of the Latin American Conference of Religious (CLAR) and the Union of European Conferences of Religious (UCESM), the presidents of National Conferences and the representatives of the Dicasteries of the Roman Curia.

Your Congress is characterized by its world-wide dimension and by the broad vision it has for having been prepared by the highest leaders of the various Religious institutes. You have certainly been able to live an intense climate of preparation for the ordinary Synod of Bishops which will take place next year. I hope that it will receive a useful documentation from your work.

2. The religious life today is experiencing a particularly significant moment of its history, because of the demanding and vast renewal that the changed socio-cultural conditions at the threshold of the third millennium of the Christian era, impose on it.

The next ordinary assembly of the Synod of Bishops will surely bring the members of the Church – pastors, clergy, consecrated persons and faithful – to an awareness of this singular hour, in order not to lose the opportunity for a true return to the evangelical sources: indeed, Jesus Christ is the supreme point of reference for every religious and for the whole People of God. To him we must look as to the Consecrated One par excellence

241

who, sent into the world, called the disciples to follow him in the radicalism of the gift of self to the Heavenly Father and to the faithful.

In the synagogue of Nazareth, as the Gospel of Luke tells us (Lk 4:16-19), Jesus applied to himself the messianic prophecy of Isaiah: "The Spirit of the Lord is upon me... (Is 61:1). In it, he is called "the consecrated one" par excellence, the "Anointed of God", the "Christ". This means a singular presence of the Holy Spirit in him that unites indissolubly his mission to his consecration. As I recalled in the Apostolic Exhortation *Pastores dabo vobis*, "the Spirit is not simply 'on' the Messiah, but he 'fills' him, penetrates him, reaches him in his being and works. In fact, the Spirit is the principle of the 'consecration' and 'mission' of the Messiah" (PdV 19).

In this light, the religious belongs radically to God and draws in the Spirit from the very source of holiness and total apostolic gift.

3. Every consecration in the Church is intrinsically linked to a radical and vital synthesis of consecration and mission. It is expressed with the practice of the evangelical counsels to witness within the People of God to the Gospel of the beatitudes (cf LG 31). This supposes a life-style which, accompanied by renunciation and sacrifice, includes a not easy commitment and requires a constant and adequate asceticism.

But the true reason for this choice does not consist in programming a life of mortification, but in the total option of Jesus Christ. That permits an authentic valorization of the Cross and the personal and fascinating discovery of the ineffable mystery of Jesus Christ, crucified and risen. The apostolic faith shows us "the Consecrated" by antonomasia in the Incarnate Word, true Redeemer of Man. Jesus, the Christ, is the measure of all. He shows man the authentic aim of life and gives him the help to reach it. In him, the new Adam, the whole human reality is enlighten by an eschatological meaning, extending his horizons beyond time.

Thus, with St Paul, we can repeat: "For me, to live is Christ" (Ph 1:21); "I no longer live, but Christ lives in me" (Gal 2:20); "If we are in Christ, we are a new creation" (2 Cor 5:17). With the Apostle, we are convinced that, in the economy of the fullness of time, God proposes to "recapitulate all things in Christ, those of heaven and those of earth" (Eph 1: 10).

This vision of faith that embraces everything, offers the true reason for the radicalism of consecrated life and clothes it with fascination and joy. If Jesus Christ is truly the centre of life and history, it is worth following him faithfully, participating in the fascinating mystery of his redemption, even when that entails difficulties and renunciations.

4. From this reflection on the mystery of Christ, dear Brothers and Sisters, there flow numerous prospectives for renewal. I would like to underline a few that might serve as useful orientations in the preparation of the next Synod.

Jesus Christ is the ultimate point of reference for every Christian, but he is so particularly for those who are called to witness "in a splendid and striking testimony that the world cannot be transfigured and offered to God without the spirit of the beatitudes" (LG 31).

The Councils exhorts: "Religious should carefully consider that through them, to believers and non-believers alike, the Church truly wishes to give an increasingly clearer revelation of Christ. Through them Christ should be shown contemplating on the mountain, announcing God's Kingdom to the multitude, healing the sick and the maimed, turning sinners to wholesome fruit, blessing children, doing good to all, and always obeying the will of the Father who sent him" (LG 46).

Therefore, this is what renewal must lead to, and with urgency. Indeed, the Church does not need religious dress in secularism and the attractions of the contemporary world, but of courageous witnesses and tireless apostles of the Kingdom.

5. That is why the first basic value to be attentive to is that of "spirituality" according to the charism typical of each institute. In the religious consecration, the intimacy, wealth and stability of a special bond with the Holy Spirit are at the base of everything.

The presence of God is transparent when the religious becomes sign and bearer of his supernatural love. Being "minister" of divine charity is the source of service. The inseparability of mission and consecration does not take away from the fact that consecration comes first, from the initiative of God who sends: "... I have chosen you and sent you so that you may go and bear fruit" (Jn 15:16).

What great need there is today for an authentic spirituality! Many, even among the faithful, feel confused and almost submerged by the ephemeral and indifference, by relativism and individualism, by lack of transcendence and the loss of the sense of sin that seem to typify the culture of our age.

From religious institutes we await a new apostolic ardor; that is, we expect that they will offer their contribution not only as individuals, but also as communities, in the demanding work of new evangelization.

For this to happen, spiritual renewal remains the first and most vital duty to which religious must devote themselves. I am convinced that the whole Church will be strengthened by it and the vocational crisis that is becoming worrisome in some parts of the world will find a valid solution.

The Council aptly recalled that the best forms of renewal of religious institute "will fail of their purpose unless a renewal of spirit gives life to them. Indeed such an interior renewal must always be accorded the leading role even in the promotion of exterior works" (PC 2).

6. Another important aspect to be stressed is the commitment of religious in the new evangelization, the great challenge of our time, to which are called the whole community of the baptized.

Economic progress, the changing social and political contexts, the expectations of the young, the radical changes in the mentalities of people: all this demands of evangelizers, and particularly of consecrated persons, that they make the proclamation of the Christ "contemporary", making every person feel that Jesus is the Redeemer of man with his concrete problems and his specific difficulties. In this effort that involves the whole Church, we have to deepen and define the spiritual and apostolic relations that exist between religious and lay people, promoting new methods and new expressions of cooperation to facilitate the proclamation of Christ in our time.

7. Finally we have to recall that our dear religious are particular gifts of the Spirit for the People of God. The extraordinary Synod of 1985 – twenty years after Vatican II – recalled that "the ecclesiology of communion is the central and fundamental idea of the documents of the Council" and that it "cannot be reduced

merely to a question of organization or to problems that concern power only" (Final Document, II, 1).

To promote a more intense ecclesial communion among religious, clergy and laity, intensifying a specific and pluriform exchange of spiritual and apostolic values would be of great help to such an ecclesiology of communion. It would bind the religious charisms more closely to the local Churches, where are expressed the vocation and mission of the laity and diocesan clergy, bringing them the dynamism and values with which religious express the universality of the Church.

8. And so, dear Brothers and Sisters, I hope that the International Congress on "Consecrated Life Today" may help you and the institutes that you represent to see your presence as a precious gift of God to his Church and to the whole world.

The religious life today is experiencing a particularly significant moment of its history, because of the demanding and vast renewal that the changed socio-cultural conditions, at the threshold now of the third millennium of the Christian era, impose on it.

May Mary, Queen of virgins, concrete model of consecrated life, guide and accompany you in this difficult and vast duty of renewal and may she intercede for the success of the next Synod. I ask her, Immaculate Virgin, supreme model of obedience in faith, to revive in the Church the testimony of the evangelical counsels, so that the beauty of the Christian image in the spirit of the beatitudes may be apparent to everyone. May the Most Holy Virgin also assist the pastors so that they may have a vision and appreciation of consecrated life that strengthens its presence and mission in the People of God.

With these wishes, dear Brothers and Sisters, I renew to all of you the assurance of my constant remembrance before the Lord, and I impart a special Apostolic Blessing to support your daily efforts in following Christ, chaste, poor and obedient.

6.

The final document
of the Congress

The term *"consecrated life"* is being used in this document to refer
to the institutes which are members of the USG. These are the
Institutes of Consecrated Life (Monks, Canons Regular, Mendicant Orders, Clerics Regular, Clerical Congregations and Lay
Congregations) and Societies of Apostolic Life.

Convictions and proposals of the Union of Superiors General

I. THE SITUATION OF THE CONSECRATED LIFE

The Congress opened with a view of the situation of the consecrated life today, thanks to the reports of the findings of two sociological research projects on the subject. The first treated the current situation of the consecrated life in the USA, while the second reflected the experience of some 200,000 religious men and women from different countries of the world.

These reports, together with the direct experience of the participants, brought to light the difficulties and the hopes, the dedication and the searchings of more than a million religious world-wide, of whom about a quarter are men.

1. A variety of situations and charisms

The work of the Congress highlighted the variety of situations which characterize the consecrated life today. In some parts of the world we are experiencing in many institutes decline in numbers and ageing as well as a worrying scarcity of new entries. In other areas, on the contrary, youth predominates and vocations are increasing. There are lights and shadows in all parts; yet despite all the difficulties there is an obvious apostolic and charismatic dynamism at work, fruit of the post-conciliar renewal.

In the brotherly and sisterly atmosphere which characterized the reflections and exchange of viewpoints, the riches of our charismatic diversity appeared evident, a fruit of the Spirit who distributes his gifts for the good of the Church. This diversity enabled us to live the Pentecostal experience of a sincere communion in plurality.

2. A variety of perspectives

We were able to observe that, as well as these charismatic riches, there was also a rich diversity of theological perspectives and of spiritual differences, born or nourished by different experiences, cultures and traditions.

The pluralism of theological approaches to the consecrated life, which gives rise to new interpretations and brings life, mission and communion into focus in different and complementary ways, is reflected in the concluding *Theological Synthesis* of the Congress. What is said here in more practical and simple language can be better understood by referring to it.

It was an experience of God in the heart of life, illuminated and interpreted by his Word and lived in the light of the founding charisms, which made this theological pluralism possible. It is something which must be preserved and promoted as a response to the Spirit who is challenging us constantly.

II. CENTRAL NUCLEI OF THE CONSECRATED LIFE

We shall pick up once again the order followed in the work of the Congress and in the Theological Synthesis: *mission, communion, identity.*

The Congress preferred to begin from mission and communion in regard to consecrated life, because it was convinced that in this way identity will appear as more vital and concrete than in following a deductive theological approach.

1. Mission

The Church is missionary by nature. It follows from this that the mission is an essential and vital part of all forms of consecrated life. Rooted in the Christian vocation, the mission is differentiated according to the charisms. The consecrated life carries it out beginning with an experience of God: in the witness of fraternal life, in the courageous proclamation of the Gospel, in the commitment to human advancement.

The challenges of insertion into new cultural situations,

planetarian communication, the emergence of the poor in the Church, the collapse of the great forms of messianism, the new thirst for transcendence, ecology, and other factors, have created new forums for the mission of the consecrated life, called today as in the past to occupy the front line of evangelization.

In the effort to discern and respond to these challenges of the Spirit, we need to keep in mind the *theological-practical* perspectives, which must be lived and deepened. Amongst them we draw attention to witness, prophecy, the preferential option for the poor, inculturation, dialogue and solidarity. All of these impel us and give us a direction in view of a responsible participation in the ecclesial commitment to the *new evangelization* in the perspective of the reign of God, seen in its multiple aspects (cf RM, 13-20).

In the light of this situation and in view of the forthcoming Synod, we wish to formulate the following convictions and proposals:

1.1 Our convictions

a. We feel ourselves impelled by the force of the Spirit to carry out, according to the specific charism of each institute, the evangelizing mission of the Church, aware as we are that the consecrated life (witness and service) is already a proclamation of the Reign (LG 44). For this it is indispensable that we religious live consciously the charismatic and prophetic aspects of the consecrated life which include: proclamation, denunciation, liberation, solidarity, hope.

b. We consider that the experience of the Spirit, gift of the Father to the witnesses of his Son, stirred into life by personal and communitarian prayer, and stimulated by the discernment of the signs of the times and of places, is essential for our mission in the Church and in the world of today. Prayer nourishes apostolic action, and this in turn vivifies prayer.

c. We wish to respond to the call to the *new evangelization* and we feel urged to carry it out, beginning with the particular characteristics of existence and service that our life as consecrated persons calls for.

d. While more than three-quarters of humankind still does not acknowledge Christ as the Saviour of the world, we feel the obligation to make an effort to increase the missionary activity *ad gentes* of our institutes and to continue the creativity and fortitude that our founders showed by their avant-garde missionary choices.

e. We are convinced that the consecrated life must remain open to the new and urgent pastoral needs that present themselves in the different cultural contexts, so that institutes can provide answers, in accordance with their own charisms, and be always sensitive to such matters as witness, dialogue, ecumenism, the preferential option for the poor by means of a life that is simple and inserted into their midst, work on the front lines and inculturation.

f. We wish to open ourselves to the challenge of new forms of poverty and situations of marginalization (AIDS, drugs, refugees...) that require a new life-style and new creative services.

g. We insist on commitment to bringing about the conversion of hearts and the transformation of the structures that generate and maintain injustices and cause the number of the poor to increase in society; we become thereby promoters of evangelical values.

h. In evangelizing activity we wish to foster openness to cultures and inculturation in the different social contexts, respecting pluralism and universality. For this we must have a deeper grasp of the conditions and the personal and collective requirements of an authentic inculturation.

i. It is necessary to strengthen the commitment to ecumenism and inter-religious dialogue, beginning with one's own experience of God and with the manifold search for his presence, recognizing and giving due value to the "seeds of the Word" and the work of the Spirit in all peoples and all cultures.

1.2 *Some proposals*

a. Members of the institutes should be recognized as protagonists and as the active subject of the renewal of the consecrated life.

b. The value of the contemplative life in the evangelizing mission of the Church should be recognized.

c. Dialogue and collaboration among all the agents of evangelization should continue to be promoted, with a view to developing a true unified pastoral effort.

d. Bishops should welcome the riches of the different charisms of the institutes of consecrated life in such a way that the collaboration of all, in the pastoral plans of dioceses, may be efficacious and in accordance with their respective gifts and ministries.

e. The members of institutes of consecrated life who are working for evangelization in especially difficult situations and in midst of great risks should be supported.

f. The experience of martyrdom in the consecrated life should be acknowledged; today it is caused especially by solidarity with the poor, the oppressed and the persecuted: such an experience enriches and enlarges the traditional concept of witnessing to the point of shedding blood and of the sacrifice of one's life because of Christ and his Gospel.

g. The importance and topicality, especially for the new evangelization, of the Institutes of consecrated life committed to the Christian education of youth, whether this is carried out in the school or in other environments, and of their family settings, needs to be confirmed.

2. Communion

The post-conciliar period has seen a new appreciation of community as communion and of interpersonal relations. The type of traditional community, based in large part on regular observance and structure, is giving way to a life of greater brother- and sisterhood. Communitarian structures are being revised in the search for greater simplicity and closeness to people. The missionary dimension of community has been rediscovered and new value is accorded to the human and Christian aspects of living together. New models of community are appearing, with a new style of spiritual animation and authority (leadership) and greater co-responsibility, which foster a new spirituality and a new apostolic sense.

Communion-*koinonia* is essential in the Church, and it is a gift and a manifestation of Trinitarian life. Although lived in an imperfect way, it does testify to the transforming and unifying presence of Christ and of the Spirit in the Church, which makes her missionary, enriching her with a multiplicity of charisms.

Although it is expressed in different models of community,

according to the variety of charisms, fraternal life in common is essential in the consecrated life. It is a process which is always open, ever unfolding in its human, Christian, religious-apostolic aspects.

Communities of consecrated life cannot be communities closed in on themselves. They live their experience of communion in openness to wider communion with the whole People of God: with lay persons, other consecrated persons, priests and bishops.

Our conviction regarding the centrality of communion in the consecrated life leads us to emphasize the following points:

2.1 Fraternal life

a. We believe that it is necessary to insist upon a communitarian spirituality, rooted in the supremacy of the Word and in the celebration of the Paschal Mystery.

b. We feel the need to give welcome to the requirements of the new type of community life in initial and on-going formation, in accordance with the different charisms. In particular, one must educate members for listening and mutual dialogue, for accountability and community discernment, for planning and evaluating the apostolate, for mercy and mutual emulation.

c. We commit ourselves to foster communities which are Gospel signs in different milieux where they find themselves, especially for young people, and which offer the riches of universality to the local Church and the riches of the local Churches to the universal Church.

d. We hold that the equality and co-responsibility of all the members of our communities should be promoted, in respect for the nature of each charism. In this perspective we see the need to undertake a possible revision of Canon Law where institutes composed of clerical and non-clerical members are concerned. The responsibilities of government within these institutes should be accessible to the non-clerics.

2.2 Communion and collaboration among the different institutes

a. We commit ourselves to foster meetings, relations of

friendship and collaboration among the diverse institutes of consecrated life.

b. It is desirable that the institutes which share the same charism or have juridical bonds or spiritual affinity find ways for greater collaboration in full respect for their own autonomy, and that they be open to an eventual convergence (fusion, union, federation) for a greater fruitfulness in spirituality, in service and in culture.

2.3 Organic communion

a. We see the need for the spirit of the document *Mutuae Relationes* to be extended to all ecclesial categories: bishops, diocesan priests, deacons, lay persons, movements, taking into account the specific nature of each.

b. We wish to foster relations that are inspired by and lead to communion: esteem and mutual respect, consultation, dialogue, subsidiarity, just autonomy.

c. We desire to see an increased participation of men and women religious in the consultative organisms of the Church (Pastoral Councils, Conferences, Synods, Theological Commissions, Regional Councils...).

d. Convinced that communion must be one of the basic concerns in the Church, we judge it urgent that relations between religious and laity, religious and diocesan priests be clarified, in order to foster ecclesial communion, in mutual respect and support of their ecclesial identity.

e. We feel the need to clarify relations between religious and ecclesial movements by seeking to formulate criteria and orientations which will be helpful in promoting a constructive dialogue.

3. Identity

Profound socio-cultural and ecclesial changes have radically transformed the vision of the world, culture, models of the Church, theology, actors. The experience of such changes together with theological reflection have given rise to a process of discernment which calls for a new formulation of the identity of the consecrated life, taking account always of the requirements of inculturation.

Amongst the efforts to renew the consecrated life, which have helped us to find new ways of understanding and expressing our own identity, we mention the return to the original charism, the experience of General Chapters, the renewal of Constitutions, opening towards new experiences, greater missionary awareness and dialogue between different institutes.

The Church is a *"Holy convocation"* which *"lives in Christ"*. She is continually renewed by means of the pluriformity of charisms which the Spirit distributes in order to rejuvenate her and to enable each person to live, as a protagonist, his or her call to holiness in the common dignity of baptismal consecration. It is within this reality that the consecrated life finds its place and is to be understood; founded on the baptismal consecration, it must be lived in communion the other vocations in the Church.

The tradition of the theology of the consecrated life has emphasized diverse nuclei that help us to interpret this charism and its ecclesial identity. We recall, amongst others: the radically lived *following of Christ*, public *profession* and the practice of the *evangelical counsels*, the life of *prayer* and search for God (*quaerere Deum*), the active presence of the Spirit who transforms the person in Christ, *consecration* as absolute belonging to God, the *eschatological* perspective, the commitment to tend towards evangelical *holiness*, the intent to renew the *apostolic community* of the Christian beginnings, ascetical renunciation inspired by the Gospel, various forms of *service*.

A significant theological category which seems capable of unifying the variety of perspectives today is that of *charism*. Each institute arises from a charismatic impulse of the Spirit offered to the founders and transmitted by them to their disciples. The charism implies a specific mode of being, a specific mission and spirituality, style of fraternal life and structures of the institute at the service of the ecclesial mission. This gift of the Spirit is dynamic impulse and it unfolds continually in harmony with the Body of Christ in constant growth; it is entrusted to the institute to be lived, interpreted, made fruitful and witnessed to in communion with the Church in the different cultural contexts.

We express some convictions concerning our identity

a. The specific character of the charisms must be respected, fostering their discernment and the opportune initiatives for a creative fidelity and for their incarnation in time and in different cultures.

b. We should cultivate attitudes and use the means necessary so that the charism may be welcomed, interiorized, re-interpreted and made to grow during initial and ongoing formation, in communitarian relations and commitments, in animation and in Chapters.

c. History shows also that the institutes which have their origins from a charism do not possess a monopoly of its incarnation nor of its permanence in time. New experiences and historical situations, impulses of the Spirit, can lead to new and hitherto unrealized expressions of the charism, to the point of allowing us to speak, in some cases, of a form of "re-foundation".

d. The priority given to the *quality* of life, without any dichotomy between action and contemplation, will greatly foster charismatic identity.

III. FORMATION AND VOCATIONS

The renewal of consecrated life, especially in a time of profound changes, necessarily passes by way of initial and ongoing formation of members; that is so whether in the *missionary* commitment of the Church, in the felt need of an ever greater *communion*, or in the search for a new *identity*. Formation itself in this time of transition and research has highlighted clear values and proven ways (PI).

Formation is an invitation to undergo a living process, centred on the person of Christ, and to deepen the baptismal commitment to follow him, in a particular form of Gospel life. In such a process the way formation leaders and candidates relate to each other is essential, keeping in mind always the riches proper to each culture and nation.

The need for continuity between first and on-going formation is clearly necessary, in terms of a constant process of maturation and discernment; an adequate, integral and specific formation is the condition for the authenticity of the ongoing renewal of the consecrated life.

In the light of this, we express the following convictions and proposals.

1. Convictions

a. We affirm the importance of an integral formation in accordance with one's own charism. This formation must be centred on the experience of God, nourished by his Word and must find its summit in the Eucharistic liturgy. Formation for the following of Christ and under the action of the Spirit must be human, progressive, inculturated; it must "initiate" into the community, understood as communion in the Church, and must prepare the candidates for mission, in contact with experiences of real life.

b. Formation recognizes the following urgent requirements: the radical following of Jesus, which has typical expressions in the consecrated life, spirituality, dialogue and mutual witness, education for affectivity and for interpersonal relations, personal and communitarian discernment, respect for persons and the understanding of social dynamisms, the preferential option for the poor and the knowledge of the mechanisms of oppression.

c. We believe that it is urgent to attempt new forms of initiation into the consecrated life for young persons coming from ethnic minorities and from marginalized groups.

d. We need to build formative communities, to prepare persons for responsibility in formation work who are capable of team work, and at one and the same time are witnesses, masters, educators. We believe that, whenever it is possible, formation should be carried out locally and that the formation directors be native, rooted in their culture of origin. A transcultural experience will enable them to be able to "transcend" (discern, give value to, purify) the local culture.

e. An ongoing formation that respects the individual and that takes into account the different stages of life and the different socio-cultural and ecclesial contexts is indispensable for the growth of persons and for the inculturation of charisms.

2. Proposals

a. Given the decisive importance of formation for the future of the consecrated life in all continents, we suggest that the Synod recognize the service of formation as a priority ministry, and that it support those responsible for formation in their necessary search for a formation responding to the new exigencies of the consecrated life.

b. Candidates for the consecrated life abound in some countries and are scarce in others: the quality of the persons and the consequent need of a true vocational discernment should be confirmed as an indispensable principle in every case.

c. The preferential option for the poor is a characteristic of the consecrated life; the suitability of formative periods spent in communities inserted in the poor environments should, therefore, be recognized (PI 28).

d. In a world rich with changes and marked by intense communications, inter-religious contacts should become ever more frequent. We propose that ecumenism and inter-religious dialogue have an indispensable place in formation.

e. The consecrated life should be presented to youth as a permanent life option and as a response to God and to the challenges of today. For this we must insist on the responsibility of every member of our institutes to be a credible and challenging witness of the charism received, so that young persons can feel its attraction.

f. Formation requires esteem for other ecclesial vocations. For this we propose that there be greater collaboration between institutes of the consecrated life and Bishops in the formation of all vocations; we propose in particular the creation of centres of study and the holding of meetings of collaboration among members of the institutes of consecrated life, of the diocesan clergy and of the laity.

g. We propose that there be courses on the theology of the consecrated life in diocesan seminaries and in theological faculties, and that studies on the diverse vocations be promoted in our houses of formation (PDV, MR).

IV. SOME MORE GENERAL EXPECTATIONS

a. We ask the Synod to take an approach that begins from the lived experience of the consecrated life, which is a living, dynamic and diversified reality in the Church, always animated by the Spirit who challenges it and inspires in it a witness of fidelity to Christ and to his Gospel.

b. The persons heading organisms responsible for accompanying the consecrated life should be invited authoritatively to defend and to foster before all else fidelity to the will of the founder and to the correct historical journey of institutes, maintaining or recovering the initial identity and developing it with a creative fidelity. In this way the identity and the charisms will not be disavowed or deformed by particular juridical and theological positions.

c. We ask the Synod to offer a word of esteem and of stimulus to live in fullness the vocation and the mission to which we have been called in accordance with our diverse charisms. It is our desire, therefore, that the Synod foster the knowledge, the authenticity and the constant renewal of the consecrated life so that it can, in consistency with its own identity, give an answer to the expectations and to the challenges of our contemporaries, in the various cultural, social and ecclesial contexts.

d. The charisms of the consecrated life should be accepted and fostered in respect for the plurality of forms of the consecrated life, in their specificity and complementarity, in communion with all the realities of the People of God, encouraging their creativity and their new ways in freedom and in discernment according to the Spirit, without fear of changes and of the unforeseen.

e. The evangelical inculturation of the consecrated life should be promoted in every local Church with due attention for the culture of the place, with an open legislation that provides support for its actuation with the help of some directive criteria, together with an appropriate initial and ongoing formation.

f. The Synod should help us to discover and to open up new paths of dialogue between bishops, consecrated persons, priests and the laity in the spirit of organic communion as developed in recent Synods so that the gift of the call and of ecclesial communion can be better incarnated in an exchange of the gifts of the Spirit.

g. It is our desire that the *"Propositiones"* which the Synod will present to the Holy Father at the end of its work adopt the expectations that came out of the present document and it is suggested that, in view of the post-Synodal document, they have a tone that is inspiring and practical, encouraging and challenging.

Conclusion

The Congress proved to be very attentive to the historical situation of the consecrated life. We feel encouraged by the words the Holy Father addressed to the members of the Congress:

> The religious life today is experiencing a particularly significant moment of its history, because of the demanding and vast renewal that the changed socio-cultural conditions, at the threshold now of the third millennium of the Christian era, impose on it.

The conclusions and the proposals presented here are offered as part of the contribution of the USG to the forthcoming Synod. They reflect an awareness that is widespread today of the need to arrive at *"a radical and vital synthesis of consecration and mission"*, as the Holy Father reminded us in a timely way.

We express the hope that the Synod may be a significant moment in the journey of renewal of the consecrated life and that it contribute to a better knowledge of this gift of the Spirit to his Church, to a recovery of vocations and to a renewed vitality.

The Pope captured well the aspirations of very many members of the consecrated life, when he said to us in the final part of his discourse:

> Your Founders knew how to incarnate the evangelical message in their time with courage and holiness. Their spiritual sons, faithful to the breath of the Spirit, must carry forward this witness in time, imitating their creativity, with a mature fidelity to the charism of the origins, in constant listening to the needs of the present moment.

We offer our willingness to collaborate with our pastors in preparing, participating in and implementing the Synod on the consecrated life, and we rely upon the prayer of the Virgin Mary, and of our founders and saints of East and West, asking them to intercede in favour of a new spiritual and missionary creativity in view of the great task of the new evangelization.

SECOND PART

Theological synthesis

Making a synthesis has something in common with the Reign of
God. It involves tension and reconciliation, plurality and unity.
Nor is there any such thing as the perfect synthesis; for new
elements are always coming to light and have to be integrated, so
upsetting the pattern of what had gone before. There is an ecology of ideas, which are in continual motion. Those of us who
have worked on this synthesis (I would like to mention, above
all, Fathers Jesus Castellano OCD and Michael Amaladoss SJ, without forgetting the suggestions made by Fathers Secondin, Zago
and Maccise) have had a very rich experience of dialogue. So too
has each one of us here in this hall, dialoguing interiorly with the
multitude of words that have been spoken over these days, words
rich with wisdom and experience. We have taken into account
the conferences and communications and the results of the work
done in the groups and constellations. In this final edition we
include as well the reactions that were shared in the hall after the
reading of the theological synthesis.

It was not our intention to make a summary. Nor did we wish
to highlight the contrasts in ideas. We sought to create a dynamic
synthesis in which one could get an idea of how the consecrated
life is journeying towards the future, even though, at times, with
different rhythms and styles – yet all together. This synthesis too
will be called in due course to die in order to give place to a new
one. Such is life. Spiritual growth means being open to life.

I. HOW MANY ARE WE?
AT WHAT POINT DO WE FIND OURSELVES?

1. If we contemplate the consecrated life in the Catholic
Church we see that it is formed by a tiny minority of Christians:[1]
a mere 0.12% of the total[2]. The great majority of the members of
the Church, in fact, is made up of lay women and men, who

constitute 99.88%[3]. However, this tiny minority which is the consecrated life has a multi-faceted appearance, composed as it is, according to the data provided by the 1992 *Annuario Pontificio*, of 1423 institutes of consecrated life of women[4] and 250 institutes of men[5]. These same data make it clear to us that the consecrated life is in its overwhelming majority lay (82.2%) and feminine (75.5%) and is only in a minority way masculine (27.5%) and clerical[6] (17.8%). It is a striking fact that this minority group has a widespread grass-roots presence in the majority of the particular Churches and on the frontiers of the mission, and that it assures a large part of the services of the Church.

2. In the countries of the northern hemisphere the consecrated life is ageing and noticeably diminishing. In the countries of the southern hemisphere, on the other hand, the opposite process is occurring: there consecrated life is becoming ever younger and is growing in number. The consecrated life is migrating from the North to the South and from the West towards the East. It is plunging its roots in new cultures and peoples. The process, however, is not yet consolidated. There is a serious concern to arrive at a type of charismatic initiation or first formation which is able to conjugate fidelity to the founding charism and fidelity to the culture. When this process has gone further ahead we may assume that the consecrated life will have cosmopolitan features and will be less determined by traditional patterns.

3. The sociological analyses which were presented in this Congress show that in recent years the consecrated life has been undergoing a very great process of transformation[7] or of change[8]. Its traditions, its symbolic and cultural world are being transformed; old institutions are disappearing while new forms of presence are emerging. The moving force behind this change has been the Holy Spirit, by means of Vatican Council II, with two basic postulates: return to the charismatic origins and *aggiornamento*, or conformity to the signs of the Spirit as perceived in each historical moment and in a given geographical place. The way in which change has been welcomed and carried through has been different for each institute, community and person. It presented itself as an unexplored and hazardous road[9].

4. To the degree that the consecrated life has entered upon the ways of renewal it has seen itself confronted by situations of chaos[10] and has been submerged in uncertainty. It has been

affected too by its own inconsistencies and sins. All of this has had its impact on government, and on formation. The lack of *"role clarity"*, doubts respecting the traditional definition of our identity as consecrated life, new life experiences, as well as our failures and mistakes have been a prior and necessary condition for taking a step towards a new model of consecrated life, a new symbolical model, which is already beginning to take shape. With all this, the temptation towards restoration continues to be there. It is a threat for the impatient. It is encouraged, besides, by those who least understand the consecrated life and its historical cycles. It is not enough, however, to reaffirm the process of renewal. There is a renewal pending which must affect in a more radical way the institutions, the excessively complicated systems of life and government, the drift towards middle class comfort and the loss of faith which affects all of us. Some venture to speak of it as *"re-founding"* or *"revitalization"*[11]. In any case, it is a matter of a return to that which is fundamental, in charismatic terms.

II. THE WORLD IN WHICH WE LIVE AND HOW IT CHALLENGES US

5. We are arriving at a new stage not as a result of pressures that are merely internal to the consecrated life, but simply because we are part of the history of our world. That history challenges our creativity and is perceived as a voice of the Spirit. The Church, and the consecrated life within it, make their own reading of this historical moment. They recognize, in the first place, how God's Reign is advancing and is becoming present in our peoples and cultures. The breath of the Spirit and the seeds of the Word are at work and come to expression in our nations, in their peoples and in their cultural creations. We grasp too a constant tension between the forces of doom and those of happiness[12]. This can be synthesized in the following points:

a. The poor are increasing and are becoming progressively poorer; the rich ever richer, less in solidarity and more warped; new forms of poverty are emerging; yet, despite it all, the poor are the ones who preserve the richest human values and it is from them that a regeneration is possible.

b. Violence is ever more cruel, more omnipresent in institutions, groups, persons; it is the non-violent who introduce a different logic and one that will overcome in the end.

c. The great religions have an enormous potential for giving birth to a new future for those who live without meaning; however, fundamentalism is closing them in on themselves and converting them into manifestations of sacred violence; those who establish dialogue, based on life and experience, those who are enriched by their moral teaching and their expressions of faith are purifying the heart of the world so that God can be seen.

d. The phenomenon of post-modernity witnesses to the dissatisfaction people experience in the face of the tyranny of reason, of the machine, of self-sufficiency; it can, however, become a facile consolation which neglects the struggle for justice and a diluted religion dominated by the scientific-technological mentality, which is its hidden idol; those who experience hunger and thirst for justice are judged, as were the early Christians, as "the *godless*".

e. Today, a culture based on the scientific-technological mentality, which can count on powerful political and economic backing, is tending to dominate everywhere in an idolatrous way; at the same time new cultures or cultures that have not been integrated into the system and new cultural agents are emerging forcefully: women, indigenous peoples, the poor; there are too those who are struggling to promote dialogue between cultures, between civilizations.

f. The gift of freedom, as expression of the personal dignity of woman and man, is frequently held captive in societies and in religions; those who struggle for freedom are persecuted and silenced.

6. It is the human communities, people themselves, whether in Latin America, Africa, Asia and the Pacific, or in North America and Eastern and Western Europe, who are the protagonists of the present historical moment. Tensions and conflicts between North and South, East and West, place our world in a situation in which it is necessary to cry out for the urgent coming of the Reign and of the Lord. This is the challenge of the Church's mission.

III. CONSECRATED LIFE:
PROPHETIC ESCHATOLOGICAL STIMULUS
IN THE MISSION OF THE CHURCH

7. Those of us who belong to the consecrated life are involved in the Church's mission. Many indeed are the charisms and ministries through which we are making our particular contribution in the five continents. So impressive and so complex are the challenges of the mission, and so mysterious is the mission itself that we can never say that we are satisfied.

The mission that comes from God

8. The mission is a mystery because it is not the Church's property. The mission proceeds and comes from God. In it the mission of the Holy Spirit is actualized in a visible way, the same mission, in fact, which in a mysterious way, energizes the march of the nations towards the Reign of God. The Spirit is the great missionary of the Father and of Jesus, the Lord. With inexpressible groaning, with signs and prodigies the Spirit testifies to the love of God Father-Mother for his people and his creation and actualizes and re-interprets the mission of Jesus in the time of the Church. By means of his Spirit, Jesus who is the Word, by whom the world was created and is carried forward to its fulfilment, makes himself present in every word of revelation which has been granted to men and women, but – above all – he makes himself present in his Church. Consecrated by the Spirit, Jesus not only walked amongst us doing good with signs and prodigies, proclaiming the Gospel of the Reign, giving his life for all on the cross and being raised up, he also continues to be present and active now in the Church, of which he was constituted Lord, which is his Body in the world.

9. For this reason we are aware that the mission is not an activity that is simply added to the being of the Church. It is its very being. The Church is called to be sign and docile and humble instrument of the mission of the Spirit: to be a witness to the love of God for the world, to proclaim Jesus Christ and to make him present, to commit itself to the task of reconciliation and of making all men and women of the earth brothers and sisters.

The Spirit grants a charism to each person in the mission

10. To be part of the Church, to be *Christifideles* is to be *missionary, a creature of the Spirit*. Each one receives his/her gift, his/her charism in the order of the mission. To put it in another way: each person who is baptized-confirmed is consecrated by the Spirit, by means of the charisms that the same Spirit grants, in order to be mission in the Church.

a. Some are consecrated by means of an untransferable *personal gift*.

b. Others by means of a *double gift*, which is shared, for example, in the conjugal or spousal relationship.

c. Others are consecrated by means of a *communitarian charism*, in so far as many different persons meet and communicate in it. The self-same Spirit has raised up in the Church an admirable variety of collective charisms, by means of persons and/or groups (founders, founding groups).

– There are collective charisms within the ordained ministry, with the lay-secular life (ecclesial movements) and within the consecrated life.

– Some collective charisms are granted by the Spirit to persons of different forms of life; for this reason they can be lived and translated into lay-secular, ministerial and consecrated forms of life.

– The gift of the consecrated life belongs to this type of charism. By means of it the Holy Spirit creates and represents in the Church Jesus celibate, poor and obedient for the Reign. The counsels, or better, the *evangelical charisms*, are three aspects of a single charism which constitutes the gift of the consecrated life. We respond to it in a personal and communitarian manner by bringing to completion in ourselves, in this way, a covenant of love.

d. In their complementarity they give visibility to the memory of the Lord that the Spirit creates in time in view of the mission. For even though the charisms are many, the mission is but one. Charismatic differences are not to be measured by the standard of more or less, but by their *"mutua relatio"* within the one mission.

11. In this present phase of the Church's history, all the forms of the consecrated life recognize that their *raison d'être* is to trans-

late into their action, passion and witness the Spirit's mission from the specific perspective that has been granted to them.

a. *Contemplative life* is mission of witness and radiation of that human source-experience of God which was granted to Jesus by the Spirit during his life's journey, and which continues to be granted to believers today.

b. *The apostolic consecrated life* recognizes that communitarian action and passion for the Reign belong to its own being and thus experiences the call and empowerment to live in unity of life as Jesus did, without any sort of dichotomy.

c. *Societies of apostolic life* and *missionary institutes* highlight more his being mission towards those who are outside, to the point of waiving any institutional bond which would in some way limit this thrust; they thereby represent Jesus on the move towards other places where he can preach the Reign.

d. *Secular institutes* are mission in diaspora and from the standpoint of the individual person. In the midst of the secular situation they make Jesus present by means of the evangelical charisms.

Our sense of what the Spirit is asking of us in the mission

12. Each form of consecrated life must endeavour to place itself where the Spirit is seeking to lead its Church today. It must collaborate there with other charisms and ministries of the People of God, without renouncing its own ministerial identity, yet at the same time without prejudice to the unity of the mission:

a. The *proclamation of Jesus Christ*: in the mission *"ad gentes"*, where a first evangelization is necessary (Asia, Africa); there where many take their distance from the faith and a second or a new evangelization (for those who have abandoned the faith) becomes necessary; or the on-going evangelization of the believing people, especially abandoned Christian communities, without priest and without Eucharist. Consecrated life carries out this evangelization by drawing on its manifold possibilities: communitarian and personal witness, ministry of the Word, *diakonia* of charity, according to its own charism.

b. The *option for the poor* (in as much as charism of compassion, accepted and progressively developed) must be a determining factor in every missionary project for the Reign. By means of this charismatic and compassionate poverty the consecrated life will overcome its attachment to middle class comfort and will announce the beatitude of the poor. Consecrated life has discovered, as significant expression of the option for the poor, the *mission carried out in the form of insertion*: communities living amongst the poor show that they are a way of the Spirit for re-living the experience of Jesus, evangelizer of the Reign, and for becoming truly incarnate in the condition of the brothers and sisters who cry out for the coming of the Reign. Thus the option for the poor is converted into prophecy for the non-poor and a drive to evangelize them by means of denunciation and proclamation.

c. The *option for non-violence and for life* gives new features to the consecrated life. It denounces wars, armed conflicts, forms of violence that have become a daily affair in social and family life. It appears as an ally of life, of peace: for this it takes care of old people, of abandoned and maltreated children, of those who feel alone and whose lives lack meaning; it cares for and helps the sick and the handicapped; it commits itself to the struggle for justice, peace and the safeguarding of the environment, and defends the maltreated and those who are discriminated against sexually.

d. The *option for the dialogue of life:* with religions, with cultures, in order to keep open the increasingly closed circle of the forms of fundamentalism and dogmatism. In dialogue the consecrated life makes itself servant of the Word: in order to be servant it listens to and welcomes it from others and proclaims it with humility and fraternally for others. It does not aim at conversion, but at walking together with others on the pilgrim way.

IV. CONSECRATED LIFE:
A GIFT FOR COMMUNION

13. Those of us who belong to the consecrated life are involved also in the communion of the Church. Our presence in very many particular Churches and ecclesial communities of the five continents, by means of thousands and thousands of communities or fraternities, enables us to offer to God's people a great service in bringing about communion. Communion is complex and difficult. Communion is, above all, mystery.

14. Communion is mystery because it comes from God. The Trinity is the first community; and with its hands, so to speak, the Trinity makes us community. It is for this that Abba sent his Son and the Spirit, namely to create communion on earth. Jesus handed over his Spirit to the Church making himself body given and blood poured out for all; the Spirit was poured out at Pentecost so that we all may be one in Christ Jesus (Gal 3,28). Thus the Church is the body of Christ in growing movement of communion, to the point of having but one heart, one soul and everything in common (Acts 4:32-34). All the charisms are called to achieve integration in communion.

15. Charismatic communion is a consequence of self-giving. It is not born spontaneously. It passes by way of the Cross, by the forgetting of self in order to affirm the other as person. The communion of wills between Jesus and the Father reached its most difficult and dramatic moment in Gethsemane and on Calvary. Nor does communion spare us tensions and conflicts that are conditions of mutual concord. The death and resurrection of Jesus gathered together the dispersed children of God; thus it is that there are elements of both death and life in every event of re-union. A constitutive element of communion is compassion, the willingness to forgive *"seventy times seven"*; as indeed is also mutual openness, the establishment of authentic personal relationships, the power of friendship.

Charismatic communion

16. A collective charism calls for an especially intense experience of communion. Formation, initial as well as on-going, should prepare the members of an institute to live in permanent communion, to work as a team and to plan together. This was Jesus' teaching to his disciples on the way to Jerusalem, this was the style which he adopted: to learn to leave everything behind, to be the least and the servant of all, to love one's neighbour as oneself. It was not exempt from internal conflicts with Judas, with Peter. Finally, *"having loved his own who were in the world he loved them to the end."* As the tendencies towards individualism become stronger, this type of formation is all the more necessary.

17. Charismatic communion makes the path to faith easier when it is perceived by non-believers. Thus Jesus asked Abba: *"that they may be one so that the world may believe."* Each form of consecrated life is a charismatic and existential mode of the *"communio"* in the Spirit. It is *"communion for the mission and in the mission"*. The charismatic mission is carried out together. Only thus is the Reign made credible.

a. Some live in monastic stability in order to be communion as permanent liturgical assembly, or existential liturgy.

b. Others on the basis of evangelizing itinerancy in order to be communion in the dispersal and in re-union.

c. *Charismatic communion* is lived in an especially intense form in each local community. There fraternity is experienced, our being family in the Spirit. Communion is created day by day in docility to the Spirit, making love the most powerful arm and seeking to be an authentic group of friends and brothers/sisters.

18. The dynamism of communion and of the con-vocation is regenerated in listening to and welcoming the Word of God (*lectio divina*), in the celebration of the Eucharistic Presence and of the Paschal Mystery, in fraternal living together, in discernment, in the sharing of a journey of spiritual life, in the reciprocal communication of one's own experience and feelings, in mutual help, in joy and good humour, in welcome and hospitality, especially towards those who approach us in their need, in the community mission project.

In the communion of the Church

19. Each community is a gift for others:

a. In the first place for the other communities of the institute. For this reason the community does not close itself in around its own interests; rather, it shares its goods, it is available for service and help, it welcomes fraternal correction, humbly and gratefully accepts the forms of mediation of communion between communities. It is aware that all the other communities are a gift for it.

b. Each community is thus itself a gift for other ecclesial communities, with whom it must maintain relations that are fraternal and mutually enriching. It can and must, however, be a gift for the people, for men and women, to whom it offers the best of itself, knowing that, by so doing it will receive much more than it gives.

c. Each community is principally a gift for the particular Church in which it has its place. It is a charism for the universal Church, cultivated in the particular Church. And for the community this is the environment where it experiences the mystery of the whole Church. The community of consecrated life can offer to the particular Church the riches of the tradition, of the universality of the Church.

20. The consecrated life recognizes with gratitude the vigilance of the universal Church and of the particular Churches and of its ministers in view of its renewal and of its existence. The pontifical and episcopal magisterium has been an especial grace to which the consecrated life owes much; however it is also very grateful to the People of God from whom flows a permanent energy and vitality which maintains the consecrated life in a state of vigilance and generosity. Mutual relations with the hierarchy have been and continue to be difficult at times. This is almost always due to lack of mutual knowledge, to a different perception of the elements that are important for the Church, to the lack of experiences of communion in pain and always to failures in the dialogue and discernment which should be characteristic of brothers and sisters in the faith. By virtue of its identification with Jesus' obedience, consecrated life should be committed to communion, aware that the last word belongs to the God of history.

The service of authority

21. Service of communion and of communion for the mission corresponds in a special way to charismatic authority in the consecrated life. This service has as its grave obligation to watch over the growth and continued formation of the institute and of its communities, in creative fidelity to the charism. The one who fulfils this service has to be endowed with the charism of a certain leadership capacity, exercised in communion and for communion. The one who carries out the function of guidance in

the community needs to have moral and evangelical authority. This is given to him not by the mere fact of being named, but rather by:

a. his enthusiastic identification with the charismatic project of his own institute, understood as *sequela Jesu* and mission of the Spirit;
b. the ability to *"sentire cum ecclesia"*;
c. compassionate love and the option for the poor;
d. sincere love for the brothers and respect full of veneration for their freedom, their charisms and their rights.

V. HOW WE EXPLAIN OUR CHARISMATIC IDENTITY IN THE CHURCH

22. Those of us who belong to the consecrated life have not always explained our theological-spiritual identity in the same fashion. Vatican Council II spoke of us in the Constitution on the Church; it affirmed that we belong to the structure of life and holiness of the Church; it highlighted our charismatic condition in saying that we are a gift of the risen Lord to his Spouse, the Church. This perspective leads us, not only to change the theoretical patterns, but, above all, to initiate ourselves into a richer experience of ecclesial life and of *"mutua relatio"* with other forms of life and ministry within the People of God and even beyond the Church. These experiences together with a broader knowledge of our traditions and roots lead us to express the distinctive traits of our charismatic identity, avoiding simplification and describing it from different perspectives: history, religions, option for Jesus, place in the Church, prophecy and symbol.

That which history tells us

23. We learn what the consecrated life is, in the first place, through its history.

a. *It is not a uniquely Christian phenomenon.* Already in pre-historic societies there were wise men and holy people who exercised an important function in the spiritual life of the people.[13] In Hinduism a strong monastic orientation appeared from the beginning, which was crystallized in the figure of the *sannyasi*[14] or in the women ascetics *sannyasini*. Buddhism arose as a monastic religion.[15] The monastic movement was also present in Judaism (*Therapeutes*, Essenes, Rechabites, Nazarines). Shortly after the birth of Islam *Sufism* appeared (in the eighth century) and functioned as a critical force in its culture.[16] There are groups in the "new religions" of our time which express similar tendencies[17].

b. As a *Christian phenomenon* the consecrated life has been present in the two thousand years of the Church's history, already from the beginning, and it has assumed very diverse forms[18]. Charismatic men and women – founders and founding communities – perceived by intuition the great spiritual and missionary needs of the Church and of the society of their time and place; they gave a response to them by means of minorities and significant life projects and works of service. Although the projects in question were limited ones, they felt the need to have them inserted into the social fabric of the Church, and to ask for its approbation. By means of the hierarchical authorization the different institutes belong publically to the life and holiness of the Church; they arise from her and are oriented towards her, avoiding any tendency towards sectarianism. Today many of these forms continue to subsist and other new ones are emerging.

c. It is an *ecumenical phenomenon*. In the Eastern Churches monasticism is deeply rooted and constitutes a very important presence, as visible expression of the monastic dimension of the whole Church. Likewise in the Anglican Church and in the area of the Reformed Churches different forms of monastic and religious life are arising with increasing force.

The perspective of the world religions

24. In questioning ourselves regarding the identity of the consecrated life in the Church we sense that behind the different expressions of the consecrated life, in the world religions as in the Church, there is in all ages and cultures a basic common inspiration and a shared aspiration. These minority and marginal groups exercise a symbolic, critical and transforming function over the society in which they are born. They respond to a

tendency, proper to human culture, to incarnate in a radical and profound form the most deeply appreciated values, especially the sacred values. They are minority and radical groups. The society sees its hopes, dreams and aspirations embodied in these groups. The consecrated life in its varied forms and through the different religions is one of the primary and most authentic expressions of the symbolic-transforming function of minorities in the midst of the majorities. We believe that these forms of life – not only in Christianity, but also beyond it – are not on the margin of the mysterious action of the Spirit of the Lord and of the "seeds of the Word" in the nations.

The option that explains everything: Jesus, the Lord and the Gospel

25. The great *raison d'être* of the consecrated life in the Church is the following of Jesus, the Lord, from the standpoint of a particular inspiration of the Spirit. In this sense it has a unique newness with respect to the forms of religious life in other religions: the inescapable reference to a historical person, Jesus of Nazareth, and to his message.

a. Those of us who form part of the consecrated life in the Church know that we have been elected and empowered (consecrated by a charism of the Spirit) to be with Jesus and to be sent as those of the pre-paschal community were; we feel that we are called to give visibility to the dream of community – of being of one heart, one soul and having everything in common – which appears in the summaries of the Acts.

b. The experience of the centuries makes us understand that God the Father wants the consecrated life in the Church so that the most significant features of the humanity of his Son Jesus may continue to be present and attract all towards the Reign. And for this the Spirit graces some followers of Jesus with the evangelical charism of celibacy, poverty and obedience.[19]

c. The plurality of charisms in the different forms of consecrated life is interpreted by us as the intention of the Spirit to recall some existential gestures of Jesus,[20] evoke some of his teachings[21] or represent some of his mysteries.[22] Each institute of consecrated life highlights charismatically, emphasizes some feature of the Mystery of the Lord, and is converted into a living memory of him for the Church. We members of the consecrated life are the symbol-memory of the Lord more by our style of life than by our activities and achievements.

d. We follow Jesus who also followed a spiritual path of growth. He did not experience everything in his life simultaneously, but in an historical way. He went through different stages: from infancy to the Cross, from the opening discourse of the beatitudes to the final eschatological-apocalyptic discourse[23]. For us the following of Jesus is a process of continual formation, directed by the Spirit and by the Word, which progressively identifies us with our Lord. The reading of the Gospel, and from its perspective of the whole of the New and Old Testament, has always been the great inspiration, the first rule of the consecrated life. The consecrated life intends to be thereby a living biography of the following *"sine glossa"*.

e. All the options that define our style of life are centred on and concentrated in one only: the option to follow Jesus, to live the mystery of the historical Jesus in our time and in our place.

The perspective of the beginning and the end

26. Whereas the forms of Christian secular life incarnate the normal creation-based modes of the historical living out of faith, the forms of consecrated life, such as are emphasized, above all, in its monastic origins, intend to be the memory of the original plan of God, expressed in the first pages of Genesis, and prophecy of the eschatological plenitude. Since the integrity and cosmic unity of God's plan for human beings has been broken and rendered impossible by sin, the consecrated life, moved by the Spirit, feels that it is called, like Jesus, to represent in this fallen world those aspects of the original project of God that sin has obscured; for this reason it renounces those goods that are most frequently abused. Celibacy-virginity, poverty and the service of obedience are thus converted into prophetic invitations of a creative-eschatological project, that has been seen so many times in the past, and that we continue to see today, contradicted in human history. In that way the prophetic forms of the consecrated life aim at giving balance to the historical existence of secular believers by evoking the memory of the origins and of the end.

We share the impatience of the Lord Jesus and of the Church-Spouse for the in-breaking of the Reign as soon as possible in its plenitude, so that the climactic moment of God's covenant with his people might come upon us. This desire becomes more impatient when we enter the desert, the frontier, the fringes of the world and suffer with those who are experiencing these as times of condemnation, death, disappointment, torture. The Gospel charism of celibacy, poverty and obedience is converted in this context into denunciation and proclamation.

The perspective of the forms of life in the Church

27. In the Church we confess that the Spirit, first and permanent Founder of the consecrated life, is the one who shapes its identity and makes it possible. At various times theology and law have had to have recourse to new and broader expressions in order to be able to make room within their concepts for all the riches of the new forms of consecrated life that the Spirit brings into being.[24] The emergence in our time of a new awareness of the lay-secular vocation and of its spiritual and missionary possibilities obliges us also to modify our theological understanding of the consecrated life.[25] It indicates that the definition of the identity of the consecrated life becomes correlative to the identity of the common and secular Christian life and to all its forms, and at the same time becomes interdependent in regard to them. Whatever each life-form is existentially will re-define the other.

28. Consecrated life is a mode of shaping a common and pre-existing reality, shared by all the members of the Church: being *Christifideles* (common condition of the children of God, followers of Jesus Christ, consecrated and anointed by the Spirit, active subjects of the life and mission of the Church). The sacraments of initiation confer on all a common dignity, a fraternal equality, and direct and impel them towards the perfection of love. The forms of Christian existence are the peculiar modes whereby, under the action of the Spirit and the guidance of the Church, each particular person individualizes his fundamental vocation.

29. When one takes account of the hierarchical structure of the Church and one distinguishes between ordained ministers and laity, the consecrated life appears as in majority lay. Only a minority are members of the ordained ministry. Being lay or

ordained minister from the standpoint of the consecrated life implies offering to others one's own gift: the life-style that buds from the charismatic and prophetic condition.

30. Through all that we have just said, it becomes clear, as the Council recognized (LG, 44), that the consecrated life exercises a symbolic function. It is a symbol within a Church which is itself all symbol in relation to the world, since it represents for her the existential prophecy of Jesus. Its symbolic function does not raise consecrated life above other forms; it makes it subsidiary and less. This form of life becomes all the more necessary wherever Christian existence is affected by the disintegration and corruption that sin produces. It is there that the exaggerated signs of the original order and of the eschatological order are all the more necessary.

VI. THE FUTURE IN THE SPIRIT OF THE CONSECRATED LIFE

31. It is not unusual for us today to raise the question of our future. We know that it is in God's hands. However we must, for our part, work with the talents that have been given to us, as faithful servants, for as long as the Lord wishes. For his sake we must seek and re-light the charismatic fire of the origins, we must return continually to the first love.

32. Spirituality, born in different cultures, will lead us to feel the experience of God in the midst of the shattering experiences of our brothers and sisters in the world, from the standpoint of the situation of the poor, from the standpoint of the experience of meaninglessness of those who suffer and are in despair, from the standpoint of the new values and interpretations of the world.

33. Each institute will have to rediscover and make its own its unique path of spirituality within the larger spiritual journey of the People of God. Charismatic revitalization will make it necessary to re-shape the formative processes of initiation and will give to ongoing formation the character of authentic charismatic re-initiation. Providing formation on the basis of vibrant and pedagogically effective experiences in line with the charism will allow the consecrated life to rediscover its identity in a new epoch and culture. In that which concerns us, a significant part of our future will be played out in formation. Formation must

translate the values of mission and communion that have been discovered in a process of charismatic initiation. It is called to make contact with the fire of their evangelical and charismatic origins possible for members.

34. The consecrated life hopes that the Church will grant it an open statute which will allow it to be faithful to the eschatological prophecy that characterizes it and that stimulates it to situate itself in the deserts, on the margins and at the frontiers of the mission in order to be *"evangelica testificatio"*. Consecrated life must not be allowed to be converted into a ready resource for resolving ordinary pastoral problems.

35. In this historical moment of cultural change, when we ready ourselves to celebrate the 2000th anniversary of the birth of Jesus, we re-read the great sign of the Woman which appears in the sky, yet which is of earth (Apoc 12) as a message of hope, also for us. She is the Woman who will give to the light. It is the Church. It is all of us, our communities and fraternities. It is our dreams at the critical point of becoming reality. Yet we cry out in pain. We long already for the darkness to be overcome and the day to dawn, because the pains are the pains of birth. The dragon is before us, ready to devour the new being with a human face. The dragon represents so many negative forces, both outside of and within us. It is the seed of the Evil One who has not as yet been overcome. Yet we hear already the prayers of the saints who are singing the hymn of victory, for the Reign of God is being consolidated. The consecrated life feels itself consoled by its Lord who says to it: *"Do not be afraid, my little flock, I saw Satan fall like lightning."* Thus can it also console others with the same consolation that it receives from God.

36. In this context how can we not evoke Mary, the woman symbol of every Nativity, the *"perfect model of the disciple of the Lord"* (MC 37)? The charismatic-consecrated life called to be prophecy of a different world feels itself inspired by Mary[26] and receives from her a mysterious spiritual force. It feels itself consecrated by the Spirit in order to form part of the offspring of the Woman. Mary is for the consecrated life a model of total self-giving to the Reign of God: in her it has discovered what it means to listen to that Word in the Scriptures and in life, and to believe in it in all circumstances in order to live what it requires; drawing inspiration from the Word, the consecrated life lives near at hand to the needs of its brothers and sisters (Lk 1:39-45; Jn 2:1-12; Acts 1:14).

NOTES

1. Since the following data were not made available to us by the sociological studies presented during this Congress, we have had to have recourse to some of the data which we had at hand, which however correspond to different statistics covering these last three years. The information concerning the number of members of institutes of consecrated life was made available to us thanks to a telephone call to the *Congregation for Institutes of Consecrated Life and Societies of Apostolic Life*. For the other data, we will indicate the sources. That which was of interest to us was to have an approximate idea of the proportion between persons of consecrated life and laity. In any case, to have greater exactitude it would be necessary to bring the statistics up to date with the latest information, which we do not have access to.

2. According to the latest data from the *Congregation for Institutes of Consecrated life and Societies of Apostolic Life*, the members belonging to it are currently 1,116,332 (which obviously does not include those belonging to institutes of diocesan right). Of these 870,344 are women and 240,988 are men. The total number of male and female novices is 28,340: 19,340 female novices and some 9,000 male novices. If the overall number of Catholics is 906,400,000, this means that we religious are 0,12%. For a comparison, the 1989 statistical Yearbook of the Church counted, in a world population of 5,165 million inhabitants, 908.3 million Catholics; of these, 281.6 million in Europe, 80.7 million in Asia, 85.6 million in Africa, 451.5 million in America and 7 million in Oceania.

3. The ordained ministry is likewise, and strikingly, a minority: according to the data provided by the 1989 statistical Yearbook of the Catholic Church religious bishops in the world were 1,114, non-religious bishops 4,159; in all, 5,273. Diocesan priests number 255,240.

4. *Women*
   - 1,370 religious institutes;
   - 59 Orders and autonomous houses;
   - 1,311 centralized institutes;
   - 42 Secular institutes;
   - 11 Societies of apostolic life.

5. *Men*
   - 6 institutes of Canons Regular (1 Federation, 6 institutes among them);
   - 11 Monastic institutes (21 Congregations in the Benedictine Federation; 2 Congregations of the Mequitarists; 12 Congregations of Cistercians; 4 Orders within the Antonians; 5 Orders within the Basilians);
   - 17 Mendicant Orders;
   - 8 Clerics Regular;
   - 89 Clerical Religious Congregations;
   - 33 Lay Religious Congregations;
   - 10 Secular institutes;
   - 28 Societies of apostolic life.

6. We must observe, nonetheless, that in the Institutes defined as clerical there is usually a considerable number of lay brothers.

7. *"While this term* transformation *has been used in a variety of ways, in the organizational real it refers basically to qualitative discontinuous shifts in organizational members' shared understanding of the organization, accompanied by changes in the organization's mission, strategy, and formal and informal structures. In contrast to carrying our comparatively simple incremental changes, organizations undergoing transformation come to understand themselves and their mission very differently than they originally had."* D. Nygren, C.M. & M. Ukeritis, CSJ, *"Future of Religious Orders in the United States"*, in *"Origins"*, September 24, 1992, Vol. 22, No. 15, p. 259.

8. *"Change is deeper and more transforming than we had believed, and less spectacular than at times we might hope. To change does not consist in taking on the new external facts, the new innovations in society... That which readily transforms men and women, institutions or society and the religious life is the change in the* hierarchy of values." J. López García, SJ, Mª Begoña de Isusi, MMB, *La realidad actual de la vida religiosa*, p. 9.

9. The most important aspects in regard to this process of change which is taking place are:

    a. The centrality of the figure of Jesus, the Christ, and of the Word of God as fundamental inspiration for a new model of the religious life.

    b. The recovery of the charismatic prophecy of the founders and of their communities to render it possible for the Spirit to re-found or revitalize them in new cultural and human contexts. There is too much readiness to welcome new forms of consecrated life born in other cultures or in moments of cultural change, without having recourse to a facile promotion of the known forms of the consecrated life.

    c. The pride of place which is accorded to the evangelical option for the poor as determining life-style and mission in the consecrated life and as inspiration for a new type of theology and spirituality.

    d. The new value accorded the human person with all his/her charisms and possibilities within an open and dialogical model of community and as an element that must never be given second place in relation to norms and institutions; this brings with it a new model of authority and leadership which is more complex and calls for new strategies.

    e. The new role of women in society and the in the Church, which is found in a special way in the charismatic leadership of the consecrated woman in the most dangerous initiatives of the mission, in her original and creative contributions to theological reflection and in her resistance in regard to theological and ecclesiological models which are found to be discriminatory and ideological.

    f. The new value attributed to the lay person as a subject of ecclesial life in the face of a clericalism that is excessively concerned to play a leading part and monopolizes roles; this has its repercussions in the lay consecrated life and in its legitimate claims to autonomy and to charismatic recognition, on the one hand, and in the necessary revaluation of the secular lay person as an authentic co-subject of the mission.

    g. The theological-spiritual revaluation of secularity and with it of the whole process of inculturation, insertion and dialogue.

    h. The rediscovery of the symbolic form of ministry which the consecrated life is called to exercise in the midst of the great ecclesial community and the society.

10. The adjective *chaotic* or the term *chaos* refer to a reality that is unformed, confused, yet in which there are possibilities, seeds. In Biblical thought it is said that the Spirit hovers over the unformed reality in order that from there he might begin his new creation.

11. These terms are most commonly used in English-speaking areas.

12. The correlation between the forces of doom and those of happiness in Luke's Sermon on the Plain (chap. 6) and the unfolding of the Beatitudes in Matthew 6 have provided us with a framework which enables us to interpret the present day situation. The situation of doom is seen as a contrast to the happiness of those who choose an alternative style of life. Neither the former nor the latter are necessarily Christians.

13. Amongst them were the religious shamans – numinous personalities – in tribal peoples, in contact with the sacred and with healing powers.

14. A monk who lives alone, or in a community – *ashram* – or in a monastery - *matha*.

15. The Buddha was a monk and he transmitted to his followers a monastic system, taken fundamentally from the Hindu *sannyasi*. The three great virtues of the Buddhist monk were non-violence, chastity and poverty.

16. Later on they organized brotherhoods, today called orders (*tariqahs* [followers of the way]).

17. Such as ISKON (Krishna consciousness), those who affirm the world like scientology, and those who accommodate to the world like the pentecostal/charismatic groups. Many of these groups take on a monastic/religious-consecrated orientation.

18. Consecrated life, whether male or female, has been taking shape in the life patterns of the early itinerant missionaries, the ascetics, the continents and the virgins, the monks (heremitical as well as cenobitical), the canons regular, the mendicants, the members of apostolic societies, societies of common life without vows, and congregations of apostolic life or secular institutes.

19. It is a question of a single charism in three dimensions, as the tradition of the consecrated life has always said.

20. His mercy towards sinners, his closeness to the least and the marginalized, his continuous prayer, his evangelizing activity, his miracles for the sick and the possessed.

21. Charity, Hospitality, Forgiveness.

22. Birth, Life in Nazareth, Passion, Death and Resurrection.

23. Luke, Mark highlight this perspective of the way, the journey.

24. The emergence of the minority charism of the consecrated life in each of its principal forms forced the thinkers of the Church to re-situate the remaining ecclesial group in relation to it. Thus, for example, did the Fathers in relation to monasticism (John Chrysostom, Basil, Augustine), or the great mediaeval theologians in relation to monasticism and the mendicant orders (Thomas Aquinas and Bonaventure), or the Renaissance theologians in relation to all the forms of the religious life, including those forms emerging at that time (Francisco Suárez, Bellarmine).

25. The Synod on the consecrated life gets meaning within this perspective;

it deals with the consecrated life following on the three earlier synods which dealt with the theme of the ministerial priesthood (*De sacerdotio ministeriali et de Iustitia in mundo*, 1971), of the Laity (*Christifideles Laici*) and of formation for the ordained ministry (*Pastores dabo vobis*).

26. The Virgin of the *Magnificat* announces the ending of an old and corrupt world and proclaims the dawn of a new history in which God casts down the mighty from their thrones and raises up the poor. Mary chose the side of the Reign of God as the Woman of the Apocalypse (Apoc 12) and against the Woman, the prostituted City (Apoc 17), and the empire that she served.